ZERO
═══ TO ═══
HERO

FROM BULLIED KID TO WARRIOR

ZERO
=== TO ===
HERO

FROM BULLIED KID TO WARRIOR

ALLEN J. LYNCH

Medal of Honor Recipient, with

RICHARD ERNSBERGER, JR.

Introduction by Colonel (IL) Jennifer N. Pritzker, IL ARNG (Retired)

PRITZKER
MILITARY
MUSEUM & LIBRARY

2019

Published by the Pritzker Military Museum & Library, Chicago, Illinois. No part of this book may be reproduced in any manner whatsoever without written permission except in the case of brief quotations embodied in critical articles, reviews, and educational papers. For more information about permission to reproduce selections from this book, write to Permissions, Pritzker Military Museum & Library, 104 South Michigan Avenue, Suite 400, Chicago, Illinois, 60603, or to info@pritzkermilitary.org. www.pritzkermilitary.org

Library of Congress Cataloging-in-Publication Data
Title: Zero to Hero: From Bullied Kid to Warrior
By: Allen J. Lynch, with Richard Ernsberger, Jr., introduction by Colonel (IL) Jennifer N. Pritzker, IL ARNG (Retired)
Description: 384 pages; with black and white photographs; includes index.
Identifiers: ISBN 978-0-9989689-2-6 (Hardcover) ISBN 978-0-9989689-3-3 (e-book)
Subjects: LCSH: 1. Vietnam War, 1961-1975 — Veterans — United States — Biography. 2. Medal of Honor — Biography. 3. Bullying. 4. Post-traumatic stress disorder — Treatment. 5. United States — Illinois — Biography. 6. United States — Army — Cavalry, 12th — Battalion, 1st. 7. Vietnam War, 1961-1975 — Campaigns — Vietnam — Binh Dinh (Vietnam : Province) 8. Vietnam War, 1961-1975 — Personal narratives, American. 9. Veterans — Mental Health — United States. 10. Veterans — United States — Psychology. 11. Military spouses. 12. Families of military personnel. 13. Lynch, Allen, J., 1945 -
Names: Lynch, Allen J., author | Ernsberger, Richard, Jr., author | Pritzker, Jennifer, N., contributor.

Classification: LCC DS559.5.L96 2019 | DDC 959.70438'

Executive Editors: Colonel (IL) Jennifer N. Pritzker, IL ARNG (Retired), Kenneth Clarke
Designer: Wendy Palitz

To access the Pritzker Military Museum & Library's collection of more than 100,000 cataloged artifacts, posters, prints, and books, go to www.pritzkermilitary.org. To access the Vietnam War microsite, go to www.pritzkermilitary.org/vietnam. Or, visit the Museum & Library in person at 104 South Michigan Avenue, Chicago, Illinois, at the corner of Michigan Avenue and Monroe Street across from The Art Institute of Chicago and Millennium Park.

The trade edition of *Zero to Hero: From Bullied Kid to Warrior* was preceded by a limited edition of 50 numbered copies with a unique tip-in page.

First Edition

Cover Image: An officer and his RTO at the An Lao Valley LZ, Vietnam, under an arriving wave of 1st Cavalry helicopters, May 1967. Getty Images, Patrick Christian.

Endpapers: LZ English. Near Bong Son, Vietnam, approximately 420 miles northeast from Saigon (now Ho Chi Minh City), Vietnam, 1967,U.S. Army.

All other images taken by or used by permission of Allen J. Lynch.

CONTENTS

INTRODUCTION   vii
By Colonel (IL) Jennifer N. Pritzker, IL ARNG (Retired)

PREFACE   ix
The Meaning of a Medal

1. My Test Time   1

2. Stalwart Parents   5

3. Good Times in Roseland   23

4. Eli's Trailer Camp   32

5. Lake Eliza: Growing up Bullied   41

6. Better Days: High School and Work   67

7. In the Army Now   93

8. Duty and Boredom in Germany   129

9. Going to War in Vietnam   153

10. First Combat   181

ALBUM
A Hero's Life   204

11. Moment of Truth at Tam Quan   224

12. Coming Home   258

13. My Family and My PTSD   282

14. Path to Recovery   304

15. Career and Change   328

Epilogue   345

ENDNOTES   351

ACKNOWLEDGMENTS   353

INDEX   359

INTRODUCTION

By Colonel (IL) Jennifer N. Pritzker, IL ARNG (Retired)

W hen I first saw Medal of Honor recipient Al Lynch at drill in the early 1990s, I was a captain and he was a master sergeant with the Brigade S2 Section—Intelligence, 33rd Separate Infantry Brigade of the Illinois National Guard. While Lynch's reputation preceded him, he didn't look or act like a war hero. The fact that he was a master sergeant was prestigious enough for me and my fellow soldiers because we knew how long it took to earn that rank. Commissioned officers listen to master sergeants.

Today, if you meet Al Lynch on the street he comes across as a regular middle-class Illinois guy. You'd never know he was a Medal of Honor recipient and it's not likely he will mention it. And yet, Al Lynch did something so extraordinary that the president of the United States personally gave him the Medal of Honor, the nation's highest military award for valor in combat, during a ceremony at the White House, with his family proudly watching.

The things that people do to become a recipient of the Medal of Honor are the things that the military wants all its people to be able to do. But these individuals somehow take the ordinary and turn it into the extraordinary. That is what Al has done his whole life, including writing this poignant, honest, and insightful book. Al got to live when others never came home from war, and he has dedicated his whole life to serving his fellow veterans, and thus our society as a whole.

The Pritzker Military Museum & Library is dedicated to the exploration of military history and affairs, and it is important that we publish Al Lynch's autobiography so that he can impart his battle- and life-tested wisdom to the rest of us. His story is very important because it is exemplary and accessible. He has struggled, like all of us have, and he has overcome his struggles—like the rest of us can. It is also important for those of us who have not experienced combat, which is mostly everybody, to understand what combat does to people. If we are to have a civilian-controlled government and military, then we all need to understand what we are asking people to do when they serve in the military.

I remember the 1968 riots and how divided the country was at the time. To a certain extent, we remain divided today. In this book, Al writes, "Hell, we didn't like the war any more than they [the protesters] did." It is our hope that this book provides us with a way to reflect on the Vietnam War with the hope of coming to some kind of reconciliation as a society. On a perhaps less grand scale, I hope this book inspires others to live a life of service. And I hope that for those of us who need a helping hand, Al's example inspires the courage to seek that help.

THE MEANING
OF A MEDAL

Sergeant Allen J. Lynch, *U.S. Army, Company D,*
1st Battalion (Airmobile), 12th Cavalry, 1st Cavalry
Division (Airmobile)
Place and date: *Near My An (2), Binh Dinh province,*
Republic of Vietnam, 15 December 1967
Citation:

For conspicuous gallantry and intrepidity in action at the risk of his life above and beyond the call of duty. SGT Lynch (then Spc4.) distinguished himself while serving as a radio telephone operator with Company D. While serving in the forward element on an operation near the village of My An, his unit became heavily engaged with a numerically superior enemy force. Quickly and accurately assessing the situation, SGT Lynch provided his commander with information which subsequently proved essential to the unit's successful actions. Observing 3 wounded comrades lying exposed to enemy fire, SGT Lynch dashed across 50 meters of open ground through a withering hail of enemy fire to administer aid. Reconnoitering a nearby trench for a covered position to protect the wounded from intense hostile fire, he killed 2 enemy soldiers at point blank range.

With the trench cleared, he unhesitatingly returned to the fire-swept area 3 times to carry the wounded men to safety. When his company was forced to withdraw by the superior firepower of the enemy, SGT Lynch remained to aid his comrades at the risk of his life rather than abandon them. Alone, he defended his isolated position for 2 hours against the advancing enemy. Using only his rifle and a grenade, he stopped them just short of his trench, killing 5. Again, disregarding his safety in the face of withering hostile fire, he crossed 70 meters of exposed terrain 5 times to carry his wounded comrades to a more secure area. Once he had assured their comfort and safety, SGT Lynch located the counterattacking friendly company to assist in directing the attack and evacuating the 3 casualties. His gallantry at the risk of his life is in the highest traditions of the military service. SGT Lynch has reflected great credit on himself, the 12th Cavalry, and the U.S. Army.

1SG (Ret) Allen James Lynch was awarded the Medal of Honor by President Richard M. Nixon on 4 May 1970 in a ceremony at the White House.

LIFE IS UNPREDICTABLE. THAT'S WHAT MAKES IT SO FASCINATING. Every life takes twists and turns—some random and beyond our control, others the result of our own decisions. I served out my one-year tour of duty in Vietnam and returned to my hometown of Dolton, Illinois, on June 1, 1968. After a stint at Fort Hood in Texas, I was discharged from the army on April 25, 1969. A day short of one year later, on April 24, 1970, I got word that I was to receive the Medal of Honor. Talk about timing! I was to marry Susan Gronholm, the love of my life, the next day. But that news about the medal did not stop us from our wedding and honeymoon.

I didn't know how to react to being a Medal of Honor recipient. I was proud and shocked. Within weeks of our wedding, I was standing in the White House in Washington, D.C., waiting for President Richard Nixon to put the medal around my neck. It was hard for me to believe what was happening: I was the most average of people, a Midwestern working-class stiff, a grunt in a war in which tens of thousands of guys just like me served honorably and heroically. Over fifty-eight thousand American troops were killed in that conflict and many more died of wounds years after the war. Somehow, I came out of it with the Medal of Honor, which brings to the recipient both great respect and great responsibility. There are only seventy-two living MOH recipients at this writing.

The Medal of Honor represents something greater than myself. It isn't really mine, in fact. I believe that I have a duty to wear it to represent all American service members, especially those killed in action, along with all those who were never recognized for their heroism. The Medal of Honor represents selfless service, sacrifice, honor, and duty. In that sense, it is a symbol of the best of America. It has given me a sense of mission, of involvement, and, most importantly, a deep sense of my responsibility to reflect its values every day.

I never wanted my life to be defined by my service in Vietnam or by the Medal of Honor. I was in Vietnam for just one year. I have lived seventy-one other years. There is no disputing the fact that the MOH altered my life. It made possible a good career that I may not have achieved otherwise. I was asked to become a veterans benefits counselor and eventually I became a veterans advocate. I stayed in those roles for over forty-five years, and spent the last twenty years of my career as chief of the Military and Veterans Bureau within the Illinois Office of the Attorney General.

I've been fortunate, but like so many veterans I have suffered for many years from post-traumatic stress disorder (PTSD). It is a pernicious dragon—not easily defeated. I tried for a long time, not very successfully, to fight stoically through my PTSD symptoms. I had anger, depression, and drinking issues and disturbing intrusive thoughts. Eventually, I came to my senses and sought real help. I put my lovely wife, Susie, and my three children through a lot, but they stuck with me, and I am grateful for their love and devotion.

This book is my attempt to make sense of my life and my journey from bullying victim and ordinary guy trying find his place in the world to honored Medal recipient. How did I get from there to here? I overcame difficulties, which takes mettle—but how? What lessons, if any, might be found in my background or character?

If there is one idea that I want to stress in this autobiography, it is that one must persevere. Perseverance is a good and essential quality. I wrote this book primarily to give hope to people who feel that their lives are meaningless. There are many children who are bullied and who feel that no one understands their shame—the hurt, the pain, the lack of self-worth. Lots of young people feel trapped by situations that appear to have no escape. Lots of adults struggle to cope with the lasting effects of childhood traumas suffered at the hands of bullies, abusive parents, or dysfunctional families.

So many people get a bad start in life and give up on themselves. They've come to conclude that their lives will never improve. I believe I can show that life can be turned in a positive direction. Being bullied in school made me a survivor. It gave me an inner strength that I believe got me through life-or-death combat situations, and later helped me battle PTSD for more than forty years. I persevered. Bad things do happen in life. They are unavoidable. But I have come to see that it is how you deal with them that matters most.

I wrote this book almost completely from memory. I've tried diligently to be accurate, but most of the events and situations are decades old. Memory plays tricks on us, and the older one gets the more tricks it plays. I sought the input of family members, friends, and veterans to ensure the accuracy of episodes, but it is possible that I got some things wrong.

I dreaded writing the battle chapter in this book. Doing so awakened traumatic memories I tried to bury many years ago. I also dreaded it because my memories of what happened on December 15, 1967, don't match some of the material written about the battle on that day—including the account in my Medal of Honor citation. It is probably impossible to recount a battle with anything close to complete accuracy because combat is so chaotic and stressful. Every soldier involved in a battle will have different recollections. The discrepancies troubled me for many years, but I also reviewed and relied upon U.S. Army after-action reports, daily staff journals, and morning reports, along with accounts prepared by other soldiers, most notably the journal of the late Company D commander Donald Orsini and *Summary of Maneuver: Second Battle of Tam Quan* by Tom Kjos, who took part in the firefight at My An.

The Medal of Honor carries with it a tradition of sacrifice, courage, personal honor, and integrity—traits that make up our warrior ethos. Like all those who have received it, I have tried to represent the many soldiers who should have gotten this medal. I haven't always been a perfect citizen, especially in my younger days, but I have never stopped trying to meet the high standards it demands.

CHAPTER 1

MY TEST TIME

W HEN I ARRIVED IN VIETNAM ON MAY 31, 1967, I WAS A twenty-one-year-old replacement infantry soldier, facing a twelve-month combat stint. I was a specialist (fourth class) (Sp4.) and a member of 2nd Platoon, D Company, 1st Battalion, 12th Cavalry, 1st Cavalry Division. Only weeks earlier, I'd been in Germany, working as a platoon clerk/ammo bearer for a 4.2-inch mortar platoon.

My life certainly has been a surprise. If you were to examine my first twenty years, you certainly wouldn't peg me for a guy who would receive America's highest military decoration. Nobody who knew me as a boy or a young man would imagine that I would become a war hero. I was not destined for success.

I grew up in the 1950s, in a working-class family, not far from Chicago. My parents were good, hard-working people, but neither my mother nor my father graduated from high school. My dad was a mechanic and factory man who often worked multiple jobs to keep food on the table. My mother was a diligent, caring homemaker. I was a good kid, thanks to my dad's tough disciplinary standards and my mother's guiding hand. But I had a variety of problems.

I was bullied for years—from third grade through junior high school—which had a profoundly negative effect on my life. I developed a poor self-image, lacked confidence, and became a loner, all of which contributed to mediocre grades. I had a bad attitude in high school and struggled academically. I had few friends and didn't participate in sports or many school events.

I didn't even think about going to college. I assumed I'd work in a factory like my dad, and had a couple of factory jobs after high

 "It's for real over there, Lynch, and unless you change your attitude you won't last a week."

school. But I got fired from one and quit the next and then worked at another until I decided to join the army. Nothing was easy in basic training but I got through it and through advanced infantry training.

I was a middling soldier—competent but not exemplary. I did get into Officer Candidate School, but dropped out, and during a yearlong stint as a Pfc. and a Sp4. in Germany—mostly as a platoon clerk—I reenlisted. But I also got a couple of disciplinary reprimands that reflected my boredom and lack of direction. I was floundering. But the good news—if you can call it that—was that I knew I was floundering.

Then, out of the blue, I got an urge to prove that I could do something more than muddle through my enlistment as an underachiever. I felt like I needed to go and fight. Vietnam was the singular event of my generation and I wanted to be needed, to be involved. So in February 1967, I requested a transfer to the 1st Cavalry Division in Vietnam. I'll never forget my first sergeant's response when I handed him the 1049 (transfer) form. He read it, looked up at me, and said, "You know, it's for real over there, Lynch, and unless you change your attitude you won't last a week."

Several weeks later, I was in a C-130 transport plane making a combat landing at An Khe, Vietnam. I was a Sp4. with Company D, 1st Battalion, 12th Cavalry, 1st Brigade, 1st Cavalry Division. I had gotten my wish—infantry! First, they taught us everything we needed to know about fighting in Vietnam. Then I was in the field for months and tasted real combat.

Operating mostly out of Landing Zone English, a forward base in the Central Highlands, we spent months trying to find and kill the North Vietnamese and Viet Cong in our area. When we couldn't find them, we destroyed their caches of food, weapons, and other supplies. My platoon probably performed more than a hundred search-and-destroy missions. It was harsh duty but I had wanted to test myself.

My real test finally came in December 1967, when my company and other units got into a two-week series of firefights with the North Vietnamese Army's 22nd Regiment. On December 14, a U.S. reconnaissance helicopter spotted what appeared to be a major NVA force near a collection of hamlets known as My An, in an area called the Bong Son Plain, not far from the coast of the South China Sea. Early the next morning, Huey helicopters flew my company into the area with the intention of confronting the 22nd Regiment. The next day, December 15, would be my "come to Jesus" moment.

Along with two other companies from the 1/12 (1st Cavalry), and the 1st Battalion (Mechanized) of the 50th Infantry, we became engaged in fierce battle with elements of the NVA's 22nd Regiment near the village of Tam Quan.

At that time, I was the radiotelephone operator (RTO) for D Company's 2nd Platoon. Not long after we landed, one of our sister companies, C, got hit hard by the NVA. The battalion commander ordered us to relieve C Company by coming up alongside it near

My An. My platoon was working the point as we moved through rice paddies and palm trees toward the enemy's position. Suddenly, we were caught in a fierce blitz of bullets from three sides. One of our point men, Sgt. Irving Wilhelms, got shot not far in front of the platoon leader, Lt. Southerland, and me. Without thinking, I ran out to him, calling for the medic as I ran. Wilhelm told me that Sgt. Javier Casares, the other point man, had been shot in both legs and couldn't move. I remember telling Lt. Southerland that I was going to get Casares and would be right back. I dropped my radio, took my M16, and dashed across an open area. Casares was down in a long trench and I dived into it. That was the beginning of a very long afternoon under fire in no man's land with two wounded troopers.

At some point, someone in my company yelled at me to leave the wounded and get back to our lines. I remember yelling, "F**k you!" Lord knows I wanted to get the hell out of that trench. I wanted with every fiber of my body to run. I wanted to leave the wounded and get back to friendly lines.

But I didn't.

CHAPTER 2

STALWART PARENTS

I WAS BORN IN ROSELAND COMMUNITY HOSPITAL, CHICAGO, Illinois, on October 28, 1945, shortly after the end of World War II. The country was in a happy mood. My parents, LeRoy and Viola Lynch, were in a happy mood, since I was their first child. My sister, Nancy, would be born in 1953. It seems to me both sad and ironic that males born in that year would come of age during the 1960s, when America was involved in yet another brutal conflict

Roseland is an official "community area" of Chicago located on the Far South Side about fourteen miles from downtown. In the late nineteenth century, a lot of skilled tradesmen from Europe came to work at George M. Pullman's factory, in the town of Pullman, Illinois, making luxurious Palace train coaches. Many workers settled in an area near the factory, which became known as Roseland. It's always been an ethnic working-class area with a population of Dutch residents, an Italian neighborhood just east of Michigan Avenue and a little south of where we lived, and Altgeld Gardens on 130th Street, a public housing project originally built for African American veterans returning home from World War II.

There were two major employers in Roseland in the 1940s. One was the Electro-Motive Diesel plant that made locomotive engines, where my dad worked for a short time after he was discharged from the army in 1946. There was also the Sherwin-Williams paint factory. When the wind was blowing in our direction, we could smell the sickening paint fumes. There were also steel mills in the area, including U.S. Steel's South Works plant, as well as Union Carbide and Standard Oil in Whiting, Indiana, just across the state line. My dad would spend some of his happiest times working at Union Carbide in the 1950s and 1960s.

My parents met while roller-skating at a rink in Roseland. Dad asked Mom out, and she said, "If you can remember my telephone number I'll go out with you." He did, she did, and the rest is history. They got married in Roseland on November 8, 1944. My father was twenty-three, my mother twenty-one. Dad was still on active duty and got married in his uniform. He was stationed in Florida, where he served as a dog trainer on an army air corps base. My parents had contrasting personalities—they were yin and yang. Mom was shy, calm, and steady. Dad was outgoing, but could be tough and impetuous. He was a complex man: He could be confident and self-assured but suffered self-esteem issues. He had a hard side but felt personal slights deeply, and he didn't forget them. He had an infectious laugh and loved practical jokes, yet suffered bouts of depression. He had problems with alcohol but never quit trying to control it. There were plenty of rocky times, but my parents pushed through them, stayed together for fifty years, and were happy.

LeRoy James Lynch, my father, was born in Chicago to Laura Trilsch and Alva Lynch on July 18, 1922. He was the youngest of six children—four boys and two girls—in a family that had more than its share of dysfunction. Dad frequently talked about being of Irish descent, and loved to tell a story that we got the name Lynch because a sheriff in Ireland lynched his own son for stealing horses. But that was just family lore. My dad also claimed regularly that another side of the family were descendants of Mary, Queen of Scots, but that was probably a tall tale, too. Neither of my parents had any real connection to the "old sod." We were Americans of European descent, but first and last Americans.

Laura, my grandma, divorced Alva in early 1930 and on December 7, 1931, he died of gangrene. Laura remarried a man named Sytsma—I can't recall his first name—who delivered milk in a horse-drawn cart. He and Laura had one child, Simon. Mr. Sytsma died not long after I was born.

Grandma Sytsma was a Victorian woman, who passed her values on to her children. Whereas Mom's family was quite open about such things as nursing babies and changing diapers, Dad's family was prudish. The women always went to the back room to nurse, closing the door and shuttering the windows. I thought my dad would pass out when, years later, he spotted my wife, Susie, very discreetly breastfeeding one of our children in the living room.

My dad was often left alone for hours when he was young, and throughout his life, and especially as he got older, he hated being alone. Dad told me that when he was a boy, he'd spend hours sitting in the front window of his house, waiting, and sometimes praying, for his mother or a sibling to come home. It makes me sad to think about that. I remember Grandma as something close to a saintly woman, but apparently she was a bit of a "flapper" who liked to go out dancing and socializing and didn't worry much about leaving Dad on his own.

Dad was a man of medium height (five feet ten) and slender build. He was strong, though, and muscular from his years working in factories. During World War II he served in the U.S. Army

Air Corps. However, a chronic health issue, bleeding ulcers, kept him from being sent overseas, so he never saw combat. His air wing fought in Europe and suffered casualties, which left my dad feeling guilty for years about his contribution to the war. He felt that he hadn't done his part.

In the late 1950s, Dad sought treatment for his ulcers. Surgeons at the Hines Veterans Administration Hospital in Cook County, Illinois, removed three-fourths of my father's stomach to help relieve his pain. The operation was a success; he never suffered bleeding ulcers again. Even better, he could eat as much as his stomach would tolerate and never gain an ounce.

When I was growing up, we didn't see much of Dad's family. They were not a close-knit group, and my mom didn't much like their company. That hurt my dad, who always treated my mom's family like his own.

Grandma Sytsma lived at Lake Eliza, Indiana, but most of Dad's brothers and sisters lived in other cities, and for various reasons there were strains among them. For example, Dad's older brother Bob was dishonorably discharged from the U.S. Marine Corps in the late 1930s or early 1940s because of loan sharking. He was an alcoholic and would come in and out of our lives until he died of an alcohol-related illness somewhere in Ohio in the early 1970s. The last time he came to visit us, he beat up his mother and tied her to a chair. He was jailed and we never heard from him again until we were told he was dead. He is buried in a pauper's grave somewhere in northern Ohio. Dad refused to assist with Bob's burial and didn't want to know where he was buried.

Art, the oldest brother, was said to be a successful businessman, but nobody seemed to know exactly what he did. "He's a big shot at some large company," said Dad. He and Art didn't get along. Grandma doted on Art—he was her favorite—and that rankled my dad. Art intimidated my father, maybe because he was a white-collar guy who made more money. When Grandma Sytsma got older, we'd take her to visit Art and his family in Waukesha, Wisconsin. We'd spend a few minutes there and then leave Grandma in Waukesha and drive home.

Dad was closest to his sister Ruth, who lived in Lowell, Indiana. Ruth and her husband, Vail, had several children, a few of whom were adopted. We saw them on holidays, but even that relationship was strained because my mother did not like how Ruth treated Grandma Sytsma. Over the years, we lost contact with Ruth as we did with nearly all of Dad's siblings except for Simon, the youngest. He was a truck driver, married with three children. I liked playing with his kids, but I saw them only rarely. I never had much of a relationship with any of my cousins on Dad's side.

Dad never graduated from high school and felt that some family members looked down on him because of it. To his credit, he earned his GED in 1962, just before turning forty. After working as a rigger and journeyman welder for many years, he started an apprenticeship to become a journeyman machinist for Union Carbide. It took him four years to complete the program; by that time, he was forty-four and I had graduated from high school and was in the army. He was so proud to receive his journeyman's card. It gave him a deep feeling of accomplishment, something to counteract his chronic feelings of inferiority.

My DAD'S MILITARY EXPERIENCE INFLUENCED HIS ROLE AS A parent. Throughout my youth, he woke me up in the morning by whistling "Reveille." He was an advice-giver without equal. He lectured me constantly on morals, individual responsibility, women, work and study habits, education, and just about everything else. Dad was a natural teacher and loved to hold forth on any subject, even those he knew little about. What he lacked in topical expertise he made up for with very confidently expressed opinions. My mother, sister, and I had the same confidence about the world and how folks should handle life's twists and turns. In our own minds, we were a family of experts. The most valuable idea that my father gave me had nothing to do with practical matters. It was about one's basic character—that every man had a responsibility to live honorably. "Life," he said, "can take everything from you—your family, your friends, and your money. But only you give up your honor. Nobody can take that from you. Honor is something you never want to give up." I did not pay much heed to that lesson until later in life, when personal honor became one of my core values.

World War II wasn't the only thing that shaped my father's worldview; he regaled me regularly with stories of the Great Depression. He told me, for example, how Grandma took in sewing and ironing to earn a few extra dollars, and how he would help his stepfather on the milk wagon early in the morning for a couple of hours before school. He also helped his stepfather with odd jobs, such as wiring old houses in Beverly, a suburb of Chicago. All his stories ended with the same lesson about making do with what you have and not wasting anything.

WHEN I WAS A YOUNG BOY, IT WAS MY JOB TO WASH THE DISHES after dinner. Dad often told a story of how he got sick for days in the army because someone on KP forgot to properly wash the mess trays, and the whole company got the "runs." I don't know if the story was true, but the idea of being thorough was drummed into my head. That is why I was, for a long time, Chicago's best dishwasher.

Another idea hammered into me was that children did not challenge or talk back to adults. Adults were right, kids were wrong. It was an ironclad rule in our house, one that I had trouble following. I was punished frequently—and sometimes severely—for questioning the authority of my mother or father. I'd be ordered to sit in a chair facing the wall for a long time or I would get a quick spanking, either a heavy hand or a belt to the backside. My dad believed in the curative effects of corporal punishment. I eventually learned to stop testing my parents, but it took years.

I learned what I could get away with and what I could not. I pushed the envelope by coming home late, being slow to follow a re-

 "Life can take everything from you...but only you can give up your honor."

quest, that kind of thing. Which would prompt Dad or Mom to say, "Shall I get the belt?" To which I always responded, "I'll be good." Their duty was not to be my friend, but to make sure I could survive in the world after I grew up.

Dad had traditional ideas about marriage and the roles of men and women. He used to tell me: "Men provide for their families—it is your responsibility. If you don't provide for your family, you are not a man. Plain and simple!" Men brought home the bacon; women cooked the bacon, raised the children, and took care of the house. We didn't have a lot of money, but I never felt poor. My parents always managed to provide. Dad's favorite metaphor for marriage was a cart being pulled by two horses. The cart is the family and the two horses are the mother and father. I can hear his voice: "The cart can only move straight if both horses pull together. When one horse goes one way and the other goes the other way the cart cannot move or it will fall apart." Mom didn't like being compared to a horse, but Dad was proud to have happened upon such a clever analogy. He viewed my mother as being an equal partner in the marriage—but he was the head of the household. When upset or challenged, he was quick to assert his lead role. When annoyed he'd often say: "I put a roof over your head, food on the table, and clothes on your back." He usually said that to my sister and me, yet there were times when my mother felt the remark was meant for her as well.

A FACTORY AND FIX-IT MAN

My dad was a factory man, one of the many men who help build America's formidable industrial sector during and after World War II. They were guys who worked hard in harsh environments, and could do anything with their hands. When I was a toddler, Dad worked as a laborer at Electro-Motive. He later worked for Union Carbide as a journeyman welder, then as a machinist. Sometime in 1963, Dad's union went on strike against Union Carbide and he found part-time work at Tetco Metal Products in nearby Riverdale, Illinois. Dad was the plant's "can do" man. He fixed machines, hatched timesaving production techniques, and generally improved the efficiency of the plant. When the Union Carbide plant closed in the late 1960s, my dad went into sales, but that didn't last. He then found work as a machinist with Standard Oil. That was his last job before retiring.

My dad could build anything, wire anything, repair anything. He fixed cars for our extended family and friends. He put a new roof on our house on Lake Eliza Road. And he got me involved, at an early age, in his home improvement projects, despite the fact that I wasn't enthusiastic about them. Once he and I laid a new septic field for our house. He supervised while I performed the malodorous labor. Dad wanted me to become as self-reliant as he was and to have the same confidence that he had. He taught me the basic rules of carpentry—"measure twice, cut once"—and how to do maintenance work on cars. He taught me about electricity and how to rewire lights. "Son," he said, "the first rule of electrical work is never let the two wires touch. And never, ever touch the two wires at the same time." I only shocked myself once.

Thanks to my father, I became a self-reliant man. That is the greatest gift he ever gave me. I developed my own can-do attitude and used it to fix up the first house that Susie and I bought in 1973. I could do it all because my dad taught me. He forced me to learn as a kid, whether I liked it or not.

BEER AND THE BIBLE

My dad could be tough and feisty, but he was sensitive about certain things, especially his lack of a formal education. One of my aunts had a way of talking down to him. She'd make fun of his poor spelling or the way he pronounced certain words. She and others in the family thought the jibes were funny, but they cut my father deeply. They didn't notice that he rarely laughed in response to their teasing, and so on it went and he suffered in silence.

But he didn't just fume—he tried to improve himself. That's one of the things I admired about him. Seeking to boost his knowledge, Dad read constantly. He had a mathematical mind and plowed through technical manuals and how-to books. After becoming a Christian, he read several versions of the Bible. He used *Strong's Exhaustive Concordance* to teach himself the meaning of both Greek and Hebrew words. He also liked comic books—until a family member made fun of him for it and he stopped. Sometimes I caught him reading mine. When in his sixties, he even read a book on how to be humble. Like the rigid person he was, Dad thought if he followed the checklist at the end of the book, he'd become more modest. It didn't work.

He wasn't all rough edges. He had a romantic side. He wrote poems for Mom on her birthday and anniversaries. He planned romantic dinners to make her feel special. She beamed every time he prepared a special meal.

Dad, like most postwar blue-collar men, liked to drink. But over time it became a serious problem. After a day at the plant, Dad often stopped at the neighborhood bar before coming home. He'd drink a couple of beers, but that would cause him to drop his social filters. He'd start to get surly and out would come the bitterness. He'd growl about people who'd slighted him in the past. He resented everybody who had ever wronged him. He held grudges for years. He could forgive but never forget.

When we lived in Roseland and Dad wasn't home for dinner, Mom knew where he was. She sent me down the street to the bar to get him. When I walked in the pub, I was always struck by the stench of cigarettes and stale beer. Those smells come back even now when I see a bar. I can still see the haze of cigarette smoke hanging like a shroud. Dad was always in his spot, about halfway down the bar, chatting with friends—typically other fathers from the neighborhood.

At age eight or so, I could have a Coke at the bar with Dad, and nobody cared. It made me feel important. And I liked the fact that the bartender knew his name. My dad knew everybody in the bar. Before we left, Dad would sometimes order a bucket of beer for the road—a real bucket. Beer was drawn from the tap into a little pail that had a metal cover, allowing for easy transport. Dad would drink the beer at home and then bring the pail back to the bar a day or two later for a refill. I remember he loved Schlitz or Old Style.

Mom hated Dad's drinking and it was an issue throughout their marriage. Over the years, his drinking gradually overwhelmed him. But when I was young, it didn't yet seem a problem. He was simply exercising his right as a workingman and breadwinner to have a few beers at the end of a hard day in the factory.

In most situations, Dad knew the right thing to do—what would be the wise decision. But sometimes he just couldn't follow through. He couldn't live up to his own value system. Each time he failed—by having one too many beers, which caused him to start hurling insults or saying hurtful things to my mother—he felt less a man.

Despite his faults, he fought all his life to be respectable. He wanted to be a good husband and father. When I grew older, I could relate to what he went through. Growing up, I was put down and made fun of at times. I later realized that a lot of the verbal digs were not meant to be hurtful. But to a young boy who, like his father, lacked a positive self-image, they hurt, and I had to fight to overcome a lot of issues myself.

Despite his flaws, my dad had a deep and positive influence on me. He was one of the great men I've known in my life. Despite facing a variety of life obstacles, some self-inflicted, he never gave up on himself. He was stalwart. That is what I loved about him.

He died of lung cancer on May 29, 1994, at seventy-two. He was under hospice care at my parent's home in Schererville, Indiana. We were washing him, getting him ready for his last breaths. He always had a fear of being put in a nursing home, and at one point he regained consciousness and looked at me, and said, accusingly, "You're going to put me in a home." I told him, "My dad wouldn't say that." He replied, "Oh, yes, he would." Those were the last words he ever said to me. He went back to sleep and never woke up, passing away later with his family gathered around his bed, saying prayers.

MOTHER'S QUIET STRENGTH

My mother, Viola Van Heel, came from a poor family of Dutch descent. She was one of seven children born to Harry and Alida Van Heel. Mom was born on June 7, 1924, but I don't know where. She often spoke about her family being descendants of Dutch Huguenots. She said she had relatives in upstate New York, but that was as far as it went. Harry Van Heel, whom I knew as Grandpa Van Heel, was a tall, balding man who rarely smiled. He was well-read and was idolized by his children. They considered him an expert on almost every subject. That wasn't the case. He knew a lot about the things he cared about, such as socialism and unionism, and little about topics that held less interest for him, like religion. I grew up listening to family discussions on everything from politics to religion to baseball, and they helped me learn how to argue effectively. Grandpa was at the center of every discussion. His opinion was valued and accepted, even when his reasoning was suspect.

Grandma Van Heel was a short, stocky woman who was gentle and kind. She loved her family and her grandchildren, and saw the good in most everyone. In the 1950s, I remember her and Grandpa taking clothes and food to the poor. She was an amazing cook and passed those skills on to her three daughters. Harry and Alida both died in the 1980s.

My mom was fairly tall, five eight, and had dark brown hair. One might think that her height would have given her a certain confidence, but she was very shy around people outside of our family. She was self-conscious and very self-contained. She wasn't stiff or without humor, but there was a reserved dignity about her.

Mom was no shrinking violet around our family. She was strong and assertive, and said what was on her mind. She had a sharp tongue. She didn't often use it, but when she did it could cut. She'd zing me regularly when I said or did something that bothered her.

In many ways, my mother was a typical 1950s housewife—meaning that she was caring, generous, and diligent. While Dad was busy "putting food on the table," Mom stayed home and took care of my sister and me. Stay-at-home moms are often ridiculed for having it easy, but, in my opinion, they do an extraordinary amount of work.

 I grew up listening to family discussions on everything from politics to religion to baseball.

Being a housewife and mother is a tough job. Mom bought groceries, cooked, and cleaned. She made sure we did our homework and our chores every day. Besides the practical duties she faced, Mom served as role model and mentor for my sister and me. She taught us to be obedient and honest.

What's remarkable about my mom was that, like Dad, she had a chronic health problem. She suffered from severe migraine headaches for most of her life. The headaches would keep her in bed in the dark for hours or days at a time. Yet, somehow, she almost always managed to make dinner and get everything else done. I, too, had migraines for years and know a little about how she suffered. Even today, it amazes me that she was able to do anything during those times when she felt bad.

Mom, like her parents, was a giver. She was the one of the kindest people I've ever known. When Mom made friends, they were her friends for life, and she'd go the extra mile to maintain good relations with anyone she cared even remotely about. In her later years, when some of her siblings had drifted away and failed to stay in touch, she would get in her car and visit them. Visitors to our home were always offered coffee (the family drink) or some other beverage. And if a visit went on, she'd offer a snack, lunch, or dinner. Nobody left hungry.

She had a knack for accepting people as they were without judging them. One of her great friends was a Spiritualist who was always getting involved with the wrong type of man. Mom, a devout Christian, never judged her and was always there for her when the woman's latest relationship ended. Where my father was judgmental, a trait he passed on to me, she was accepting. She was a very moral woman, but she respected people with all of their frailties and failings. I loved her for her open spirit. "It's not my place to judge other people," she would say. "That's the Lord's work."

On a couple of occasions, my mother took jobs to help pay bills. Not long after I was born and we were living in Chicago, she worked on a production line in a cookie factory. She didn't make much money, but from my perspective, she had the best job in the world. When my dad and I picked her up from work, I could breathe in the wonderful aroma of chocolate and baked cookies blocks before we got to the plant. Her company couldn't sell broken cookies, so Mom and her fellow workers got to take the "defective" treats home. Lucky me. I learned immediately that broken cookies tasted every bit as good as whole ones. That started my addiction to cookies and milk at bedtime—a habit that I still have.

While Dad was the "hands on" enforcer of family rules, Mom was the steady, less emotional family disciplinarian. If I cursed, she'd wash my mouth out with soap. And she wasn't shy about putting a little fear in me, if necessary, to change my attitude. When I misbehaved, her typical response was, "Wait until your father gets home." It was code for: "I'm going to tell him what you did, and he is going to spank you." Growing up, I heard that phrase a lot, and it never failed to strike terror in me and spark an immediate improvement in my behavior.

My mom was a phenomenal cook. Her specialties were pot roast, meatloaf, chicken and dumplings, and pigs in a blanket—one of my all-time favorites. It was truly comfort food, and just thinking about her meals brings back comforting memories—and makes me ravenous! She made the best apple pie, along with a variety of fried pies (dessert pastries) that were delicious.

Like many people raised during hard times, she could economize. She knew how to stretch a meal. Sunday's chicken dinner became Monday's casserole and Tuesday's soup. Our leftovers never seemed like leftovers, however, because Mom, with a few extra ingredients and a little kitchen magic, could turn them into a different meal.

Nothing was wasted in the Lynch household. Being children of the Great Depression, Mom and Dad knew what it meant to go without, as the expression went, to not know when the next meal was coming. I was raised with stories of "depression soup" (throwing anything left over from the week's meals into a pot and heating it up) and "depression bread" made with flour, yeast, and water.

My mother was a compulsive cleaner. She did not like the house being dirty or things out of place. In their later years, after my sister and I had moved out and were raising our own families, Dad would often have lunch in the TV room. During a commercial break, he'd get up and leave the room for a couple of minutes. When he returned, his lunch would be gone. Mom had put his sandwich and Coke in the refrigerator and the chips back in their bag.

MOM WAS DEVOTED TO HER FAMILY. EARLY IN MY LIFE, WE LIVED close to her parents and siblings, and we saw them a lot. They often came to visit us on weekends. Even when we lived in Indiana, and they in Illinois, we visited. Vacations were always with one or more uncles and aunts. She loved them as much as she loved us. Even when some of her closest family members treated her badly, she would make excuses for them; it was just her loving way.

As a boy, I sometimes decided that she loved her parents and siblings more than she did me. It wasn't true—but occasionally, when she was frustrated with me, she'd ask: "Why can't you be more like...?" and then name one of my uncles or cousins. The name she picked depended on the circumstances. If I got a bad grade on a test, she'd mention my aunt who was about a year and a half older than I was and who was a good student. Or if I'd misbehaved in some other way, she'd mention an uncle who never seemed to put a foot wrong. As I grew up, I frustrated my parents in more than a few ways. I didn't have a lot of friends, I was bullied for years, and my grades were poor. All of which drove them to distraction. So in a way, I understood my mom's wishing I were more like some of the well-adjusted people in her family.

Mom was a pacifist. When I was bullied in grade school and junior high, she convinced me not to get into fights. She worried that if I hit someone, I could hurt him. She always said, "What if you knock his eye out? How would you feel then?"

ANSWERING THE CALL

My mom's charitable nature showed in times of crisis. In the early 1980s, when my parents were living in Dolton, Susie's mother, Mary, broke her wrist. She suffered from rheumatoid arthritis, and the wrist injury caused her arthritis pain to become acute. Mary's condition worsened and eventually became debilitating. It was slowly killing her. Mom came to Mary's aid. Several times a week, she drove a few miles to neighboring Riverdale, where Mary lived, to give her a hand. She cooked meals for her, cleaned Mary's house, and helped her with daily needs. Toward the end, when Mary could no longer feed herself, Mom not only prepared meals but fed her as well. She was happy to help.

She stuck with my dad through some rough times. Many women would have divorced a man who drank too much and was often depressed, but she stayed with him and loved him with all his faults. It was never easy for her; she endured a lot. But she never gave up on him. My father smoked a pack or two of cigarettes a day for most of his adult life and was sick with lung cancer in the months before he passed. During that time, Mom was the only person he felt he could rely on for help. She answered every call. She fed him, helped him to the bathroom, and sat with him all day and night. During Dad's last months, Mom rarely left the house. When he passed away, she walked to a maple tree we planted in her yard and breathed a deep sigh of relief. After months of strain, her body finally relaxed. "I can walk out to the tree and not worry that I'll miss his call," she said. Mom was the strongest woman I've ever known, and a wonderful example of sacrifice and love.

One day in January 1997, about two and half years after my dad's death, I got a phone call while I was working in the Illinois attorney general's office. I'll never forget it. It was Mom, and she told me that if something happened to her we should just let her go. I thought it was a weird call, and told her I'd call her again when I got home. But as soon as I walked into the house, my sister called and said, "Mom's had a massive stroke!" My wife, Susie, and I got in the car and headed to the hospital in Schererville, Indiana, where Mom had been taken. A doctor there updated us on her condition. It didn't look good. He said he could save her life but there would be debilitating effects from the stroke. For one thing, she probably wouldn't be able to speak again. Or, he added, we could "just let her go." At that moment, I remembered Mom's words from earlier in the day—how eerie—telling me to do just that.

But my sister and I weren't ready to let her go. We chose life, and it was a mistake. Mom lived another ten months, but never regained her ability to speak or communicate. For decades, Mom had dyed her hair light brown; it was the only color I knew. After her stroke, her hair came back to its natural dark brown and gray. I was stunned by the fact that she suddenly had gray hair. I visited her every weekend at the nursing home, and each time I couldn't help recalling her last request to "just let me go." I wish I had. She died November 8, 1997.

My parents had their individual faults and their difficulties, but they also had one of the strongest loves I've ever seen. Dad's love for Mom was unfailing, and she was his rock. They couldn't imagine being apart from each other. Each taught me essential life lessons that I carry with me every day. They were the greatest influences on my life.

CHAPTER 3

GOOD TIMES IN ROSELAND

WHEN MY DAD WAS DISCHARGED FROM THE ARMY IN 1946, the three of us lived in a two-story apartment building on East 111th Street in Roseland, on the edge of Chicago. East 111th is a very busy street, about half a block from the Illinois Central Railroad commuter stop, which locals call the IC. I didn't see much of 111th Street, but I know it had mom-and-pop stores and a streetcar line that my mom took to visit her mother, who also lived in Roseland. My first friend when I was a kid was Gary Struck, whose family lived in an apartment above ours. He and I were the same age and we spent a lot of time outside playing with trucks and army men in the backyard. The yard was small and mostly dirt, and when it rained, we got muddy. Like me at that time, Gary was an only child and very possessive of his toys. If we were playing and he had go to the bathroom or go up to his apartment for lunch, he always took all his toys with him—all of them. I don't remember much else about him. I met him again many years later at a family reunion. We both laughed at how we'd aged and put on weight.

My mom and Mrs. Struck often did laundry together while Gary and I played. Doing laundry in the late 1940s and early 1950s was a lot different from today. Women used a washtub with an agitator that churned the dirty clothes in hot water. It had an automatic wringer into which Mom fed the clothes once they were washed. Washing one load of clothes was a laborious multi-stage process that took at least an hour before the clothes were ready to be taken outside and hung on a clothesline to dry. In those days many homes were heated by coal furnaces. Factories also used coal to make steel and to heat the plants so there was a lot of coal dust in the air. Even clean white clothes looked dingy. I remember Mom occasionally washing clothes a second time, not wanting her "whites" to look smudged.

In Roseland, going "up the Ave." was a big part of our culture. It meant getting to Michigan Avenue, which was the area's hub for shopping, movies, dining, and dancing. One of our favorite places to shop for clothing and household items on South Michigan Ave. was Gatelys Peoples Store, which was founded in 1917. We called it Peoples Store; the company called it "the biggest store on Michigan Avenue." While Mom and Dad shopped upstairs at Gatelys, I'd go to the store's lower level to watch donuts being made. I loved the sight of formed dough floating through a river of hot oil on its way to becoming a finished donut. I watched as one side of the donut would get browned in the oil, then the donut would be flipped so that the other side could be cooked. To see the sweet treat getting made was spellbinding. If I was a good boy and hadn't moved from my seat by the time my parents had finished shopping, Dad would buy me a donut and a glass of milk.

Peoples Store was the site of my first public spanking. One day, when I was about five, I was running in and out of the clothes racks, hiding from my parents. The racks were circular, so the middle of the rack was a perfect place to hide. I thought I wasn't being seen as I dodged from one rack to the other. Then, suddenly, my right arm was jerked in the air and in one motion, Dad swatted me on the behind and sat me in a chair. "You sit here and DON'T YOU MOVE!" he said. I did as instructed. I sat...and sat...and sat. I sat there for a long time. Eventually Dad came back to get me. I didn't find out until I was an adult that my parents had forgotten me and gone to another store before remembering that I was still sitting in Peoples Store. The original Gatelys in Roseland closed in 1981, and the chain went out of business in 1994.

When I was four or five years old, we moved down the street several blocks, to 123 West 111th Place. Like our first apartment building, it was a wooden, two-story walk-up, but west of Michigan Avenue. The building had two front doors: One led to our apartment on the ground level, the other was the entrance to the upstairs apartment, where a very nice older couple lived. There was a gangway on the side of the house and a garage facing the alley. But we didn't have a car to put in it. Our kitchen was off the back porch, and there was a huge pantry just off the kitchen. Our front window looked out on 111th Place, which was a residential street.

I was always sick in October and November. I had a lung issue of some kind and would get bronchitis or whooping cough almost every fall. It may have had something to do with the dust from the coal furnace. Lung problems continued to plague me all my life. I am often sick, still, on my birthday. Some years when friends and relatives came to the house to celebrate my birthday, I was confined to my room. My mom would carry me out to the living room for a few minutes to say hello to everybody, and maybe open some gifts, and then lug me back to the bedroom. I contracted pneumonia three times while in grade school and missed a lot of classes.

The upstairs neighbors in our second Roseland apartment were much older than Mom and Dad. The lady was short and plump and wore her gray hair in a bun. I have a vague memory of her infectious smile—and a better memory of the cookies she offered me every time she and Mom visited each other. Mom would have coffee with her in the mornings. I could always smell her cookies when she was baking them above us. I remember nothing about her husband, probably because he didn't make cookies.

Our next-door neighbor was a very skinny World War II veteran named Herby, who lived with his mother. He was said to be "loony" and still fighting the war. Occasionally, he would go into his backyard and dig a foxhole. He yelled at all hours of the night and sometimes he'd walk around brandishing a long bayonet. The police were often called to settle him down. Then one day he was gone. The adults whispered that he suffered from "shell-shock" and had been bundled off to the "nut house." I never saw him again. When he was rational Herby was a nice man. But when he was acting out he was very scary to a young kid.

Our apartment was spacious, with a big front living room, a dining room, a large kitchen, and three bedrooms. There were also two porches, one in the front and one in the back where I played when it was raining. One of the worst spankings I ever got was when I took it upon myself, at age five, to paint the back porch. I made a mess, and my dad was not happy.

I had my own room in the front of the house. It was small but cozy. My bedroom was under the steps leading to the upstairs apartment, and I'd often be awakened by the sound of the couple coming home at night and tromping up the stairs. The sound scared me until I got used to it.

Soon after we moved into the new apartment, Dad asked me to memorize our address and telephone number. He made me say it over and over again, until it was embedded in my head. I recall Dad telling me, "If you get lost, just go to a policeman or an adult and tell him your address. He'll get you home." It was a time of innocence—a time when adults, for the most part, could be trusted. I don't recall ever getting lost.

SCHOOL DAYS

I started kindergarten at age five. I walked with my friends about five blocks to Van Vlissingen Elementary School at 109th Street and South Wentworth. The school is still there but is now the Lavizzo Elementary School. It looked like a castle, with large rooms lit by naked light bulbs hanging from the high ceilings. Kindergarten was half a day. I have little memory of it except that my kindergarten teacher was very kind but strict, and we got warm milk and cookies in the late morning. Cookies always made an impression on me.

First grade was much longer than kindergarten; it marked the start of a full day at school. There were classes, then morning recess, then another class, and then lunch, which I brought from home either in a brown paper bag or in a lunch box with an image of Gene Autry on it. He had a TV show at the time that was popular with kids. Other kids had lunch boxes featuring Roy Rogers or Captain Video and His Video Rangers—both also on TV. My mom often filled a thermos with soup and put it in the lunch box with my favorite sandwich, peanut butter and jelly. The school supplied the milk.

Sometimes I walked home for lunch, which I enjoyed. I typically ate a peanut butter and jelly sandwich with a cold glass of milk, then watched either *Uncle Johnny Coons* or *Two Ton Baker, The Music Maker*—two popular TV shows—before heading back to school. After lunch there was a play period, then another class or two, then afternoon recess, then the final period before the bell rang that ended the school day.

Back at home, I played before and after dinner, until the street lights came on. That was the nightly signal that it was time to get ready for bed. Mom gave me a bath almost every night. We had a huge tub—it was white and very deep and my favorite place in the house. After a long day of school and play, I always welcomed my evening bath. Mom would put me in the water with my toy ships and men, and I'd soak and play for a while. Imagination is a wonderful thing. It took me to any place I wanted and let me do great

 One day I came home from school and noticed that my panda was gone.

things. My ships, men, and I had many nautical adventures in the choppy waters of my massive tub. After a while, Mom would come in, give me a good washing, and put me to bed. My baths are one the best memories of that apartment.

I got very sick in the first grade, and once stayed home in bed for a few weeks. I eventually missed so much school that I was held back and had to repeat the grade. I got to watch a little TV when I was sick, and Dad comforted me with stories about cowboys and Indians and his army experiences. Sometimes we played out his tales with my toys. When I was alone I played army on my bed by making mountains and valleys with my pillows and blankets. Great battles were fought. Some days, I was a great military commander; other days, a courageous Indian fighter.

My favorite toy was a big stuffed panda bear that Mom and Dad bought for me one time when I was sick. I don't remember what I called him, but I played with him during my days in bed and sometimes used him as part of the terrain for my battles. We had many adventures and he became my best friend. One day I came home from school and noticed that my panda was gone. Without asking or telling me, Mom and Dad had decided to get rid of it. I can't remember the reason they gave me, but it was painful to lose my bear. I still hold fond memories of him. There is an episode of *The Simpsons* in which old Mr. Burns longs for his lost teddy bear, Bobo. How true! At age seventy, I still miss my friend, the stuffed panda bear. We had such good times together, wrestling and playing like Calvin and Hobbes.

WONDER YEARS

My early years in Roseland were happy times, especially on weekends. My friends and I would roam the neighborhood on foot or on bikes. We explored and played games. I can still remember the laughter of my friends when we played "Kick the Can," "Red Light, Green Light," and "Hide and Seek," along with games we made up. We sometimes rode our bikes across 111th Street to the penny candy store. For a quarter we could fill our pockets with candy.

One of the neighbors had a Doberman pinscher that was often outside and barked wildly at passersby. He scared us, especially after we heard that he'd once eaten a rabbit in one bite. We always felt a surge of danger and excitement when we rode our bikes at top speed past his house and managed to get away without injury. It was thrilling.

One day, my friends and I decided that each of us must test his bravery by walking past the dog's house...alone. And we each did it. I vaguely recall being very nervous and walking quickly and not looking at the dog or his house. No one was attacked. Then one day all the drama ended. The lady who owned the dog introduced him to us, and we all became friendly with him. Soon we were petting and playing with him regularly. He proved to be, as the saying goes, all bark and no bite.

Because mothers were usually at home, we all played under their unseen eyes. No matter where we were, we knew that somebody's mom—or "old lady"—was watching us. For that reason, we rarely got into trouble. At the first hint of mischief, an anonymous mom, hidden from view in the urban landscape, would yell from a window, "Hey, what are you kids doing?" And we knew then that our moms would receive an update on our activities before we got home via the neighborhood network. The mom network was efficient!

We rode bicycles a lot. In those days nobody wore helmets because they didn't exist. There was no protection of any kind. Skinned knees and hands were common and treated with iodine or alcohol and a bandage, and then it was back on the bike. Sometimes, someone would get more seriously hurt—break a bone, maybe. It was all to be expected and just part of growing up—a child's "rite of passage."

I remember my dad telling me as he applied iodine, "Don't cry. Men don't cry." I always tried to tough it out but sometimes the iodine stung so much that a little yelp or tear would escape. When that happened, I always felt like I'd let my dad down and didn't measure up to his standards.

OUT AND ABOUT

We had few luxuries and personal distractions in the 1940s and 1950s. It was a simpler time. We didn't have a car. When we traveled, it was either on foot or by public transportation. Dad took a bus to and from his factory job. Mom took the bus, the IC, or the streetcar to visit her family. But mostly we walked everywhere. We knew our neighbors and spent time with them regularly, not only our next-door neighbors but people up and down the block.

There was no air conditioning. During the summer, we opened windows, or we sat on the porch to keep cool or took walks. Often, we'd walk several blocks from our house to Western Avenue to get ice cream. Dad usually let me get a three-scoop rainbow cone, with red, blue, and orange-colored ice cream. My other three-scoop favorite was chocolate, vanilla, and either strawberry or another chocolate scoop on top. As we walked home, I hurriedly lapped up the ice cream before it melted. Along the way we would stop and chat with people sitting on their porches—sometimes, people we didn't know. They'd offer us a glass of lemonade or cold water, and we'd accept. Everything was more communal—that's the way we lived.

America was in the "postwar period." A sort of quiet euphoria coursed through the nation following our triumph over, first, the Great Depression of the 1930s and then the Germans and the Japanese. My dad and my uncles Jack and Dick, on my mother's side, all served during the war but none saw combat. Jack, one of my favorite uncles when I was growing up, took part in the atomic testing at Bikini Atoll. He was aboard the USS *Panamint* in the Pacific Ocean. Years later, he claimed to have seen his bones during the blast. He got cancer and died in 2015. He was convinced it was caused by radiation from the atomic bomb.

There were some problems in the country. Veterans struggled to find jobs or housing, and schools were overcrowded. But the economy was booming, and there was a general feeling that Americans were special people who held a special place in the world. The future seemed bright. Our family was employed, we had a little bit of money, and the horror of war and the miseries of the Depression were behind us. I grew up hearing stories of rationing and financial hardships, but my parents' generation did its part and persevered.

CHAPTER 4

ELI'S TRAILER CAMP

IN THE SPRING OF 1951 WHEN I WAS SIX, MY FAMILY MOVED TO Eli's Trailer Camp in Homewood, Illinois. It was to be our home for about two years. Homewood is a suburb of Chicago, about sixteen miles from Roseland. Like Roseland, the Homewood trailer park was a close-knit community. But it didn't have the access to stores we had in Roseland so we had to drive to town to go shopping.

We moved to Eli's Trailer Camp for several reasons. According to Mom, it was because Dad's favorite bar was just a block away from where we lived in Roseland and Dad visited it too often in Mom's opinion. According to Dad, it was to move a little farther away from Mom's family. I was sad to leave my friends but Grandma and Grandpa Van Heel moved into our old apartment. So whenever we visited I got to see my friends.

At that time, Harry Truman was nearing the end of his presidency, and the United States was involved in two new conflicts. One was the Korean War, which was a lot nastier than most people remember, and the other was America's Cold War with the Soviet Union. With its threat of mutual nuclear annihilation, the Cold War was a sort of U.S.–U.S.S.R. stare-down. For big thinkers and makers of foreign policy, it was an uncertain time, but nobody we knew talked much about Korea or Russia or nuclear war. Families were busy chasing the American dream—working, making money, having kids, trying to get ahead. Everyone wanted to forget about war. My dad was working as a rigger for Union Carbide in Whiting, Indiana; Mom was taking care of me and soon to be pregnant with my sister. Life seemed fairly good. America was the best country in the world, and this was our time.

NEW DIGS

Looking back, the move to a small, rented trailer was inconvenient. I didn't have my own room anymore, but I didn't view it as a hardship. I was just a kid following my parents, so I rolled with the new lifestyle and the new location. For me, it was just another adventure.

Our trailer had only two rooms, a combination living area and kitchen and a bedroom. It had a very small bathroom, but we couldn't really use it because there was no "dumping station" for waste in the park. The camp had a communal toilet with showers and that's what we used. Several times a week, Mom, Dad, and I walked there with our towels for a shower. Dad and I would enter one side of the building and Mom went in the other side. On each side, there were several open showers with no privacy, and stalls for each commode. When it was time for bed, one of my parents escorted me to the communal toilet and that was it until morning.

My uncle Dick (my mother's brother) and his wife, Jay, also lived at Eli's Trailer Camp with their children, Ricky and Debbie. Their trailer was located nearby. Uncle Dick had a white-collar job at Electro-Motive and they had a bigger, better trailer than ours. He opened a Tastee Freeze in Chicago Heights, where I got free frozen custard. I didn't play much with my cousins because they were quite a bit younger.

Going to bed in our new home was, for me, a two-stage process. My bed was a pullout sofa in the living area, but because my parents stayed up later than me and needed the sofa for sitting, I always fell asleep in Mom and Dad's bed. Later, when my parents were ready to sleep, they'd pull out the sofa bed, put the linens on it, and then Dad would carry me out to the living room. Most of the time, I did not wake up.

I did wake up every morning at 5:30 because that's the time my dad got up to get ready for work. When Dad got up, everyone got up. Mom made his breakfast, usually bacon and eggs, before he walked to the park entrance to meet his buddy for the ride to his job. Even

 We did duck-and-cover drills throughout my school years. I was never afraid.

on weekends, he got up at 5:30. It was his lifelong habit and became my habit as well. I didn't like getting up before the crack of dawn but got used to it, and I ate a lot of good breakfasts. To me, there is no better breakfast than bacon and eggs—unless it's steak and eggs.

I attended second grade and part of third grade at the Homewood Elementary School. My friends and I walked about a mile to the school. We could have taken a bus, but we liked to walk. I wore my yellow rain suit on stormy days. It was a long trench coat–like jacket with a broad-brimmed rain hat. I also wore galoshes. In the winter, I wore a heavy coat and galoshes plus a winter hat and gloves.

While nobody we knew was worried about the possibility of nuclear war, the government and the school districts believed that vigilance was needed. At school, we were shown movies that explained the potential horrors of atomic blasts and that demonstrated how citizens should "duck and cover" should one occur. We did duck-and-cover drills throughout my school years. I was never afraid; I don't think anyone was. I don't know why anyone thought that ducking would offer protection from an atomic explosion.

I hate to admit it, but I was bored by school. Recess was the only part of the school day that I liked. During class, I often stared out the window and daydreamed. Sometimes I got so lost in my reveries that I leapt from my seat when the teacher called on me to answer a question. I mumbled a response, usually wrong, and was soon daydreaming again.

ADVENTURES

Eli's Trailer Camp was a huge playground for me. I had a lot of friends, and there were many good places near the camp to hang out in and play. There was a creek, a swimming pond, and a real playground near the trailer park office. Sometimes, we'd venture to the other side of a busy street that bordered the park, where there was a cemetery, woods, and a horseracing track. During the racing season hobos, or "bums" as we called them, got work at the track and made a "bum town" of small tents, cardboard boxes, and such. I think the police and the Izaak Walton League, which owned the area, turned a blind eye to it because the track needed the workers. But to us kids it held adventure. We were warned about Bum Town, which only made us want to explore it more.

One day we did the unthinkable—we crossed the busy street and went into the woods. We were looking for Bum Town and we found it. It was hard to miss since there were cardboard houses, tents, fire pits, and clotheslines with newly washed clothes hung on them. Did we dare walk into the town? We were afraid but the lure of adventure pulled us in. Then we heard someone talking and suddenly the stories of kids who got caught in Bum Town—told by our parents to scare us—leaped to mind. We ran and we didn't stop running until we got to the busy road and then got back home. Never again did we cross that road.

The creek was one of our favorite places to play. People dumped old stuff in it like broken furniture, appliances, and cardboard boxes. Other people's junk became our forts, boats, and anything else we could imagine. A big tree had fallen down near the creek, exposing thick roots and a stump several feet in diameter. For us it became a great rocket ship, or an airplane, or a tank, depending on what mock adventure we had conjured up on a particular day.

When we weren't outside, we'd watch television. Television was still new in those days. It was stimulating but not addictive—maybe because there were only two or three networks. A lot of the children's programing seemed to feature good guys fighting bad guys, and we learned that the good guys always won—but never before there was a climactic fistfight or gun battle. We learned about the American West through programs featuring the Cisco Kid, Gene Autry, and Roy Rogers and Dale Evans. We also watched *Captain Video and His Video Rangers*—a live broadcast with very cheesy acting and storylines. The captain and his rangers fought evil across the planet. Of course, there was an evil scientistwho wanted to rule the world.

Every TV show stoked our imaginations, and afterward my friends and I would dash outside to play, brimming with energy and ideas about characters we could pretend to be—pirates, bandits, space aliens, or soldiers fighting Nazis and "Japs" (a term commonly used in the 1950s). Every day was an opportunity for new feats of daring and new conquests by the brave young heroes of Eli's Trailer Camp—and with our big tree stump serving as an all-purpose super vehicle, we could go anywhere and do anything.

LASH LARUE I'M NOT

Our imaginary adventures occasionally created real-life problems. One day I watched a cowboy show in which the hero used a whip. Soon my friends and I were carrying "whips"—whatever long, thin, flexible ropes or cords we could find. Mine was an extension cord with the ends cut off. We whipped everything—lampposts, trees, and anything else that caught our fancy. We placed a bunch of bottles and cans on the stump and had a contest to see if we could whip them off, one at a time.

I decided to kick things up a notch. One day at the creek, as one of my friends got on his bike and started to ride away, I let my whip fly. The cord went around his neck, and I, acting like Lash LaRue (star of Western movies and "king of the bullwhip"), gave it a sharp tug. The cord yanked my friend off his bike and he fell to the ground. He started crying. When I got to him, there was a bright red mark around his neck and glistening drops of blood were starting to leak out of the wound. Still crying, he hopped back on his bike and pedaled for home. Oblivious to the trauma I'd caused to my friend, I went back to playing. I had no idea that I'd screwed up.

A short time later, I heard my dad yell my name. That wasn't unusual. Dad always yelled when it was time for me to go home. But that day, I detected something different about his tone. There was more urgency in his voice than normal. I ran home as fast as I could and just as I rounded one of the trailers, I saw my friend with his dad, talking to my dad. Uh-oh. I got a sick feeling in my stomach. As soon as Dad saw me, his face contorted into a look of controlled rage. I can still see it.

When I walked up to the group, my friend's father told me to look at his son's neck. It was bandaged but the boy's father slowly took the dressing off so I could see my handiwork. The red mark had grown from a small red line into a huge red welt, with gloppy areas where blood had oozed out. Dad told me to apologize, which I did, and my friend forgave me. But I wasn't relieved; something told me that my reckoning for being reckless with my whip was not over. Dad looked at the boy's father and told him I would receive proper punishment for my crime.

I knew what that meant. As my friend and his father walked away, Dad grabbed me, sat down on a picnic bench just outside the front door of our trailer, put me over his knee, and gave me a serious spanking. The jeans I was wearing were stretched tightly across my butt, so that when Dad's hand hit my backside it made a sound like a rifle shot—crack! crack! *crack*! On and on the spanking went. The noise—the spanking plus my blubbering—prompted people to pop out of their trailers to see what was happening.

Today, if any father were to spank a child that severely in public, the police would probably be called. But sixty years ago corporal punishment—spanking—was a very common method of disciplining wayward young people. So no one rescued me. And my punishment wasn't over when the spanking was done. I was grounded for a week and had to work for both Mom and Dad. Mom, who was usually my champion, showed no mercy. It was a tough punishment, but I learned to think before acting. In the future, of course, I continued to make mistakes, lots of them—but none involved the use of a whip.

I'm old school, and I often wonder if today's kids are disciplined enough. I've seen countless incidents in which children speak disrespectfully to their parents. I see kids making demands and parents almost afraid to say no. When we were growing up, nobody my age was coddled. Quite the opposite. I realize that I'm generalizing—the classic "things were different in my day" comment.

VACATION TIME

During our first summer at Eli's Trailer Camp, we took the first of what would be many vacations to Lake Saint Germain in northern Wisconsin. That lake and a neighboring lake would be our vacation area until I left for the army. It was a time for fishing, long walks down wooded trails, and horseback riding—but most of all fishing.

We had a travel routine. We always left very early in the morning, when it was still dark. Dad packed the car the night before our departure, and fixed a makeshift bed in the back seat. When it was time to leave, Dad carried me out to the car and placed me gently in the back seat. Even now, whenever I drive a long distance, I leave very early, when it is still dark outside, just as we did when I was a boy.

There were no superhighways or toll roads, so our trips were rather slow. The drive from Illinois to northern Wisconsin usually took at least ten hours. Sometimes I woke up and looked out the window as we passed through darkened towns. All I could see, if anything, were streetlights. Then it was back to sleep. I remember sometimes waking up alone in the car; Dad had stopped at an all-night diner, and he and Mom would be inside drinking coffee and eating pie. I would walk in the restaurant and join them, and they'd buy me a piece of pie and a glass of milk. Then we'd get back on the road. When the sun started to rise, we'd stop again and I would switch places with Mom. She'd get in the back seat and sleep and I'd sit in the front seat and talk with Dad. I felt so big at those moments: Just me and Dad, talking.

Vacations were a thrill for me. We stayed at a resort with lots of cabins and kids to play with. In the early morning, before daylight, Dad and I would quietly gather our gear and take a boat to go fishing. He'd start the outboard motor and off we'd go. Around 7 or 8, we would go back to the cabin for breakfast. Then I'd stay and play, and he'd go back out fishing. Sometimes at night we'd walk down to the lake and fish off the long wooden pier. Dad also taught me how to row a boat, and I could go fishing or just exploring by myself.

We took long drives in the country to see deer. But the most exciting part was going to the dump to see bears. Each vacation lasted a week, but as Dad gained seniority at work, he earned more vacation and our trips grew from one week to two. I remember them fondly.

I'M NOT NUMBER 1 ANYMORE

The summer of 1953 was a busy time. My sister, Nancy, was born in July and suddenly our lives were different. At age seven, I was no longer the only child. It was a bit of a shock, really. I no longer got all the parental attention. My new sister did. I must be honest and say that I didn't like the change. I resented Nancy because my parents were totally focused on taking care of her, and because she was an adorable, special baby! And it wasn't just my parents; everyone doted on her. When relatives came to visit, I was no longer the big man. I was just the other kid, taking up space. It wasn't long before I started to ignore Nancy.

CHAPTER 5

LAKE ELIZA: GROWING UP BULLIED

OVER TIME, I CAME TO SEE THAT DAD HAD STRONG BELIEFS about the roles of boys and girls: Boys are raised by moms until they are ready to work outside and learn manly skills. Girls, on the other hand, are to work side by side with their moms and learn womanly skills. Girls are special and never get spanked, while boys need the discipline of the spanking so they will learn to stay on the straight and narrow path through life.

Because of our age difference, Nancy and I didn't spend much time together. As she grew up, I shelved my resentments and we became as close as any brother and sister can be. Nancy was a neat kid once she got over being cute and cuddly. I started to realize early on what a smart kid she was turning out to be. I especially love that she learned at a very early age to cook like mom. Nancy was inquisitive about everything. After we moved to Dolton—when I was fourteen and she was seven—we started spending more time together. We played games, talked, and hung out. And I tickled her unmercifully.

Nancy grew up to become a wonderful woman. She loved to cook and bake. When I was in Vietnam, Nancy sent me homemade cinnamon rollups. They are simple to make, but as a soldier in faraway Asia, I remember them as treasures—the best thing from home.

She got married in 1972, when she was nineteen, about two years after I got hitched. She and her husband, Thomas ("Beau"), have two children, Rebecca and Tommy. Nancy is a wonderful mother and grandmother. She now has five grandchildren. She is tall and slender and careful about her appearance. She is a focused woman who likes to learn, and we've grown closer as we've grown older.

Nancy's birth made my parents happy. But the change didn't alter my dad's habit of stopping for a drink after a hard day's work. He drank too frequently and too much for Mom, even when he did not get drunk. All she had to do was smell beer and she would be angry with him. Mom decided that the only solution was to move again—to a place where there were no nearby bars to tempt Dad every day on his way home from work. Dad agreed with the idea of moving because he wanted a house in the country. He loved the peace and quiet at night. So in 1954, my parents started looking for a new home and found one on Rural Route 2, Lake Eliza Road, in Lake Eliza, Indiana. It was a little over thirty miles from Homewood, and it came with an acre and a half of land for a garden. Mom and Dad fell in love with the house, and Indiana was a link to Dad's family history. My great-great-grandfather Daniel Lynch fought in the Civil War for both an Indiana regiment and an Illinois regiment.

Lake Eliza would be our home for the next five years. I would attend grade school, from third to sixth grade, at Union Center Elementary School and seventh and eighth grade at Wheeler High School. It would be the "best of times and the worst of times." And living there would forever change my personality.

Lake Eliza was a resort area centered on a small lake. It was a popular summer vacation destination for Chicagoans in the 1950s. Visitors could rent cottages or stay at a large rustic lodge that featured a dance floor and a bar. The lake was about three miles from our house on Lake Eliza Road. My family and friends swam in the lake a lot in the summer.

COUNTRY ADVENTURES AND COUNTRY CHORES

I was seven or eight when we moved, and life in Lake Eliza started out great. I spent most of my time outdoors with friends. There was a field we used for playing baseball and the outdoor games called "piggy move up" and "knockout flies." We started a large vegetable garden on our property. Across the road was a hilly pasture that was ideal for sled runs in winter and for downhill bike races in summer. When we moved to our home we got a dog that we named Duke, a mixed-breed collie and setter. Dad taught me how to train and care for him. Taking care of him taught me the meaning of responsibility. He and I became best friends, and Duke's loyalty helped me through some of the worst times of my life. Duke loved to chase me around the yard and play fetch.

I found out quickly that when you live in the country, you've got more chores than you do living in a city. During the spring and summer, it was my job to cut about an acre of grass once a week and to tend to our half-acre vegetable garden every day. I had to weed, cultivate, and water. We grew squash, tomatoes, cucumbers, corn, beans, peppers, and more. It was hard work but I learned to make it fun.

One day I happened upon a timesaving idea. I was watering the garden and noticed the water coming out of the hose had collected on the ground, making a big puddle. I took my hoe and started making a path for the water. Soon I had an irrigation channel going down one of the vegetable rows, and with a little more spadework I had the whole garden channeled. Instead of having to carry buckets of water around the whole garden, all I now had to do was move the hose from one channel to another. I felt brilliant. I still had to weed and cultivate, which took me a good part of the morning, but I'd found a way to get my garden work done more quickly.

Our next-door neighbor was an odd person. He worked in a factory and raised chickens and roosters at home. He entered the roosters in cockfights—a barbaric hobby that was illegal in Indiana at the time, but the authorities did little to stop it. We'd often be awakened late at night by the screeching of his injured roosters when he brought them home from a fight. He had a son named Ed who was around my age, eight or nine. Ed and I became friends.

My dad didn't like the man, cockfighting, or the way he treated his roosters, but he tried to be neighborly. It wasn't always easy. One day, as I was getting ready to cut the grass, Ed came walking over to me. I noticed his father and uncle were watching. Before I knew it Ed hit me and we started fighting. I wasn't yet afraid to fight. I was getting the worst of it before my dad broke it up. Later, I asked Ed why he'd started a fight with me. It seems his dad and uncle had bet him that he couldn't beat me. They just wanted us to fight for their entertainment. That seemed weird to me, but Ed's father had a backwoods mentality. He beat Ed regularly; at night we'd sometimes hear the boy's screams. It was awful but, thankfully, not long after we arrived, that family moved back to Tennessee.

I found other friends, including a couple of kids named Tommy and Eddie. Tommy's dad owned a farm; Eddie lived fairly close to me. On weekends, once our chores were done, Tommy, Eddie, and I would meet up on our bikes, and for the next few hours our time was our own. As long as our parents had a general idea where we were, we were free to go anywhere or do most anything, within limits. We rode to Lake Eliza to swim. We explored the woods up and down Lake Eliza Road, playing army or cowboys and Indians. We got so good at building forts that people could walk right past them on trails and not notice us. Sometimes we pedaled several miles to Wheeler, a small town, or even several miles farther to Valparaiso, where we would ride around Valparaiso University and into town. Sometimes we'd have enough money to buy ice cream or a soda pop.

The woods became my sanctuary, especially when I began to get bullied at school. I loved to play and hunt in the forest. I could take my .410 shotgun or my .22 rifle into the woods and shoot cans or bottles. Sometimes I'd hunt rabbits or squirrels and none of the

 The woods became my sanctuary, especially when I began to get bullied at school.

neighbors would freak out—their kids were hunters, too. My time in the forest taught me to love nature. I built a fort in the forest near our house, along a well-traveled path. When the bullying at school started I escaped to my fort, where I could go and be totally alone. I kept comics there and stashed them in a large Mason jar to protect them from the weather. Sometimes my dad would try to follow me on my walks in the woods to see what I was up to. But I usually noticed him and hid in my fort; he never found me. Even when I had no friends, the forest was there for me. Much later after my tour in Vietnam when I suffered from severe PTSD, I found peace in the woods.

There were three ponds and a lake in the woods behind our house. The smallest of the ponds was an ideal swimming hole. It was in a beautiful meadow, and there were a couple of oak trees beside it that provided shade. My friends and I often skinny-dipped in the pond and in late summer, we'd build a fire near it and cook fish we caught and corn plucked from a nearby field.

Then there was the new lake. It was a farmer's cornfield when we moved in, but after a hard rain the next year it flooded and became a sizeable though not very deep lake. It was, for a short time, our wonderland. Surprisingly, there were bullheads, catfish, bass, and other fish in it, which we'd catch and bring home for dinner. We built rafts, fished, and swam and in the winter, went ice-skating on the lake. We felt that we took our lives into our hands when we walked across its thin ice. It was terrifying to be in the middle of a lake and hear the ice crack, and then see the crack spread like a spider's web. Yet we ventured out on the ice again and again just for the thrill.

One day, as we started to cross the lake, the ice cracked and Tom's right leg went into the water up to his knee. Thankfully, we were near the shore. All our mothers were home so we couldn't go in a house to get him dry for fear of punishment. We decided to go into my garage and use one of my dad's spotlights to dry his jeans. It worked, but only after hours of keeping the light directly on the wet leg. Unlike my irrigation idea for the garden, this one was not very efficient.

The lake dried up for a short time the next summer. Tommy and I walked through the muddy lakebed and found tiny bullheads—a species of catfish—in little ponds. We reached down to scoop some up and found out that bullheads have a spike on the side of their heads, and if you pick them up the wrong way, they will stick you. We figured out how to handle them and brought a few back to the house.

When my dad saw our bullheads, he grabbed a couple of buckets and asked me to take him to the ponds. Soon we had two buckets filled with bullheads. That night, after we cleaned them, we had bullheads for dinner. Once or twice a week, Dad and I took our buckets down to the lakebed and collected the fish. Usually, we cooked them on the grill. Grilling was just starting to be popular in the 1950s. We got so we could skin and clean the fish in just seconds. Mom's family usually came to visit on Saturdays, and soon we were having huge fish frics. Our families loved fish of all kinds, and we especially loved them cooked on the grill. I still love properly grilled fish.

Just beyond the new lake and through a small wood was another pond. We wanted to fish there but bramble bushes encircled it. One day we decided to hack our way through the brambles with machetes and establish hidden fishing spots. As we started to whack the bushes, we made a pleasing discovery: The brambles were blackberry and raspberry bushes. After that, we spent our summers picking berries. My mother put fresh berries in pancakes and pies, and canncd a lot of them.

My mother's brother Dick and his wife, Jay, lived just four houses south of us. They moved into their house shortly after we moved. After they moved they had a baby, Laura, who died of pneumonia when she was a year and a half old. It was my first death and it hit me very hard. My cousins, Ricky and Debbie, and I played a lot together. Debbie and Nancy got very close. One day we found a strawberry patch, which I never mentioned to my friends. That patch added to our berry trove and we had delicious canned blackberries, raspberries, and strawberries throughout the winter.

BATTLING BEES AND WASPS

I considered myself a country boy who wasn't afraid of anything. But bees and other flying and stinging insects were my nemesis. I went into a shameful panic when they were anywhere around me. One summer I was cutting the grass and ran over a nest of bees. I left the lawnmower and ran into the house. After the bees settled down, I went back and finished cutting the grass. My cousin Rick found out where they were and, one day, decided to rile them up. Debbie,

Nancy, and I were in the breezeway when Rick rode his bike through the bees' nest and then zoomed straight toward us with a swarm of bees on his tail. I dove into the house while the girls ran away and got stung. Rick and I were unscathed but our parents gave us both a good talking-to after it was over—me, for going in the house and leaving the girls to get stung, and Rick for riling up the bees.

The worst incident happened after we built a new room off the breezeway. Dad and I had used a long pipe to fix the water well several months before and then left it on the roof of the house. In August 1955, a big refinery fire broke out at the Standard Oil plant in nearby Whiting. Mom, Dad, and I went up on the roof to catch a

 These days, I think young boys rarely have the kind of freedom I had at Lake Eliza.

glimpse of it. As we were looking, I absent-mindedly picked up the pipe and immediately heard a very loud buzzing sound. Then I saw a swarm: "Wasps!" Yelling in terror, I jumped off the roof and ran into the house. After about fifteen minutes, I went back outside and saw Mom and Dad still standing on the roof, motionless. I could hear my dad saying, "Vi, don't move." Wasps were landing on my mom's head. She was frozen as they crawled over her face, neck, and arms, but she didn't move and didn't get stung. Neither did Dad. After almost an hour they finally were able to get off the roof.

I thought I was going to catch hell. But dad told me it wasn't my fault and that I couldn't have known there were wasps in the pipe. He laughed at how fast I jumped from the roof, then told me I needed to control my fear. I wish I'd learned that lesson then as fear, when given a place to incubate, grows like a cancer.

WHEN BOYS COULD PLAY GUNS

Being young boys, we sometimes did dumb things. Across the road in front of our house there was a hilly cow pasture. My friends and I had dirt-clod fights in the fields and, in the summer, rode our bikes down the hills at breakneck speed. Each of us got thrown head over handlebars a least once. Sometimes we'd get firecrackers and stick them in cow pies and then watch them explode. We soon learned—again, the hard way—that one should get away from a firecracker once it has been lit. Especially if it is stuck in a fresh cow pie.

We played army with our BB guns, thinking that would make it more real. My friends and I eventually concluded that wasn't a smart thing to do. Getting hit by a BB is painful; it can embed in the skin. When one of us got hit, we'd sneak into my garage and pull the BB out with a pair of dad's needle-nose pliers. Mom never found out until I got back from Vietnam and accidently spilled the beans one night. Even then, she was not happy with me. These days, I think young boys rarely have the kind of freedom I had at Lake Eliza. But that was life in rural America in the 1950s.

FIXING OUR HOUSE

Our Lake Eliza home was a one-story frame house. Needless to say, it was a lot bigger than the trailer we'd lived in previously. It had a large living room, dining room, kitchen, two bedrooms, and a very small, basic bathroom just off the kitchen. Soon after moving in, Dad divided the master bedroom into two rooms and one became Nancy's room. An oil stove in the living room kept that part of the house warm in the winter while the rest of the house remained cold. I slept with several blankets to keep warm. My room had a huge closet and, unbeknownst to Mom and Dad, there was a passage between it and their bedroom. I could get in my closet then pass through to my parent's closet. It was a great way to sneak up on my sister, and when we played hide and seek in the house with my cousins, it was a neat place to hide.

A breezeway led from the house to an old wooden garage. Dad and I later closed in the space between the kitchen and the garage by building a new room that encompassed the breezeway. The garage had a dirt floor, and it was my job to sweep it. I thought it weird sweeping a dirt floor but, surprisingly, a hard-packed dirt floor can actually be swept clean.

Dad felt more comfortable in the garage than any other place in the house. Over the years, it became his fortress of solitude, though I spent a lot of time in there with him working on family cars and making things for the house. One year he got very ill after spending too much time lying on the cold dirt floor while he fixed my uncle's car. I never liked helping dad fix cars, but I didn't have a choice and eventually learned how to fix cars myself.

Our house was served by a water well and a septic system. Septic systems feature clay tiles that serve as drainage pipes from the toilet, bathtub, and sinks. If septic tiles are not deep enough in the ground they can freeze, get clogged, and stop working. One cold winter some of the tiles froze and blocked waste from moving through the pipes to the septic field. Dad asked me to help fix the problem. He wanted me to find the tiles that were clogged. I dug down through the frozen ground to uncover the tiles. When I found one, I had to carefully lift it out and inspect it, knowing it might have "stuff" in it. If the tile was dry and clear, I put it back, and moved on. Meanwhile, Dad sat in the warm house drinking coffee and occasionally coming out to provide guidance.

When I found a clogged tile, I had to clean it out. Thankfully, only three needed cleaning. Now I know why gloves and soap were invented. Several times during that winter, I had to go out and fix a sewage blockage. The next summer we laid a deeper sewage line, which did not freeze. It was hard, but dad and I worked as a team, and we grew close from working together on home-improvement projects like that.

One summer, we put a new roof on our house. Dad bought shingles and tarpaper, and every day after he came home from the plant we worked on the roof. I carried the stacks of shingles up a ladder and placed them all over the roof. Dad and I then took off all the old shingles, laid new tarpaper, and spent a weekend laying new shingles. I got so good with a hammer that I could sink a nail with one hit. At lunchtime Dad would take me to town for a hamburger. He'd have a beer and a burger, and I'd have a Coke and a burger. Sometimes he'd let me take a drink from his glass. I felt so grown-up. At the end of the day, after the work was done, Dad took us to Lake Eliza for a swim.

HORSES, CANNING, AND MOM WORKING

Tommy Fitzgerald, the owner of the Lake Eliza resort, was a major farmer in the area. The resort had cabins, a petting zoo, and riding horses. We were able to rent a horse for two hours for about a dollar and a half, and we could take the horses without a guide. We could ride anywhere we wanted as long as we got back within the two-hour period. The money for horse riding, the petting zoo, comics, and other things that I bought came from my allowance, which was a dollar and a half a week. I had to earn my allowance, like the other kids. Sometimes I could add to my allowance by picking up beer and pop bottles I found alongside the road and turning them in for the deposit. Sometimes I helped my grandma, who lived nearby, with tasks and she would reward me with a quarter.

We attended church sporadically in Valparaiso. During the school year I had to attend Sunday school but didn't have to attend church. While my parents were at church, I'd head to the local drugstore-soda shop. Dad usually let me buy an ice cream sundae and the Sunday paper. I loved, and still love, the Sunday cartoons. Mom and Dad and my sister, still very young, joined me at the drugstore after church. My parents would have coffee and, usually, a piece of pie.

Coming home from church, we drove down country roads. Gas was super-cheap in the 1950s—fifteen or twenty cents a gallon. One Sunday we discovered several apple trees with their branches hanging over the road. We stopped and picked a few. The following week, Dad put baskets and buckets in the trunk of our car, and on the way home from church we stopped at the apple trees again and filled the baskets and buckets with fruit. Mom and my aunt Jay canned the apples in the fall. We had canned sliced apples, applesauce, and apple jelly—all homemade. They canned all the vegetables from our garden plus our berries and whatever else we could pick.

My family, you could say, was enterprising. We had to be because we had very little money during the 1950s, but I don't remember feeling poor or downtrodden. We adapted and did the best we could, like everybody else. Thanks to our garden, for example, we never had to worry about food. Dad had one simple rule about food: If Mom cooked it, we ate it. There was no "I don't like this." If we didn't like what Mom cooked for supper, then there was nothing to eat until breakfast.

One night, my mom broached the idea of getting a job to help make ends meet. Dad didn't want to hear it—it was humiliating for him to acknowledge that we lacked money. A "discussion" followed that was so heated it woke me up. Mom, when she was determined, could get her way, and she won that argument. She took a job at a factory in Valparaiso working in the office as a typist. There was more money, but Dad turned sullen and reclusive. He felt he'd not fulfilled his chief duty as a husband to support his family. In his view, a man who can't do that is not a man. Owing to that belief, my dad worked two jobs most of his life. On weekends, he worked as the area handyman, putting in electrical wiring, doing plumbing, pouring cement, and just about anything else to make a few extra dollars. I learned from him, and have never been afraid to take on a project at home. He told me repeatedly, "All work is honorable, Allen, as long as it is honest work. Never be afraid to get your hands dirty." When the bills finally were all paid, Mom quit her job—and Dad became his old self.

THE BULLIES

I attended third to sixth grade at Union Center Grade School two miles from our house. After that I attended seventh and eighth grade at Wheeler High School, which was a combination junior high and high school about five miles away. Space was so limited at Union Center that there were two classes per room, and one teacher for both classes. I enjoyed third grade and fourth grade. I was initially placed in the second grade because I didn't know cursive writing. But Mom and Dad didn't want me to be a year behind my peers and pushed the administrators to put me in third grade. They agreed. I took the bus to school, and usually arrived a bit early. We had classes, along with a couple of fifteen-minute breaks, until lunch was served at 11:30. After lunch there were more classes and a couple of brief recesses until school ended at 3:30.

Recess, for the first couple of years, was fun. In the fall we played "knockout flies" and "piggy move up" on the big hill by the playground. Sometimes we found cardboard panels and slid down the hill on them. Come winter the big hill became a popular sledding site. Winter recess meant sledding, building snow forts, and massive snowball fights.

We were a busy group. We built lean-to shelters along the fence line behind the school. Our shelters were often warmer than the school. Sometimes we snuck under the fence and played in the woods or in a farmer's barn behind the school. The barn was off school property and off limits for students, but the temptation was too much for us. Getting caught meant standing at the blackboard with your nose in a chalk circle until the teacher felt you had been punished enough. In cold weather, the air from our noses would create a trickle of water that ran down the blackboard. We thought it was cool but the teacher, upon seeing it, made us wipe it away then put our noses back in the chalk circle. Being boys, all we could do was giggle, which got us a smack on the back of the head with an eighteen-inch wooden ruler.

We learned not to irritate the teacher. She had many little punishments that would probably shock parents and teachers today. One day, after she caught me chewing gum, she had me spit the gum into her hand, and then she put the sticky wad on the tip of my nose. She caught me a second time a few days later and put the gum in my hair. When I got home, Dad shaved the gum out of my hair. For weeks afterward I went to school with a bald spot where the gum had been. It all reinforced School Rule Number 1: The teacher is always right.

One day when I was in third grade, I got into a fight. Again, that was before I was afraid to fight, and I don't remember what we were fighting about. We were both grabbed and taken to the principal's office. The principal, Mr. Albers, took out a paddle, which he called "the board of education." It was about a foot long with a handle, and holes had been drilled through it. He had us bend over and touch our toes. That tightened our jeans across our butts, ensuring maximum pain. It also enhanced the sound of wood meeting backside. The effect was a crack that sounded like a rifle shot. Ten swats was the usual punishment. They hurt but were tolerable for me because I'd been spanked more than a few times before and knew what to expect.

Early in fourth grade, three bullies joined our class and what had been a happy period in my life turned dark. The bullies were two brothers and a friend of theirs. I don't remember much about them

 It's hard to explain why people are unkind or mean, because bad behavior isn't rational.

personally—just the emotional and physical pain they inflicted on me. They weren't that big—I may have even been taller—but they were three, I was one, and they would make my life hellish for parts of the next four years.

I don't remember why they decided to pick on me. I wasn't the most popular kid in school, but I wasn't unpopular either. It's hard to explain why people are unkind or mean, because bad behavior isn't rational. I rode the bus home for a while—until the bullies began pushing me to the back of the bus every day and harassing me during the trip. They'd each give me a good punch before getting off at their stop. No one ever stood up to help me, and the bus driver pretended he didn't see what was going on. Sometimes other kids would emulate their behavior and push me to the back of the bus. That was their way of trying to get on the good side of the bullies. I felt alone and ashamed. Eventually I started walking home. Oddly, I could get home faster on foot than on the bus, which meandered around the area dropping kids off. I liked to walk because I could be by myself. I walked along Route 30, and sometimes I'd squat and walk through storm drains just for fun.

My parents had different reactions to the bullying. Mom was a pacifist and didn't believe in fighting or violence. Dad, on the other hand, was a "punch 'em in the nose" type. He believed that when pushed, you push back. He asserted that fighting and losing was a far better response than not fighting at all. If you can bloody your opponent a bit, even in defeat, he won't be eager to fight you again. But my dad wasn't around much; he worked days and nights and many weekends. Mom was at home in my early years, and she was my greatest influence. I was a fairly big kid, and she did not want me to fight and possibly hurt somebody. "How would you feel if you knocked out someone's eye or really hurt someone," she'd say. I imagined what it would be like to literally knock somebody's eye out of his socket. That horrible mental image stuck with me, created fear in me, and kept me from fighting. In retrospect, I believe the pacifist approach of taking the high road was not the right reaction. It only emboldened other kids.

I should have listened to my father, because not hitting back only made things worse for me and I got beat up day after day. I got a lot of black eyes, bloody noses, and fat lips.

EFFECTS OF BULLYING

The bullying had a very bad effect on my life. The recess that I'd looked forward to became a nightmare. I avoided the hill on which I used to play, and I avoided the back of the school where I used to be invited to help build lean-tos. Those became danger zones for me. Day after day, I was pushed from behind. One of the bullies' favorite tricks was for one of them to start talking to me as another of the trio snuck behind and got on all fours. Then the kid talking pushed me and I fell over the kid behind me. After several times, I learned to avoid that trick. I was made fun of, and blamed for everything. If there was mischief in a class and the teacher asked who was responsible, the typical reply was "Lynch did it."

The biggest hurt was that once I became a victim of bullying, my friends dropped me. They stopped talking to me, stopped hanging out with me in school and on the playground. No one wanted to be friends with the class pushover. I no longer was invited to birthday parties. No one even wanted to be around me. In winter when we used to all have fun sledding down the school hill, I was by myself. Looking back, I don't blame my friends. Had the situation been reversed, I might have acted as they did—or maybe not.

I tried to participate in sports, thinking if I was good then maybe I'd have friends. I played Little League baseball in the summer and did OK. I wasn't the best player, but I wasn't the worst either. When we had pick-up games, I was always picked last, but at least I wasn't being bullied. However, when school started, the bullying resumed, and the friends I made playing baseball went away.

I played basketball in junior high school but quit because of the cruel jokes played on me. No one passed me the ball, even when I was open. I was on the team but not a part of the team. The coaches saw it but did nothing. One night after a game, I returned to the locker room to find that my shoes had been filled with urine. I felt so ashamed that I didn't return to the team.

The teachers knew I was being bullied, but in the 1950s there weren't many institutional protections. Kids had to fend for themselves and work out their own problems. There were no psychologists or social workers to help kids like me. Instead, I just had to adapt to being bullied. And I did adapt. I learned to be wary. If I had a feeling I shouldn't walk to a certain place, I didn't. If I took the bus home, I made sure to be the first in line and take a seat up front, ideally right behind the bus driver

My grades suffered from all the stress. I never had the greatest grades, but once the bullying started they went down. I lost the will to learn. I'd go home and just sit. I'd lie about having homework, especially if I didn't like the subject or was intimidated by it. My homework avoidance ended one night in fifth grade, when my parents and I were at school for a parent-teacher night. All the students sat at their desks, and the parents were scattered around the classroom. The teacher gave a brief talk and started complimenting some parents on the work of their children. Then she came to me. I had already been chewed out by Dad for having a messy desk, but then the teacher informed my parents that I was three weeks behind in long-division homework. I felt Dad's hand descend upon my shoulder like the talons of an eagle. His grip almost drove me under the desk as he said in his most pleasant voice, "Please give me his missing assignments and he'll catch up by the end of next week." Then he let go of my shoulder. I thought the crisis was over but it wasn't.

Every night for the next week, after I did my daily homework and chores, I had to do several of my overdue long-division assignments. One night early on, Dad saw me struggling to work the problems. I just couldn't understand how to do long division. Dad sat down beside me and proceeded to show me how to do it. He was an amazing teacher—patient, soft spoken, and easy in his instruction. Before long I had a good idea of how to solve the problems.

Or so I thought. The next night Dad had to work late and wasn't home to check my homework. I went to bed without reviewing my calculations. Around 11:00 p.m., Dad woke me from my sleep. He'd checked my work after getting home and found mistakes. I soon was sitting at the table. Gone was the patient instructor; back was the hardened taskmaster. Lesson learned. If you are doing work, do it right. Later, my army drill sergeants would impress the same lesson on me.

PUNCH 'EM IN THE NOSE

Dad tried to teach me to fight. He took an old mattress, rolled it up, and made a heavy punching bag out of it. Night after night he'd take me out to the garage and show me how to jab, dance like a boxer, and deliver a "Sunday punch." He also taught me several kinds of judo flips, and how to turn and hit someone who is pushing me from behind. "If you hit 'em right between the eyes, you'll blacken 'em both," he said one night. "Don't be afraid of being hit."

But my fear was overpowering. I wanted to fight. I wanted to push back, but when I tried, fear overcame me and I was helpless. Yet there was one night in sixth grade when I made a stand. It was another parent-teacher night, late in the winter. I was walking down the hall and a kid, a friend of the bullies, tried to persuade me to go outside. I knew what would happen if I went with him. He grabbed me and, without thinking, I grabbed him and pulled him down to the floor. Then I put my feet in his belly and monkey-flipped him all the way down the hall. When I got up he had a strange look on his face. He never bothered me again. You'd think I would have been emboldened by my fight that night, but I didn't learn. My unhappy life went on as before.

My mom and my dad were not proud of me, and I deeply felt it. They had tried to help me. In Dad's mind, real boys don't get pushed around. He would have preferred that I fight and have poor grades rather than have good grades and not fight. I wasn't as manly as he thought I should be. Mom didn't know what to do. She didn't want me to fight but had no other solutions. Often in her frustration she would ask why I couldn't be more like one of my uncles. Looking back, I was probably very depressed. My self-image and confidence hit rock bottom.

One day as I was getting ready for school, I got a terrible pain in my stomach. It was so bad I started to cry. I had had stomach pains before, but this one was the worst ever. Mom asked if I needed to stay home. I mumbled yes as I ran to the bathroom. As I was sitting there, a thought came to mind. Stomach pain might be my ticket to getting away from the bullies. I was smart enough to know that I couldn't claim illness every day, but for a long time I was able to "get sick" once or twice every couple of weeks. Then one day I went too far and Mom took me to the doctor. She told him school issues were giving me stomach problems.

The doctor put me on a tranquilizer, something I only learned years later. I was on the drug for a month or so, until Dad noticed how passive and "lazy" I'd become. He took me off the medication. I was taken to the doctor several more times because of my stomach pains. On one visit the doctor asked to speak to me alone. He asked me several questions and listened to my answers, thoughtfully. We talked about the bullying, and as our visit came to an end, he said, "Son, everyone has his day to shine. These kids who are pushing you around are shining now. But one day it will be your turn." I never forgot those words. For years, through the rest of school, then into the army, those words kept coming back to me. They helped.

Summer was my respite from the bullies. They lived in Wheeler and I rarely if ever saw them. After my chores were done, I was free to roam. Grandma Sytsma, my dad's mother, lived in a community on a hilltop that overlooked Lake Eliza. I often visited her during the warmer months. At the back of her house was a very steep hill with a walkway that led to some streams that ran off the lake. There were two benches halfway down the walkway. Sometimes after helping Grandma, I'd sit on one of them and read. Reading was, at that time in my life, an escape from everything. I could read for hours.

A WRONG ROAD

One Saturday in 1956 when I was eleven, I went shopping with Mom at a supermarket in Valparaiso. While she shopped for groceries, she gave me permission to go to the five-and-dime store. As I wandered up and down the aisles, I saw a pen and pencil set I wanted. The set cost $1.50, and I had $3.00 in my pocket. No matter: I picked up the pen and pencil set and stuck it in my pocket. As soon as I put the package in my pocket I noticed the store detective looking at me. I panicked and started to walk around the store. He followed me, and I got even more panicky. I could have simply paid for the pencil set, or put it back, but I stupidly did neither. I was not thinking clearly. I saw a screen door at the back of the store and thought I could make a break for it. Just as I opened the door I felt the guard's giant hand grabbing me by the shoulder. I was caught.

The guard took me through the store, and everyone knew what I had done. I started to cry. He took me down the street to the police department. By then I was in the grip of terror and regret. I remember it like it was yesterday. The police station had four towers, one on each side of the building. I was taken up into one of the towers to an interview room. It looked like something out of a Mike Hammer mystery: The room was small, dark, and dank, with one light hanging from a long cord. There was one bare table and two chairs. I sat in one and waited for what seemed like hours but in reality was only a few minutes. A police officer came in and asked me where my home was and where my parents were. I told him where my mom was shopping and was left to wait again.

The officer came back in and asked me several questions. He accused me of being a part of a ring of shoplifters. I told him that I was not part of any criminal ring and that this was the first time I'd shoplifted. That was a lie; I had actually stolen from stores four

 As students moved from one class to another, I feared being pushed down the stairs.

or five times. When he was done, I was taken down to the waiting room, where my mother sat. I was turned over to her, and we left. She said nothing—NOTHING!—all the way home. I tried to explain my action but she told me to shut up—and then sealed my fate with the dreaded words: "Wait until you father gets home from work." When we got home I was sent to my room.

As soon as I heard the front door open, I shuddered. I was a thief and would be severely punished for embarrassing my parents. I heard Mom and Dad talking in low voices but could not hear what they were saying. Soon Dad walked into my room. "Here it comes," I remember thinking. "I'm going to get such a spanking." But that didn't happen. He simply said, "I am so ashamed of you," and walked out. Over the next few days, Mom and Dad said very little to me. Each day the shame of what I had done weighed heavily on me. There was no lecture, no spanking, no grounding, nothing. Except for the occasional "It's time for supper" or "Cut the grass," they gave me the silent treatment. Finally, I couldn't stand it any longer. When Dad got home one night I apologized and tearfully told him and Mom how sorry I was that I had disgraced our family.

They both gave me a hug and it was forgotten. Over the next several years, whenever I walked into a store I put my hands in my pockets and vowed never to shoplift again.

I finally graduated from sixth grade and moved into junior high school at Wheeler High. Since the high school was farther from home, I had to take the bus both to and from school. The bullies continued to heap misery on me. My books were shoved out of my hands, and as I bent down to pick them up I got a kick in the behind. Sometimes my books were kicked down the hall. As students moved from one class to another, I feared being pushed down the stairs or over the banister.

DAD STEPS IN

The situation finally came to a head in the last semester of seventh grade. Our history teacher, a veteran who'd lost an arm in World War II, decided to teach civics by having us enact different types of governments. During class and throughout the school day, we were to act as much as possible like the form of government being taught. If we were a true democracy, everything that affected the class had to be voted on by the students. If a republic, our elected officials had to vote. The last system taught was totalitarianism, and he chose the Nazis as an example of it. Of course, he chose the three bullies to represent the Gestapo! They were given permission to act the part—in and out of class, within reason, except, apparently, when it came to me. The bullies took advantage of the situation, and for the next couple of days treated me especially roughly.

Then they made the mistake that would change everything. They began demanding that I and a few other boys give them money to avoid being beaten up. Somehow, my dad found out, though I hadn't told him anything. Not long after this shakedown started, the bullies and three student victims, including me, were pulled out of class and told to report to the principal's office. There sat my dad and the principal. We were told to take a seat, and Dad started in on the bullies. He vilified them for abusing me. One of them responded by being a smart-ass. He told Dad they never laid a hand on us for the money, and he said it with a smirk on his face. Big mistake!

Dad got enraged. "You punk, who do you think you're dealing with?" he said. "You take money from my kid, you're taking money from me! Don't give me that crap that you never laid a hand on them. I'll back you all the way down the stairs and not lay a finger on you. If I chose to, I could break both of your legs. So here's what is going to happen. If anything happens to any of these kids, I'm blaming you."

That was it. The principal just sat there with his mouth wide open. He never said a word except at the end, when he said to the bullies, "If I were you, I'd believe Mr. Lynch." And for the most part that ended the bullying. As the seventh grade came to a close, I was no longer afraid to ride the bus. I still had to keep an eye out for dirty tricks, but a weight was lifted off me.

I wish I could write that the change drastically improved my life—that my grades got better, that I gained lots of friends, and that I became a stellar kid. But I can't. When eighth grade started, there was a new bullying victim—our teacher, whom we treated terribly. Relieved to be free of my tormentors, I took part in harassing her. I'm ashamed to say we made her life hell. Over the years I've often wished I could personally apologize to her. After the way I was treated, I should have empathized with her and stayed apart from the class bullies, but to my shame I didn't. I was too young, I think, and after years of being a school pariah, I just wanted to fit in with my classmates.

BOY SCOUTS

When I was in seventh grade, my dad volunteered to be scoutmaster of Troop 20 in Valparaiso. Dad was an immediate hit with the scouts and I was welcomed into the troop. I was assigned to a patrol and was soon working on becoming a Tenderfoot. We went camping and worked on all those things Boy Scouts are known for doing. I learned the Scout motto, "Be prepared," and the Scout slogan, "Do a good turn daily." But what really influenced me was the Scout law: "A scout is trustworthy, loyal, helpful, friendly, courteous, kind, obedient, cheerful, thrifty, brave, clean, and reverent."

When we Scouts went camping, we'd raid other troops in the area and get raided by them. We had so much fun. A raid was a good-natured attack. We might pull tent pegs out, collapsing a tent, or throw water balloons at the opposing troop. I especially liked the Scout Jamborees. We would learn the finer points of camping, hiking, and how to tie knots. We would also be tested on our skills and even earn merit badges. Some Jamborees lasted only a day, others lasted a weekend. Generally, Scouts ran the camp. We did all the cooking with adult supervision. I made it to First Class before I quit. Scouting was a safe place where I could have friends and learn what I thought were cool skills.

ALONE AND HAPPY

One day when I was thirteen, as I was coming back from a store, one of the bullies approached me and gave me a shove. I didn't have time to think or run; I just reacted, and soon we were on the ground fighting. Fighting! Me! I gave as good as I got. He won, but I fought, and we both came away from it somewhat damaged.

Later as I was walking to class, one of the high school kids asked the bully why he kept pushing me around.

"Because I hate him," he said.

"Why?" asked the other student.

"Because everyone else does," the bully replied.

I stood there and felt all my life drain out of me. The words "everyone else does" hit me like a backhanded slap. I remember just being tired.

Life went on, and at some point, I started to be very comfortable being by myself. I found I neither needed nor wanted friends. That happened gradually over all those years of being bullied. I could be around people but never with them. I learned to be alone, and even today I am more comfortable being by myself than with people. The only people I truly feel comfortable with are my wife, Susie; my children, Eric, Carolyn, and Brian; their spouses; and some wonderful friends.

One might think that being a bullying victim embittered me. I suppose in some ways it did. However, my mom's empathetic mindset and her constant reminders to think about others helped to keep me from feeling sorry for myself as I got older. My father's example of selfless service to others was also instructive. And over the years I got good advice from high school teachers, a drill sergeant, and other military leaders. Negative experiences are rough, nobody wants them, but there's some validity to the old saying about clouds with silver linings. Hard times can offer opportunities for personal growth, if one is resilient.

I was.

CHAPTER 6

BETTER DAYS: HIGH SCHOOL AND WORK

I N JUNE 1960, SHORTLY AFTER I GRADUATED FROM JUNIOR HIGH school, we sold our house on Lake Eliza Road and moved again. A few months earlier, Mom's brother Dick and his wife, Jay, who had lived with their two kids down the street from us in Lake Eliza, moved to Dolton, Illinois. We decided to follow them back across the state line. My mother and her brothers and sisters always liked being geographically close. That was one reason we moved. Another was that Dolton was said to have a good public school system. I'd had problems at school in Indiana, with bullying and poor grades. Mom and Dad thought a new start at a new high school would be a good idea.

Dolton in the '60s was a middle-class bedroom community just about ten miles south of Roseland, between Riverdale to the west, Calumet City to the east, and Altgeld Gardens to the north. It had two main streets, Lincoln Avenue and Chicago Road, where the town's main businesses were located. It had the usual barbershop, restaurant, town hall with war memorial, drugstore, liquor store, and a couple of bars. It was known for its Fourth of July festivities—a parade, a carnival that took place in Dolton Park, and a massive fireworks display. It was a safe town, where a kid could walk from one end to the other without fear.

My parents sold the Lake Eliza house before finding a place to live in Dolton. So they opted to move us back to a familiar spot, Roseland, until a new apartment could be found. We moved into an apartment on 111th Street, just a little south of Wentworth Street. It was right next to the store where I used to get penny candy when I was five. Now I was fourteen. Our new apartment was on the second floor of a wooden, two-story walk-up built in the late 1920s or early 1930s. It was a bit strange to be back in Roseland, but I was happy to finally be free of the bullies who'd tormented me in Lake Eliza.

I spent most of the summer getting used to living in the city again. Gone was the quiet of the country and the crystal-clear, star-lit nights. Gone were the quiet walks in the woods. My family and I still walked a lot, but now along busy 111th Street.

High school started right after Labor Day. Mom and Dad registered me at Thornridge High School, giving school officials my Uncle Dick's address in Dolton as my local residence. Until we found an apartment, I would make the time-consuming commute to Dolton every day.

My dad always had household chores for me. When fall arrived and the weather began to cool, Dad gave me the responsibility for keeping the heat going in our apartment building. That meant tending to the coal furnace in the basement, twice a day. Every morning, I had to dispose of the coal ash in the furnace from the night before, throw in several shovels of fresh coal, and open the damper. The simmering coals would soon burst into flame and more heat would move up through the vents and into the apartments. At night, I again filled the furnace with coal, banked it, and set the damper, so that the coal would burn steadily throughout the night.

It was simple enough, but coal-burning furnaces are fickle. Once my dad woke me in the middle of the night. The apartment was freezing. Apparently, I failed to bank the coals properly and the fire had died out. We had to reignite the coal, which wasn't easy. It involved newspapers, matches, kerosene, and a lot of new words Dad taught me when things didn't go just right. It took about an hour for us to get the fire going again. We stumbled upstairs, washed the soot off our hands, and went back to bed.

My morning routine was to get dressed, tend to the furnace, grab a bite of breakfast, and then make the six-block walk to the bus stop where I caught a commercial bus to Dolton. The trip to Dolton took about twenty minutes. The bus dropped me off three blocks from the school bus stop and I waited there for about half an hour until the school bus arrived to take me the five miles to Thornridge High School, completing my hour-long journey. At the end of the school day, I made the same trip in reverse. Rain, snow, cold, or hot I made the long trip every school day.

It was a long, arduous commute, but I liked it. Over the years, I'd learned to enjoy being by myself—it was the best way to avoid life's torments. I still enjoy solitude—not all the time, but perhaps more than most people. Walking to and from the bus stop and riding the bus gave me time to relax, shake off cares, and to think.

In November, the school learned that I didn't actually live in Dolton. We were found out! My parents were told that I had to live in town or leave the school. We needed a new plan. Aunt Marty and Uncle Chester came to our aid. They were renting an apartment on the second floor of the house Uncle Dick had bought in Dolton. They agreed to let me stay there during the week. On the weekends I'd go back to Roseland. I got along very well with Aunt Marty and Uncle Chester during this time. Dad and I had spent a lot of time fishing with Chester over the years and we had all vacationed together. I don't know what Uncle Chester did for a living. I know he worked in a factory somewhere. Kids aren't very concerned with what adults do for a living.

Living with my aunt and uncle was a lot different from living at home. I didn't have my own bedroom but slept on a cot. I did get to know some of the kids in the neighborhood. So after I got home from school and did my homework, I could hang out. We played sandlot football or baseball and walked uptown to hang out with other kids. And I rode the school bus with them. I actually had friends there, but after I moved into our new apartment, I lost contact with them.

In the spring of 1961, after about six months of living with my aunt and uncle, my parents found an apartment at 15030 University Avenue in Dolton, about ten miles from Roseland. The section of University Ave. leading to our building was a gravel road. Our apartment was in the last building at the end of street. I would live there for three and a half years.

We lived on the first floor of a two-story brick building, and not long after we moved in Aunt Marty and Uncle Chester moved into the apartment above us. (As I said, my mom's family liked to stay close to one another.) Our apartment had a large living room, dining room, kitchen, small bathroom, and two large bedrooms. Nancy and I shared one of the bedrooms. Dad divided it by hanging sheets across the room—one side for Nancy and the other side for me. It wasn't ideal, but life often isn't. Later, as Nancy got older, she got the whole room and I started sleeping in the dining room.

We lived about a mile from Thornridge High, so I walked to school every day.

THE HORROR OF ALGEBRA

High school was very different from junior high. In junior high, we switched classrooms only once or twice a day; in high school, we switched rooms for every class. The bell would ring, and we'd pour out of one class and hurry to our lockers. We had just minutes to get our next set of books and make it to the next class. It was not like today where every kid carries a backpack full of books and rarely goes to his or her locker. We went to our lockers at least four times a day.

The first two years of high school, most classes were mandatory. That's a word I've come to associate with "hard." One of my mandatory freshman classes was algebra. We had to have a year of math, and for some reason Dad signed me up for algebra. I took it the first semester and failed. Because I failed, I had to switch to general math. Little did I know that failing algebra also meant I'd have to retake it in dreaded summer school.

Dad made it very clear to me that failing had consequences. "Mom will not be punished by having to take you to summer school," he said. "So, you get your ass there and back." Summer school was not at Thornridge; it was held at Thornton High in the nearby town of Harvey, Illinois, three-and-a-half miles from home. I rode my bike there and back every day for several weeks—and on my second go I passed algebra.

Mom and Dad got some heat from other members of the family for making me get to summer school on my own. "You're being too hard on him," one said. But I thank God, even today, for parents who loved me enough to make me uncomfortable. It was hard to spend summer days in school rather than goofing off with friends. It was hard to ride my bike seven miles a day, and hard to peddle over the high bridges on Sibley Boulevard and Indiana Avenue to get to Thornton. But hard slogs can have benefits. In the end, summer school taught me a valuable lesson: There are consequences to failure, so don't fail. I came perilously close a few other times; I struggled with biology, another mandatory class. I got some Ds and even D-minuses, but fear of summer school, and having to ride my bike for miles and losing vacation time, motivated me to study at least enough to pass.

There were also consequences to not being respectful to Mom. One day, I came home and Mom asked me to do something. I gave her some choice lip. She started to say something and I popped off in my most sarcastic voice, "What are you going to do? Tell Dad when he gets home?" Suddenly the door to their bedroom flew open and out came Dad. "She won't have to," he said as he walked over and grabbed me by the shirt just under my chin and proceeded to lift me up off the floor with one hand. "I don't care how you talk to your mother. But don't *ever* talk to my wife that way again!" Each word was enforced with a little bounce under my chin. When he was done, he tossed me like a rag doll down the hallway. "Didn't know I was home, did you?" he said as he turned and went back into the bedroom. In Dad's eyes, I was a man even though I was still in high school. He had worked since he was in eighth grade and had dropped out of high school in his sophomore year to help his family during the Depression. Men of his era demanded respect from their children.

My favorite classes were history, geography, and English. I always did well in history and geography, and especially liked American history. English was another matter. I liked the subject but got terrible grades—straight Ds all four years of high school. I often wonder what my English teachers would say if they knew I would later write legal briefs for veterans in the VA appeal process, along with several books on veterans rights for the Illinois attorney general's office. I've also had essays published in a couple of books—*Lincoln Replies* and *Choosing Courage.*

I sat at the kitchen table when doing my homework. Mom was usually there, cooking, and it was a comforting place to be. She'd bake cookies, especially chocolate chip cookies, which I loved to dunk in milk. A chocolate chip cookie with cold milk was one of the things I craved when I was in Vietnam.

Our kitchen was the center of the universe for me when I was growing up. It was the family gathering spot. It was where the day began and ended, where we discussed the events of the day, where we chatted with visitors, where I learned to drink (and love) coffee.

 I was slowly gaining some personal confidence but I had not challenged myself.

And the place where we ate some of the best and most comforting food ever made by a loving mom. It was the same at the homes of my aunts and uncles. When we visited, we'd gather at the kitchen table. Uncle Dick, a navy veteran, had an especially warm, inviting kitchen. Maybe it was the smell of coffee and the warm smiles. Aunt Jay was a phenomenal baker and always had some pie or cake or brownies or cookies when we came to visit. But it was warm casual conversation served with coffee and goodies that made it special. Someone in the family even wrote a poem titled "Dick's Kitchen Table."

You've heard the expression "wherever you go, there you are." A person can change location—such as moving to a different place or changing jobs—but that doesn't change the person. Your personality, your character, your strengths and weaknesses, your quirks—they all travel with you wherever you go.

I was slowly gaining some personal confidence but I had not challenged myself. I thought changing location would create a new me. Nobody at Thornridge High School knew me when I arrived. Yet my personality and interactions with others were, to an extent, unchanged. That is to say, I got bullied in high school, too—not nearly as much as in previous years, but still bullied.

My cover was blown at lunch period one day. I walked over to a table and was about to sit when a guy already sitting at the table said something about me that I didn't like. I called him on it. He stood up from the table and challenged me. I froze. The Lake Eliza me was back. I turned and walked away. I had backed down in front of everyone in the lunch hall. I hadn't changed. My clean slate, my new Dolton identity—gone. The real me was back. There was bullying in gym class, in the hallway, at lunchtime, and after school. But it was more the occasional snide remark and not the physical abuse I often suffered in Lake Eliza. One thing helped: I had made some friends at Thornridge. Most of them shared my indifference to school. They helped to make it bearable.

I just wanted to get through high school. I had a poor attitude— and because of it, I missed out on a lot school activities. I skipped sporting events, dances, extracurricular activities, and more. Why? Because I was afraid of getting out of my comfort zone, afraid of going to an event and again finding myself in a situation where I would be bullied. I gave fear a place and it again took over.

I was also struggling to find my identity— that's not a bad thing. In fact, it can be a good thing if you're wise enough at some point to recognize your flaws and work to overcome them. If you confront your shortcomings, you can become a better, more successful person. I'm a prime example. I'm not sure if I confronted mine consciously or not. But circumstances intervened and forced me to change.

One fateful intervention came in the person of my dad. He was my no-nonsense professor of life. He was a strict disciplinarian— and while I didn't care for his hard-nosed style, I believed that it was good for me. He demanded respect for himself and for my mother, and I gave them respect. He demanded that I be accountable for my actions, and I learned to be. That acceptance of accountability kept me out of a lot of trouble. I knew that if I ever did something that got me arrested or brought shame to the family, I'd have to deal not only with town authorities but also with the authority in my family, Dad. That was something I feared more than anything else in the world.

BIKE BUSINESS

If my academic desire was low in high school, my financial ambition was high. I saw that there was money to be made if I was willing to work. Not just pocket change for chores, but real money. My first entrepreneurial effort came in the winter of 1961, when there was a lot of snow on the ground. Two friends, Jim and Paul, and I went house to house in the neighborhood, offering to shovel snow. It wasn't exactly a novel idea, just practical. To our surprise, adults sitting in their warm houses were happy to pay us five or ten dollars to shovel their sidewalks and driveways. One weeknight, the three of us made a bundle in just a few hours and went to bed that night praying for more snow.

Jim always seemed to be the guy who came up with the ideas on how to make money. Jim was the shortest of all of us but always stood tall when it came to finances. Paul was an artist. He had a talent for drawing and I believe he did some cartoons for the school newspaper. Like me, he had his problems at school especially in gym class. Later in life he would get into the martial arts. Another boy, Turk, was one of our group. I believe he was in the United States on a student visa. He had other friends but sometimes hung out with us. I think he ended up marrying Paul's sister.

When spring brought green grass, we switched from snow shovels to lawnmowers. We rolled our lawnmowers from house to house, asking owners if we could cut their grass for three dollars or more, depending upon the size of the lawn. As with the snow clearing, many were happy to give us the work. We had regular weekly customers, and the three of us made a lot of money—or what seemed like a lot of money to teenage boys. We also started washing and cleaning neighborhood cars, and that, too, became a part of our little business. We kept adding new jobs, and before long we were washing windows, cleaning garages, hauling trash—anything that needed doing.

Later, the three of us started a bicycle shop, which became our most profitable business. One day we were looking at the *Shopper*, a local classified ad publication. Jim noticed that several bikes were for sale. That got us wondering if we could make some cash selling bikes. Jim suggested we visit the local garbage dump to see what we could find. At that time, the dump was open to scavengers. We found all kinds of bike parts and carted them back to my house. Over the next three years, we'd spend quite a lot of time rummaging amid trash and junk for bike frames and parts.

There was a shed alongside the garage at my house, and it became our shop. After school and on weekends, after completing our other neighborhood jobs, we worked on bikes. We sold our first within a week for thirty-five dollars—big money at the time. Soon we were selling one or two bikes a week. Because of our entrepreneurship, we were never without funds for dates and food and other things.

THE CALL OF CATHOLICISM

In spring 1961, my family converted to Roman Catholicism. We had been nondenominational most of my life and didn't go to church very often, so maybe "convert" isn't quite the right word. But Mom had been raised Catholic, and one day she announced that we were going to be Catholic. Nobody objected, and so we took our instruction at St. Jude Catholic Church in South Holland, a bedroom community south of Dolton.

Father Naughton, the lead pastor, taught me about the religion. He was a saintly man who loved the Catholic Church. His knowledge, authority, and passion made me love the church. In the late spring of 1961, I was baptized.

In the early 1960s, Catholicism was more ritualistic and traditional than it is today. Church services tended to be more formal, especially on high holy days. The church still had the Latin mass, and the pope was still infallible. And there were rules. Meat could not be eaten on Fridays, and church members were supposed to fast from food for three hours, and water for one hour, prior to communion. That rule made communion meaningful to me.

As Catholics, we were expected to confess our sins regularly. Confession is one of Catholicism's seven sacraments. I usually went to confession and communion once every couple of weeks except during Lent, when I went every week. Confession was done privately, in a small, three-booth cabinet inside the church. There were two enclosed booths for church members on either side of a middle box, where the priest sat. You entered a booth and knelt, facing a small, screened window connected to the middle box. The window was meant only for the priest and confessor to hear each other. You, the sinner seeking absolution, were anonymous. You waited nervously in the stillness until the priest slid open the window. That was your signal to start. You then said, "Forgive me, father, for I have sinned," and itemized your transgressions since your last visit. I'd say something like: "I've taken the Lord's name in vain four times; I've had impure thoughts three times; I took what was not my own two times." Everyone was expected to not only identify specific sins, but make clear how many failings you'd had. I tried very hard to remember all the bad things that I had done during the week so that I could give a good confession.

Once you were done, the priest would admonish you briefly, tell you to improve your behavior, and then note your penance. Prayers would need to be recited or occasionally a task would be given to perform prior to absolution taking place. A task might be returning

 Father Naughton taught me that the church was traditional and historic.

something you took or apologizing if you had been disrespectful. But once the prayers or tasks were performed, your sins would be forgiven and you were free to take Holy Communion. It was all very nerve-racking, and I always left the box feeling relieved.

At St. Jude, confession was held several times during the week and on Saturday. For my friends and me Saturday was, typically, the day for confession. We always tried to get there early so we could see which priest was going into the confessional. Our reasoning was simple: The young priest, whose name I can't remember, was, shall we say, easy, usually giving only ten Our Fathers and ten Hail Marys at most. Father Naughton, on the other hand, was known to occasionally speak rather loudly and give penance that required a lot more time. I remember him telling me once that for absolution, I had to say one rosary a day for a week. I don't remember what I did but I must surely have irritated him greatly. On one occasion, he gave several of us the stations of the cross as penance. Suffice to say it took us most of the day to accomplish that.

Believe it or not, confession actually appealed to my friends and me. We liked the idea that we could date on Friday night, make out with our dates (I did not have a steady girl, but I did occasionally date), then go to confession on Saturday, do an act of contrition and penance, and take communion on Sunday. To our way of thinking, this schedule gave us quite a bit of behavioral leeway on Friday nights. If, God forbid, we were ungentlemanly on dates, or a bit raucous, by Sunday noon we were sin- and guilt-free, and good to go again. Every week, a clean slate!

More seriously, Father Naughton taught me that the church was traditional and historic. It could trace its lineage back to Peter the Apostle, who Roman Catholics revere as the first pope. The Catholic Church was the true church, he said, because it was the same yesterday as it is today. God and his church are unchangeable. Right is always right, and wrong is always wrong. That deep moral underpinning appealed to a young man struggling with teenage insecurities. I was enthralled with a holy institution that could trace its origins all the way back to Jesus.

These days, many of Catholicism's traditions and prohibitions still exist, but many church members don't pay much attention to them. The Catholic Church is far less formal today than it was fifty years ago. The changes that stemmed from the Second Vatican Council in 1964 caused me to question my belief in the infallibility of the church. How could a church that claimed to be right suddenly change its thousand years of tradition? I couldn't come to terms with it, so I left the church shortly after returning from Vietnam. I would find my faith elsewhere.

THE COLD WAR

I became politically aware during the 1960 presidential campaign, when John F. Kennedy ran against Richard Nixon. Kennedy was the youthful idealist and Nixon was the stern old man, though he and Kennedy were peers. Nixon always appeared hunched over and severe looking, while Kennedy was handsome and robust. Because Kennedy was a smart, articulate candidate, and a Democrat, my family was taken with him from the start. The fact that he was a war hero added to our infatuation.

Of course, the press was more discreet in those days. There were no "bimbo" outbreaks because personal matters were off-limits to the media. There was seldom a need for "damage control." As I recall, it was an election based upon ideas and issues. Chicago-style politics and other shenanigans might have figured in it—but in the early 1960s, most people were naïve; politicians were trusted, by and large, and there was an expectation of honesty among public officials.

The fact that John Kennedy came from money, earned by a father of dubious character, didn't matter. He spoke eloquently about his vision for our nation. We loved JFK, Jackie, and their children. He was a Democrat and, therefore, the candidate for the workingman. We were thrilled when he became president. The famous line in his inauguration speech, "Ask not what your country can do for you—ask what you can do for your country," hit home with me. It made me want to do something good for the country, though I had no idea what.

For a short time in high school, I played the guitar. Mom and Dad got me lessons with a private teacher. On October 22, 1962, I walked into my guitar teacher's house and heard President Kennedy on a radio. My teacher and I sat and listened as Kennedy explained a potential threat to America's security: The Soviet Union was shipping intercontinental ballistic missiles to Cuba. The president said the United States was not going to allow the U.S.S.R. to place missiles in Cuba, ninety miles from our shores; the weapons would have to be withdrawn. He went on to say that any missile launched from Cuba would be viewed as if it was launched from the Soviet Union.

The speech scared me and a lot of other people. I thought we were going to war. The next day at school, everyone talked about it. It was an anxious moment for America—but I think we all believed that our country and its leadership would protect us. If there were to be a war, we would win. I remember watching television and seeing the U.S. presentation to the United Nations on the Cuban Missile Crisis. I was proud to be an American and to see how strong we were. When the crisis was over on October 28, after Nikita Khrushchev backed down and ordered the missiles returned to the U.S.S.R, we had a lot to celebrate. We as a nation had come close to a major military confrontation and yet had prevailed peacefully. I had a lot to celebrate, too—it was my birthday. That was the first national crisis that I closely followed, and like everyone, I was glad when it was over and war was avoided. Then it was time to get ready for the holidays!

NO PLACE LIKE HOME FOR THE HOLIDAYS

Christmas was the most exciting time of the year in our family. The good cheer started about a week before Thanksgiving and culminated with New Year's Eve. We always had Thanksgiving dinner with the extended family. The assorted smells coming from the kitchen— the turkey, sweet potatoes, mashed potatoes, vegetables, various casseroles—intoxicated me. After the dinner feast came the aroma of pies warming in the oven—pumpkin pie, apple pie, cherry pie— plus cookies. I was always in a blissful daze during Thanksgiving. After dinner the men would settle back, while the kids—with the women supervising—would clean the table and do the dishes.

After Thanksgiving came the buildup to Christmas. There was the thrill of Christmas shopping, gifts being stashed, and searching for just the right tree. The tree would sit on the porch until we put it up two weeks before Christmas. Throughout the Christmas season, especially after the decorations were up, we'd visit our friends and family.

On Christmas Eve, we'd usually gather upstairs at my Aunt Marty and Uncle Chester's apartment before attending midnight mass. The men would smoke, play poker, and talk politics, and the women would cook—Italian dishes, Polish dishes, and desserts, as well as almond rolls and Christmas cookies. Oh, the smells that came from that kitchen! The food would be warm and waiting for us after mass. It drove me crazy that I couldn't touch it before church, owing to the fast before communion. At 11:00 p.m., we'd all get dressed for mass. Men wore suits, women put on their finest, and the children were nicely attired. It was a way we honored God.

Christmas Eve mass was always a High Mass, with incense, a choir, and the beauty of a candlelight service. There was majesty about the mass that made me feel the holiness of the night Jesus was born—though decades later I came to learn he was probably born in the early fall.

Once mass was over, we hightailed it home for a Christmas Eve feast. It was a relatively light meal if you consider Polish and Italian sausage, baked mostaccioli, and a variety of desserts a light meal. At some time during the party, as with most of our family parties, Dad, Uncle Dick, and Aunt Laurie (who was just a year and a half older than me and had a marvelous voice) would start harmonizing Christmas songs and some of the old barbershop quartet songs learned from their years in the Society for the Preservation and Encouragement of Barbershop Quartet Singing.

Christmas Day, we all awoke early, groggy but happy. We gave each other gifts and hugs and kisses, and then relaxed. In the afternoon, we would visit family and a week later, we'd have another family party on New Year's Eve. More amazingly good food would be served, songs would be sung, and a good time had by all. Then it was the long drought of no holidays until Memorial Day and summer vacation.

A BAD HABIT

I'm embarrassed to admit it now, but I started to smoke when I was a high school freshman, age fourteen. All my friends smoked, too. Everyone, it seemed, smoked. We wouldn't know the health risks associated with the habit until years later. Dad knew I smoked and occasionally borrowed cigarettes from me, always saying, "Don't tell Mom." He didn't want her to know that he knew I was smoking. It was our little secret, or so I thought.

On our way to Saint Germain Lake for vacation one year, we stopped in a little town in central Wisconsin for breakfast. When we finished, we took a little walk to stretch our legs. I lagged behind Mom, Dad, and Nancy so I could smoke. I lit up quietly and kept the cigarette cupped in my hand so Mom wouldn't see it if she turned around. What I didn't realize is that moms see everything! After we'd walked a block, she turned around and said, "You aren't fooling me, come walk with us. I'd rather have you smoke in front of me than behind my back." I would smoke and enjoy it until January 15, 1969, when I quit cold turkey. I haven't had a cigarette since, though occasionally I smoke a good cigar, especially if there's brandy.

THE DAY KENNEDY DIED

It was my senior year, and I had just sat down for my fourth period health class, just after lunch. An announcement came over the school intercom: President Kennedy had been shot while on a visit to Dallas, Texas. A hush fell over the classroom. Over the next several minutes there were more intercom announcements, including one that said the president was in surgery and doing well. The bell rang to end the period, and I moved to my next class, English. Instead of the usual high-pitched chatter of teens in the hallways, there was only an eerie quiet. A few students were crying; a few talked in hushed whispers. Most everybody was in a state of shock. Shortly after I got to English class, there came the news again via intercom: President Kennedy was dead. A short time later, we were sent home. The day Lee Harvey Oswald assassinated President John F. Kennedy, November 23, 1963, is a day I'll never forget.

After Kennedy's death, we saw Jack Ruby, on live television, shoot and kill Oswald. What the hell was happening? I started looking at the world with a different set of eyes. The TV networks showed footage of both the assassination and Oswald's killing, again and again, in slow motion. News anchors explained what we were seeing, as if we were too stupid to understand for ourselves what had happened.

I remember my mother crying softly as we watched Kennedy's funeral. We all mourned for the first family. They'd been America's family. We had cried when John and Jackie's son Patrick was stillborn. We smiled at photos of little John at the White House with his dad. They'd represented Camelot, and while it was a myth, the Kennedys were a glamorous reflection of America's vigor and promise, at least to my family and many others. And then Camelot was gone. I believe that at some level, my generation still mourns Kennedy's death.

Our family watched on television as Lyndon Johnson was sworn in as president. My mother, wonderfully positive, said that Johnson would be able to get JFK's domestic agenda passed, because of his huge clout in Congress. She was right; Johnson did get some land-mark legislation passed, notably the Civil Rights Act of 1964. My family and most Democrats were happy with Johnson, at least until he seized on the Gulf of Tonkin incident to ratchet up America's mil-itary involvement in the Vietnam War. Johnson's popularity would slide. The Vietnam War would be his crucible—and mine, but not for a while yet.

TIME TO WORK

In the early summer of 1962, my dad's union went on strike against Union Carbide. It was a rather long strike, and striking workers are not paid. Dad needed a job to bring home some money. He found one as the plant mechanic at Tetco Metal Products, a small wa-ter-heater company in Riverdale, Illinois, our neighboring town. He was in charge of the machine shop at Tetco, and loved it. When the strike ended, Tetco management persuaded him to stay on and work nights, repairing machines.

One day after I got my homework done, I told Mom I was going to visit Dad at Tetco. My plan was to walk down Greenwood Road through Dolton to Riverdale and on to Tetco, located near 141st Street and Indiana Avenue. It was about a five-mile walk. As I was ambling down Greenwood Road, I noticed a slow-moving freight train heading toward the freight yard in Riverdale. I walked over to the track, and as a car came alongside, I hopped on the ladder on the side of the car and rode the train all the way into Riverdale. I'd found a cool way to visit my dad. I would ride freight trains to Tetco for nearly a year and a half until I got my driver's license.

When the train got close to the company, I hopped off the freight car and walked over to Dad's shop window. I tapped on it. He turned and a big smile spread over his face. He opened the door and said,

"Hello, son, what brings you here?" I told him that I was done with homework and was bored, so I thought I'd take a walk. Dad showed me the shop, and over the next several months, the two of us spent a lot of time together there. Dad taught me how to weld and how to use a milling machine and a grinder. He taught me how to use a feeler gauge, which can measure tolerances, on machines or on parts he was making to within a thousandth or even a ten-thousandth of an inch. He taught me a lot in that little factory.

My senior year, Dad offered me a job at Tetco as the night janitor. I'd make a few dollars an hour, he said, and I'd work weekends, too. I took the job. The first night of my employment Dad walked me through the building, explaining my responsibilities. First, I was to clean the front office—empty some trash baskets, clean the coffee machine, and sweep the floor. Not bad. Once a week I would need to wash and wax the floor. Next came the men's bathroom and locker room. There were eight stalls in the bathroom, each with a commode. When Dad kicked open the first stall door, I almost lost it. The commode was un-flushed and disgusting. Stall number two seemed worse than the first. I was grim. Dad said, with a sly grin on his face, "Just remember, this is why soap was created. You can always wash your hands."

We went into the locker room. On the walls were pinups of women in various stages of undress, and some who were not dressed at all and posing in very unladylike ways. Now, I had looked at *Playboys* before with my friends, but never with my dad! He just smiled and said, "Welcome to the real world," adding, "Just because they're up there doesn't mean you have to look at them." I thought, "How can I avoid it? I'm a seventeen-year-old boy, soon to be eighteen, and I have urges, and you tell me not to notice them!" Yet after a couple of days the novelty of the photos wore off.

Dad showed me a few more rooms that needed cleaning and then took me to the office of the company president and owner Mr. Teters. Dad made sure I knew that it was the boss' office and required special attention. He explained precisely how the office should be cleaned. Finally, he was ready to let me get to work. He left me with a final warning: "You got this job on my reputation; don't let me down. When you are done, come get me, and I'll inspect your work." Left unsaid but fully understood was the message "and it better meet my standards."

I did all the easy jobs first. I cleaned Mr. Teters' office, then the other offices, and then inspected my own work. I was sure I'd done a great job. Next, I ventured into the dreaded locker room. I was in full panic mode. How in the name of all that is holy was I to clean the commodes and not go bug nuts? Dad had shown me the janitor's closet, and I remembered seeing a brush and rubber gloves. They will help, I thought. I grabbed them along with a bucket and a bottle of bleach. Then as I returned to the bathroom, I noticed a high-pressure hose. That will help, too. I looked for a floor drain, and found it. I was on a roll. I went back to the janitor's closet, and there was the last piece of the puzzle: a squeegee. I felt a surge of confidence—I might be able to clean the commodes without contracting a disease. Each commode got a heavy brush scrubbing with bleach and then got hit with the hose. I squeegeed the water into the drain. Then I brought in two heavy floor fans I'd seen elsewhere in the factory. I pointed one toward the stalls and set the other to blow on the bathroom floor.

I went to get Dad, all proud of myself. He came back and with a furrowed brow began to inspect my work. He checked the offices. Pass. He examined the coffee machine. Fail! I'd noticed old coffee, cream, and sugar in the coffee-machine reservoir, and thinking it foul, didn't clean it. I figured Dad would never spot it. Wrong! We then proceeded to the locker room. He inspected each stall, the floors, the windows, everything. Then he saw the hose. I thought I was in for it. But he smiled and said, "How did you think of using that?" I explained. He told me that the locker room had never looked better and how proud he was of me for doing such a great job.

His shift was over, and so was mine. I was tired and thought we'd just head home, but instead we headed to Dave's, a nearby bar. He ordered a bottle of beer for himself and a Coke for me. We sat, talked, and then played a couple games of shuffleboard. As we played, Dad told me I could have a small drink of his beer—but I couldn't let the bartender see me drinking it. I felt ten feet tall.

The next night, I got a compliment from dad. He'd gotten a note from somebody at Tetco saying that the men were impressed with how clean their locker room was. I was excited. After a week, I'd got the cleaning routine down to a science. It took me almost six hours to clean the building that first night, but by the end of the second week, I could get the job done in half the time. I learned very quickly to do all the hard stuff first. Soon I was doing my homework at Tetco, after cleaning the place, and on nights when I didn't have homework I helped Dad in the machine shop. And most nights we ended up at Dave's.

THE END OF SCHOOL

As my senior year at Thornridge drew to a close, I began to think about my future. I realized that I didn't have many options. My weak grades meant that college was out, but then I'd never thought seriously about going to college. It wasn't for me, I thought. I was the son of a blue-collar man, and figured my future would be the same. I might go to a trade school, but college? No way! Dad encouraged me to learn a trade or some skill that would make me valuable to a factory. He told me often that being a tradesman enabled him to earn a living during hard times. But I just wasn't interested in the trades or anything for that matter.

My dad often made snide remarks about "college boys" and how little they knew about factory work. He didn't realize his own class pride. The men in the family had often talked about the arrogance of the upper class, never realizing that it was a two-way street. I

 I was the son of a blue-collar man, and figured my future would be the same.

think listening to all of the talk about college boys dissuaded me from even thinking about going to college. I believed at that time the factory was my future.

Finally, the great day came: June 5, 1964, high school graduation day. I'd been looking forward to it for four years. I thought, "I am done with school forever." No more stupid homework. Never again would I worry about failing a class and report cards. Little did I know then, as I was making all those brash statements to my family and friends, I'd be back in school in fewer than ten years.

Until then, I was free! Well, not exactly. I'd gotten a full-time job at Tetco, in the shipping and receiving department, starting Monday morning. Work started at 7:00 a.m., but I'd be off at 3:30 p.m. Plus, I'd get a ten-minute break in the morning, thirty minutes for lunch, and a ten-minute break in the afternoon. What's not to like?

Then Dad dropped a bombshell. Since I was set to be a workingman, he said, he expected me to help the family by paying rent—about $75 a month, as I recall. I was dumbfounded. Rent? I had to pay rent? I couldn't believe it. It wasn't a large amount, but to me, having lived in the family home all my life, it was a shock. Looking back, it was my father's way of telling me that I was now a man and had to make my own way. The unstated message was that nothing is ever free, even at home.

My job at Tetco didn't last very long. I was fired within a week, One day after unloading a truck, I took an unscheduled break. The plant manager happened to walk by as I was sitting during work time. About twenty minutes later I was told to pick up my check—I

 I began to realize the my future was not going to be in Dolton with my family.

was out! When I told Dad, he said he'd already heard. "It's simple," he said. "They are paying you to work and not sit. You sat. Welcome to the real world. And congratulations—you've just been fired from your first job. Oh, you still owe us rent for the month so you better get another job soon." My heart sank. So, this is what it is like to be "on your own"?

Within a week, I had a new job at Owens-Illinois, a box-making company. The plant was in Dolton, just three miles from home. I ran a machine that taped the seams of boxes. Again, I didn't last long. After three weeks, I quit. I didn't get along with the foreman. One day he told me to do something, and I told him I didn't want to. He said, "So you quit?" I said, "I guess so."

Within a week I found yet another job, at Libby, McNeill & Libby in Chicago. Libby's made canned food—beef stew, sausage, fruit, and such. I started work in the shipping department, unloading trucks and boxcars. I learned to drive a forklift. After ninety days, I was admitted to the meatpackers union and was making very good money. I loved the job and worked there until I joined the army on November 4, 1964. Little did I know how working at Libby's would change my life in the future.

By then my best friends from high school—Jim, Paul, and Turk— were all working and had bought cars. I got one, too—a candy-apple red 1960 Pontiac Catalina convertible. I think I paid fifteen hundred dollars for it. And we all had girlfriends. I was dating Gail, a sweet girl who was still in high school. Friday night was our date night, and Saturday night was guys' night. Most Saturday nights, we'd get a bum to buy us a case of beer from a liquor store on State- line Road, which divided Calumet City, Illinois, from Hammond, Indiana. Indiana was "dry" on Sunday, and so those living close to the border went to Stateline Road to buy liquor. It was also a hang- out for drunks, who, for a small fee, would buy beer for underage teens like us.

My life quickly became routine. There was my job at the plant during the week, a date with Gail on Friday, and a night of drinking beer with my buddies on Saturday. But I quickly became restless. I loved my job but I didn't want to work in the same plant, doing the same things, all my life. I wanted something more. I began to realize that my future was not going to be in Dolton with my family.

I knew that if I wanted to become something more than a gen- eral factory worker, I had to get out on my own. And yet, my op- tions remained severely limited. In the early '60s, if you didn't go to college or a trade school, you got drafted. I wanted to chart my own course after graduation, not just wait for something to happen. I decided I would join the army and get my service out of the way.

In the late summer of 1964, while my parents and sister were on vacation, I went to the local draft board, talked to one of the board members, and asked him if I could have my draft number moved up. It was not an unusual request, and he was happy to grant it because I would have been drafted in October or November anyway. I didn't want my mother to know that I'd chosen to join the army, and moving up my number was the way to ensure that I'd be drafted. Only then did I realize that even after my two years of active duty, I'd still have two years of reserve duty. But, if I did three years of active duty, I would only have an inactive reserve commitment when I got out. And I could control the date that I was going to leave. I told the recruiter I wanted to enlist the first week of November; that way I could spend my nineteenth birthday at home.

I was now a man and it was clear to me that, for all intents and purposes, I was on my own. I was responsible for my own decisions and actions like never before in my life. Dad had taught me a lot about responsibility and respect. Now at the age of eighteen, soon to be nineteen, I knew it was time for me to put all he taught me and all I learned in school to work. I had learned a lot from the many odd jobs that Jim, Paul, and I had through high school. I learned a lot during the summer working in factories. All of those experiences would help me as I entered the next chapter of my life, the army.

CHAPTER 7

IN THE ARMY NOW

THE YEAR I ENLISTED, 1964, WAS A PRESIDENTIAL ELECTION year. President Lyndon B. Johnson ran against Barry Goldwater. By the time I graduated from high school in June, the campaign was in full swing. It was a hotly contested race. Goldwater, a Republican, was billed as a brash warmonger who would blow up the world at the slightest provocation, while Johnson, who'd assumed the presidency after the assassination of President Kennedy, ran as the peace candidate.

There was no question who my family supported. We were Democrats, had voted for Kennedy, and would be voting for Johnson. My family and many others viewed him as an extension of Kennedy, even though the backgrounds and personalities of the two men could not have been more different. We wouldn't know for decades just how corrupt Johnson was, and how much damage he would cause to his country.

I remember many family discussions about how Goldwater was rallying crowds much like Hitler had done in the 1930s, and some Democratic politicians were making the same point. Nobody realized that when President Johnson asserted that "we are not about to send American boys 9 or 10,000 miles away from home to do what

Asian boys ought to be doing for themselves," there were already a lot of U.S. military advisers in South Vietnam. Johnson was preparing for a war between the United States and North Vietnam that would require many thousands of American boys to fight in Asia. Communist North Vietnam, with aid from China, aimed to defeat South Vietnam and take control of the country. The United States was determined to stop it, as part of the effort begun in the 1950s by John Foster Dulles and his brother, Allen, to roll back communism.

Earlier in the year President Johnson, unknown to voters, had authorized covert military operations off the coast of North Vietnam. Then on August 2, 1964, two U.S. Navy destroyers reported being fired upon by North Vietnamese torpedo boats in the Gulf of Tonkin. Two days later, the two ships reported another attack. There were no U.S. casualties, and the historical consensus now is that there was no second attack.

Nevertheless, the Johnson administration and Congress inflated what was at most a minor skirmish into a significant assault against the U.S. military, and then used "the Gulf of Tonkin incident" as a pretense to ramp up America's military effort in Vietnam. On August 7, Congress passed the Gulf of Tonkin Resolution, giving the president wide-ranging authority to protect American interests in Southeast Asia (meaning Vietnam), and on August 10 Johnson signed it. He informed the nation about the resolution and its implications in a televised address.

I ENLIST

I did not watch that address. Like many teenagers at the time, I had no interest in the news and only watched it occasionally while waiting for the 10:15 p.m. movie to start. Though I could probably have picked out Vietnam on a map, I knew almost nothing about the country or America's escalating involvement there before I joined the army. For me, it was a vague, inconsequential nation that was messing with Uncle Sam. We'd handle the problem. Besides, there were more important things to do, such as deciding where my friends and I were going to party on Friday nights and what we were going to do Saturdays.

 For me, [Vietnam] was a vague, inconsequential nation that was messing with Uncle Sam.

On October 28, I celebrated my last birthday at home with family and friends and got myself mentally prepped to join the military. On November 3, Johnson defeated Goldwater. Six days later—Monday, November 9—I enlisted in the U.S. Army.

I chose three years of active duty rather than two. A three-year enlistment came with no reserve-service requirement, and so seemed the shorter alternative—never mind the risks associated with a third year of active duty. One of the benefits of enlisting was that I could pick my army specialty school. I chose personnel and would go on to serve as a clerk. Personnel seemed like an easy way to get through three years of active duty. That calculation proved wrong.

At the time of my enlistment, some twenty-three thousand American personnel were already in Vietnam. Before long a lot of young guys would be headed to the dangerous jungles of that country—I among them. By the end of 1965, a year after Johnson's election, the number of U.S. troops in Vietnam would rise to 184,300. By the end of 1966, that number would reach 385,300. American boys were fighting and dying in significant numbers—by the time the U.S. military withdrew from Vietnam in March 1973, more than 58,220 American men and women would lose their lives. Thousands more would be wounded or suffer health issues from the spraying of the toxic defoliant Agent Orange. And thousands of U.S. service members would commit suicide because of the trauma of serving in Vietnam and coming home to a hostile nation that treated them horribly.

But that was all in the future.

BASIC TRAINING

On November 9, I got up at 5:30 a.m. with my dad and mom and had a nice breakfast—bacon and eggs, as usual, and a cup coffee. I was nineteen years old. When Dad was ready to leave for work, he gave me a long hug and said goodbye. I didn't realize it then, but Dad and I would never be as close as we were at that moment. A few minutes later, I said goodbye to Nancy, who was just getting up for school. Then Mom and I drove down to Chicago's Armed Forces Examining and Entrance Station (AFEES) on Dearborn Street.

Mom dropped me off at the entrance to the dingy, red brick building. We both got out of the car and gave each other a goodbye hug. She was very quiet. She told me she loved me, gave me a kiss, then got back in her car and left. I watched as her car moved away, getting smaller and smaller. When I could no longer see it, I opened the AFEES door and started up a long dark stairway. There was one light bulb hanging from an electrical cord in the ceiling. The lone bulb and the murky stairway made me nervous. I had a knot in my stomach—and with each step I took my anxiety increased.

I reached the top of the stairs and reported to a man in uniform behind a desk. He told me to take a seat in a large classroom that was already mostly filled with young men like myself. Over the next several hours we were given several tests and a very comprehensive physical examination. We were poked and prodded and tested. Strangers looked at parts of my body that I had never seen.

There were about fifty new recruits, and after the testing we were taken to a room and told to relax. On one side of the room was an American flag trimmed in gold, along with other flags representing all the military services. A short time later we were told to form ranks, which we did. After we had formed four ranks, an officer entered the room. I think he was a second lieutenant. We were asked to raise our right hand and to repeat after him. "I, Allen James Lynch, do solemnly swear that I will support and defend the Constitution of the United States of America against all enemies foreign and domestic, and that I will bear true faith and allegiance to the same." The oath went on, and we all said, "I do."

Not long after, those of us who were going into the army were taken a few blocks away to Union Station, where we boarded a train bound for Louisville, Kentucky, for basic training. We arrived in Louisville the next morning. Buses at the train depot were waiting to take us to Fort Knox, where we would spend the next eight weeks learning how to be soldiers.

Fort Knox is located amid 109,000 acres in the beautiful hills of central Kentucky. It is 333 miles from Chicago and 40 miles south of Louisville. I remember the bus ride to the base as being a very long trip, despite the fact that it lasted only an hour. It was the last hour before a major change in my life: Reality—the fact that I was about to become a soldier—was rapidly sinking in.

As soon as the bus pulled up and stopped at Fort Knox, a noncommissioned officer got on and told us in a rather forceful way to get off the bus and to place our feet on stenciled footprints on the concrete just outside the bus. The footprints were there to teach us the proper placement of our feet for the position of attention.

This was our first lesson in "falling into" formation. I was prepared to encounter officers screaming orders at us, but that didn't happen. Two noncommissioned officers (NCOs) met us. The sergeant who'd boarded the bus was in charge. His assistant made sure we moved smartly, stood where we were supposed to stand, and kept our mouths shut. The sergeant told us to get rid of any dirty magazines we might possess, along with any weapons such as knives or brass knuckles. Anyone subsequently found with a personal weapon or adult publication, he added, would be severely reprimanded. We had no idea what that meant, but we damn sure didn't want to experience it. The tone of his voice suggested nothing less than doom for any act of misconduct. If there is one thing that drives all recruits to get through basic training, it is the foreboding bellow of sergeants ready to lower the boom on anyone who fails to meet the army's expectations. It's been fifty years, and I can still hear the ominous bellowing of sergeants.

Other than that, the first hours for my group of recruits were fairly relaxed. We were taken into a classroom for a brief orientation, and then were loosely marched to a barracks-like building and told to form a single line. A medic came out and told us we were going to get a series of vaccine shots. He made a strong suggestion: "When you get a shot, look straight ahead and not at the needle. And don't flex your arm muscle to try to break the needle." He also informed us that should we flex our muscles while getting the polio shot (delivered by some sort of shotgun-like device) our arms could be ripped wide open because of the air pressure used.

At the first station we got a shot in each arm. At the next station we each got our polio shot. At the third station we again got one shot in each arm. I'll never forget the well-built young recruit who, at one station, looked at the needle going in his arm and immediately passed out. He was carried outside, revived, and put back in line to receive his remaining shots. There is no sympathy for anyone, at any time, in basic training.

For the most part, there was no harassment, though it was made clear by the NCOs that there was to be no nonsense. One recruit made the mistake of talking while we were in ranks and got barked at by the young sergeant in charge. But as long as we kept silent and did what we were told, the first "duty day," as it was called, wasn't so bad.

Even my first taste of army food was OK. We ate lunch and dinner in the mess hall, and the "chow," as I recall, was more than tolerable. Meals in the army are referred to as "chow" morning chow, dinner chow, evening chow, or just plain chow. It sounded strange at first, but I got used to it and learned to look forward to chow time.

At the end of the first day, we were released and allowed to roam around the reception station. There was a PX (Post Exchange) for shopping and a movie theater showing the new James Bond movie, *Goldfinger*. I never thought that on my first official night in the army I'd be watching a newly released movie. The only difference between an army theater and a civilian theater is that, in the army, the national anthem is played before all movies, and everyone stands for it. I began to think: How hard could this soldier stuff be?

The second day, we were issued our uniforms. Then we were marched back to the barracks and told to pack our civilian clothes in boxes, which would be mailed to our homes. We had to pay for the postage. It wasn't a problem because we'd received, as I recall, a half month's advance pay to cover early expenses. Also on that day we got the infamous military haircut—the buzz cut. We had to pay for that, too. Our second night was much like the first: After duty hours, we were free to roam about the reception station.

THE DRILLS BEGIN

On the third day, everything changed. That morning, right after chow, our basic training sergeants arrived. Life as we knew it was over. We recruits were no longer individuals who could think for ourselves. Henceforth, we would be told what to do and when to do it. Even a simple act such as smoking a cigarette could only be done when approved by the sergeant. We would be told when to sleep, when to wake up, and even when we could go to the bathroom, commonly called the latrine.

It was all part of indoctrinating us into the military way of thinking. It didn't matter what color we were, what sort of education we'd had, or where we were from: We were now all part of the same team. Still, it would take a few weeks of very hard discipline for that lesson to sink in.

We were no longer recruits but "trainees." Our unit was B-9-3, which stood for B Company, 9th Battalion, 3rd Training Brigade. To be called "soldiers" we had to graduate from basic training. It's surprising how degrading a word can be when it is said in a particular way. We came to perceive "trainee" as a derogatory term because of the condescending tone with which sergeants said it. That was part of basic training—to break down individuals and then work to build them up.

I was in 3rd Platoon, comprising about fifty men. Sgt. Wright (we never knew his first name) was our platoon sergeant. Sgt. Wright, who was probably in his mid-twenties at the time, was the classic, old-time sergeant—fit, upright, and tough. He was not to be messed with.

Most of the basic training sergeants in our unit at Fort Knox were noncommissioned officers and were not drill sergeants. As I recall, the army had just started the drill sergeant program and there were none in our unit. Near the end of our training, Sgt. Wright would get orders to report to drill sergeant school. He was very happy about it. I would later earn the privilege of being called drill sergeant myself, after going to the Drill Sergeant Academy in the late 1970s, when I was in the reserves with the 85th Division.

The barracks at Fort Knox were vintage World War II. They were two stories high, and each floor had enough living space for two squads, one on each side of the floor. There were twelve men in each squad, or about twenty-four men on each floor. Each living area, or squad bay, had six double-decker bunks. Each man was assigned a footlocker and a wall locker. We were shown how to display our uniforms in our lockers and how to make up our bunks—and, yes, the blankets had to be tight enough that a quarter would bounce when dropped on the bed. Everything, from our towels, laundry bags, wall lockers, and footlockers, had to be displayed properly. Nothing could be the least bit out of place. We were in the army now.

Each barracks had a latrine—one latrine for fifty men. Its primary feature was a lack of privacy. There were nine commodes, all right next to one another. There were no stalls. When you had to take care of business, you did so right beside, or across from, another guy. The first night in the barracks, I tried to wait until everyone in the platoon was in bed asleep before going to the latrine for a BM, but others had the same idea. I learned a basic fact of life for a trainee—there would be no privacy.

There was one communal shower, with six showerheads along the wall. It was like the commodes, up close and personal. I couldn't help remembering the long, hot showers and leisurely baths I'd taken at home all my life. No more. At Fort Knox, I took quick showers: I could wash completely and be toweling off in a minute or two. Outside the shower, sinks lined one side of a wall. Above the sinks was a long shelf on which we all put our shaving cream, razors, toothbrushes, and general toiletries.

Each platoon had a platoon guide, who was responsible for ensuring that the barracks were properly cleaned, that all the men in the platoon were accounted for, and that any other tasks deemed necessary by the platoon sergeant were accomplished to his standards. Each of the four squads had an acting squad leader, who was responsible for accounting for every man in his squad at all times. He also ensured that any assigned details were done properly. The squad leaders on each floor shared a private room and the platoon guide had his own room. Sgt. Wright had a private room on the first floor. There's a saying in all the military services: "Rank has its privileges." A private or semi-private room is certainly a privilege. What they don't add is that rank also has its responsibilities.

I was made second squad leader. Imagine that—me, high school malcontent, as squad leader. I don't know why I was picked. But, at least until I was relieved, I was able to move into one of the private rooms with two other squad leaders.

Generally, the platoon was run by the platoon sergeant (Wright), his assistant platoon sergeant, the platoon guide, and acting squad leaders. This was a microcosm of the real army. As squad leaders, we were responsible for giving an attendance report to our platoon guide at first formation and at several other formations during the day. We either said "all present" or reported those who were missing from formation ("Private Jones on sick call"). We were also responsible for making sure our squad learned the subjects taught every day and for maintaining a squad duty roster, which was kept to ensure that all duty work was split evenly among the squad members.

Sgt. Wright was a tall African American man. He wasn't married and lived in the barracks. He wore airborne wings over his right pocket, which meant that he'd been through airborne training at Fort Benning, Georgia. He was demanding—all sergeant, from the top of his head to his spit-shined Corcoran jump boots. "If Sergeant Wright ain't happy," he bellowed at us one day early in basic training, "ain't no one going to be happy." We trainees tried to keep him happy.

Before joining the army, I had never had any interaction with African Americans. Now I was subordinate to one. I didn't know what to expect. I was a white kid from a white neighborhood and had only seen African Americans or people of other ethnicities or nationalities from a distance. My family was very liberal and we talked about racial equality, but we had no black friends. In basic training, I lived

 Each man had to put away his personal biases if he expected to survive basic training.

and trained in a melting pot—African Americans, Mexican Americans, Puerto Ricans, city boys, country boys, young men who'd had some college education, and young men who had dropped out of school at a very early age. Some men were racist; some men were not. In the end, for all our personal differences, we trainees recognized that we had to work together as a team. Each man had to put away his personal biases if he expected to survive basic training.

Early on, some of the men worried that Sgt. Wright would treat black trainees better than white ones. But he soon dispelled that notion. As it turned out, Sgt. Wright was harder on African Americans than anyone else. That's not to say that he wasn't hard on all of us—he was. He simply demanded perfection from everyone in his platoon.

Our typical day started at 0530 hours (5:30 a.m.) with first call, an army term for "time to wake up." In basic training, the platoon sergeant and his assistant platoon sergeant woke the platoon by barging into the squad bay and screaming at the top of their lungs, "Get up! Get up!" Then they'd start walking down the squad bay, one on each side. If a trainee was not out of his bunk by then, the sergeant or his assistant tipped it over. That's not very pleasant if you are in the top bunk. Luckily, I was in the lower bunk. Sometimes they'd throw a garbage can down the center of the squad bay.

 The army loves push-ups and considers them to be the antidote to every failure while in training.

Once out of bed, we had a half hour to get our business done in the latrine, shave, dress, and get our area cleaning started. I was surprised at what a person can do in thirty minutes. At 0600 hours, we would fall out for the day's first formation, physical training.

Physical Training Formation, commonly called PT Formation or just PT, consisted of several exercises that were meant to build our stamina and strength. If you failed to do an exercise properly, or were out of sync with everyone else, you were ordered to do push-ups as punishment. The army loves push-ups and considers them the antidote to every failure while in training. Morning PT always ended with a one- to two-mile run. The first few PTs were exhausting for everybody, but as we got in shape they weren't as difficult. Our PT uniform consisted of fatigues and combat boots. These days, PT uniforms are different—running shoes, shorts or long pants (depending upon the weather), and shirts to match.

There was one rule during a run: No one dropped out. The rule was meant to reinforce the idea that soldiers never leave a wounded comrade behind. If someone was faltering and looked like he was going to drop out of a run, we would "hold him in formation." This meant quickly grabbing the guy and helping him along until he could catch his breath. We did this while running and singing cadence. A very old military tradition, cadence songs help soldiers stay in step while marching or running. They also help relieve the boredom of long marches and runs.

After PT, we were allowed to either fall in to the barracks or go right to morning chow. In the army, you don't enter or leave a building; you fall in and fall out. Falling in and out may sound simple, but it wasn't. We had to fall in and fall out of formation within a certain amount of time. Failure to beat the clock meant that we had to repeat the maneuver—and we did it over and over and over again until Sgt. Wright was satisfied. Many times, another NCO, Sgt. Owens, would have the entire company fall in and fall out—all one hundred fifty men. And like Sgt. Wright, Owens ordered us to do it over and over again until we moved fast enough to please him.

"AIN'T NO USE IN FEELING BLUE, JODY GOT YOUR DISCHARGE, TOO"

Nothing is easy in basic training—not even eating. Once in the chow line, each trainee had to swing through overhand bars, monkey-style, before getting his food. As training progressed, we had to earn our chow in other ways—usually by answering various questions about material we'd been taught, such as the four life-saving steps, the M14 rifle, the eleven general orders, or the code of conduct. We could be asked a variety of other questions as well. Over time, the number of overhand bars we had to swing through seemed to increase steadily. The first week we only had to go down the bars once, but as we got in better shape we had a do it twice, then three times. Failure to answer any of the questions correctly, or failure to complete the required number of bars, meant push-ups and a trip to the back of the chow line.

Once chow was finished, we left the mess hall and double-timed back to the barracks to get it ready for inspection and to prepare for the day's training. Most of our running for PT and from one point to another during basic training was done in double time, or what we called the "airborne shuffle."

The "airborne shuffle" is a term that originated from soldiers running with a lot of weight—parachutes, combat packs, and/or individual weapons. It is based upon a nine- to nine-and-a-half minute mile. It doesn't result in as much wear and tear on the knees, hips, and back as an all-out run would. It could be called trotting or even jogging—but let's face it, jogging just doesn't sound as cool as doing the airborne shuffle.

At 0800 hours we again fell out for formation, to start the day's training. We would march or shuffle to our training site. Most of our instructional training was conducted outside, on bleachers, though we'd occasionally sit in a classroom. When we filed in to our seats we had to stay standing at attention until the sergeant commanded us to "take seats," at which time we trainees screamed in unison: "B–9–3, B–9–3, we're the best that we can be!" Then we sat down in unison. Classes usually consisted of a lecture by an NCO, a demonstration of whatever we might be learning—the assembly and disassembly of the M14 rifle, for example—and then hands-on training.

I remember basic training as mostly eight weeks of marching and double-timing—from class to class, from training area to training area. One thing about basic training: You will get fit or die trying. We could airborne shuffle for miles without getting winded, especially if we were singing cadence songs.

There are many different types of cadence, and various army

units have their own. There is the airborne cadence, ranger cadence, infantry cadence, and, the most popular, Jody cadence. Jody cadences are songs about a nefarious fictional character named Jody. He's the dirty rotten scoundrel who stole our girl, drove our car, took our money, and drank our booze. And that wasn't all. As one line goes: "Ain't no use in feeling blue, Jody got your discharge, too."

Sometimes we sang dirty cadences, when there were no women around or we were marching to a training area or the rifle range. One line, in a mild version, was: "I know a girl all dressed in black, she makes her living on her back." Other lyrics were much more crass. On one occasion, Sgt. Wright made a wrong turn while marching us to the range, and we moved through a military housing enclave while singing one of the dirtiest cadences. By the time Sgt. Wright got the cadence stopped, it was too late; a few military wives had gotten an earful of sexual lyrics. We never again sang dirty cadence anywhere close to base housing.

We marched and practiced drill and ceremonies until we could do them in our sleep. Hours were spent doing the right face, left face, and about-face. Hours were spent going from at ease to attention to parade rest to stand at ease. And we all had to make the same movements at the same time—move as one person, effectively. If anyone was out of sync, didn't turn fast enough or snap into position quick enough, the sergeant noticed and we all did push-ups. Mass punishment works! It's not fun, but the peer pressure works.

Marching was the same way. We had to learn how to march in step, as a synchronized unit. We learned how to do a column right or left, a right flank, left flank, and rear march. As with facing movements, we marched and drilled until we moved as one.

There is a lot of pretty scenery around Fort Knox, but I couldn't appreciate it during basic training. No one could. That's because we spent scores of hours marching up and down the steep hills with our M14 rifles and full field packs. The names of the hills speak for themselves: Misery, Agony, and the twins, Mr. and Mrs. MF. (Anyone with a passing knowledge of curse words will get the acronym.)

Part of our training required us to go through the infamous gas chamber. The gas chamber was a rather small building. One of the NCOs would put on his protective mask, go into the building, and ignite a tablet of CS gas, commonly called riot or tear gas. Within a few seconds the entire building was filled with gas. We were ordered to line up outside the building and to put on our protective masks. We had previously been drilled on putting on and taking off the mask, and we'd been taught how to clear it in the event we had to put it on in the middle of a gas attack.

Our training was soon tested. Prior to going into the chamber, an NCO told us that we were to report to the sergeant, who would tell us to take our masks off. We were then each to recite our name, rank, and serial number, put the mask back on, and clear it.

That's what we were supposed to do, but we couldn't. Most of us were only able to recite name, rank, and maybe part of the serial number before breaking through the exit in a state of near terror—coughing, snot swinging from our noses, and tears streaming down our faces. The sergeants in charge got a big kick out of watching us poor trainees go through that. I must admit, when I became a drill sergeant with the 85th Division, a reserve unit, I too laughed as I watched trainees come bursting out of the gas chamber with snot bubbles and tears running down their faces.

During the first two weeks at Fort Knox, the only day we had off except for Sundays was Thanksgiving. On November 26, 1964, we got to lie around the barracks, everyone but those unfortunate few who drew KP (kitchen police). As a special Thanksgiving treat, we had post privileges. That meant we could go to the PX and wander around. It was a sort of confined freedom.

Our mess hall prepared a Thanksgiving dinner. It wasn't like Mom's but at least they tried. I was very homesick; it was my first Thanksgiving away from home. In the barracks, many of us talked about the Thanksgiving traditions in our families. We all knew that eating turkey and stuffing in the mess hall wouldn't be much fun, but we did get some welcome news just before the holiday: We'd all be getting a week's leave over Christmas.

TENSIONS GROW

Living with a bunch of strangers from different walks of life, from different races, and with different educational levels wasn't easy. For one thing, there were a lot of accents—southern accents, Brooklyn accents, Chicago accents, and all accents in between. Of course, we all had different musical tastes. Guys from rural areas liked country music, while those of us from the city liked rock 'n' roll. African Americans liked soul music, while Mexican Americans and Puerto Ricans preferred Latino music. Thankfully, there were no boom boxes in 1964; some of us had small transistor radios, so there were few instances of conflict because somebody was playing music that the others didn't like. I liked almost everything I heard. Basic training helped me to develop an appreciation for different cultures and a variety of music. Today, I'll listen to, and enjoy, anything from country music to opera.

For the most part, everybody in the platoon got along. But when a large group of young men live and train together in close quarters every day, there will be tensions. For example, some of the guys in our platoon didn't believe in bathing regularly, even though we worked up a heavy sweat from training and running every day. Nothing will stink up a barracks more than an individual with a lot of body odor.

Our sergeant noticed that one man in particular had that problem and suggested that we, his peers, take the matter in hand. We did. First, the squad leader told the man that he needed to bathe. He ignored the request. Next, some of the squad members left a bar of soap on his bunk. He failed to take the hint. We were left with no choice but to give this malodorous trainee a "G.I. shower." After a day of training, when the sergeant had left the barracks and everybody was in bed, a group of squad members got up, grabbed the guy, carried him to the shower, and threw him under the water. He was told in no uncertain terms to bathe. We all stood and watched as he did so. The guy got the message that a daily shower was imperative.

Bathroom habits caused other problems. One man would regularly take off his dirty underwear and place it on the shelf over the sinks, where we routinely put our toiletries. He was surprised to hear that we didn't like his skivvies sitting next to, or on, our toothbrushes. After he was "asked" to scrub the shelf thoroughly, he found another spot for his underwear and it was no longer an issue.

As training progressed and we trainees got tired and homesick, tensions rose within the platoon. There were several fights—and I made the mistake of getting into one with an African American kid from New York. I can't recall why we fought, but I do remember the fight. We went out behind the barracks, and the platoon gathered around to watch. The two of us exchanged some threatening words and then started to fight. It didn't last long. My opponent boxed like Muhammad Ali and I stumbled around like Sonny Liston. He hit me three times before I took my first swing. That's all I remember about our brawl. The next thing I knew, someone was throwing water on me. Turns out the guy had been a Golden Gloves boxer. In the end, we settled our issues, shook hands, and had no further difficulties.

Sgt. Wright had a sense of humor and it occasionally came through. He liked to mess with us when the platoon was at attention. When you are at attention, you are not supposed to move, talk, or even shift your eyes. To test us, Sgt. Wright would put us at attention and leave the formation. He'd then come up from behind and whisper a trainee's name. At first, he got away with it easily—the trainee would move and get a verbal lashing plus a punishment of push-ups. We caught on, but he kept testing us.

One day he got behind me and whispered, "Hey, Lynch." I didn't move. He said it again: "Hey, Lynch." I didn't move. He whispered my name a third time and a fourth—and I held strong. But me being me, I couldn't maintain my composure. When he whispered my name in my ear a fifth time, I turned around. Within seconds I was on the ground doing fifty push-ups.

GUARD DUTY

During our fifth week, as I recall, we stood our first guard mount. Guard mount, or preparation for guard duty, consists of a uniform inspection and a quiz on our eleven general orders and other subjects. (General orders are essentially rules of conduct. "To take charge of this post and all government property in view" is one general order. "To walk my post in a military manner, keeping always on the alert, and observing everything that takes place within sight or hearing" is another.)

If you passed inspection, answered all of the questions satisfactorily, and demonstrated exemplary "military bearing," you were declared a supernumerary (meaning, essentially, extra) and given the night off. Every soldier on guard duty, throughout the army, seeks to be designated supernumerary.

But the designation is rarely given. It's not enough to answer the questions correctly; you must also demonstrate strength and confidence when speaking and generally project an image of jut-jawed solidity—the qualities that constitute military bearing. I, like most of the other trainees, usually got the answers right but failed the subjective test of military bearing, and so got guard duty anyway. One guy in our platoon, who'd been in Reserve Officer Training Corps (ROTC) in high school, managed to present the requisite military bearing and was made supernumerary.

Once guard mount was over, the twelve of us on guard duty were marched to the guard barracks. We each had one hour of guard and three hours off. I drew first shift and had to guard several buildings. I was required to walk around them and let no one enter. "Easy," I thought. But the sergeants had a different idea. I wasn't on my post fifteen minutes when an apparently inebriated NCO, one of the platoon sergeants assigned to our unit, started wandering toward one of my buildings.

Following procedure, I told him to halt. He kept moving. "HALT!" I said a second time, half-yelling as I ran toward him. "Commander of the relief post number 4! HALT!" By then I was just a few steps from the sergeant. He finally stopped. I said: "Place your ID card on the ground. Turn and walk back ten paces and get face down on the ground." He started laughing, then gave me the password, and told me I did a good job. What a relief. That night each of us was challenged in various ways to ensure that we'd be ready for the future, when we'd be walking guard duty for real.

GRENADES AND BAYONETS

Learning how to throw a hand grenade, which we did during this middle period of basic training, is very exciting, especially when you are throwing a live one. Perhaps it's a military thing, but weapons that go "boom" always stoked me and most other trainees. There were a few guys who were frightened by the prospect of throwing a live grenade. One trainee scared the bejesus out of all of us when he threw his hand grenade only a short distance in front of his foxhole. A sergeant threw him to the ground and dove on top of him just before the grenade exploded. Once the range was made safe, that poor trainee did more push-ups than we could count while half a dozen sergeants screamed at him simultaneously for endangering everyone's lives. I loved throwing the hand grenade, and though I didn't hit the target (a bunker slot), I got close.

During range week, as it was called, we were issued our M14 rifles. We learned how to assemble and disassemble the weapon, clean and oil it. We also learned the manual of arms. For two weeks, we were marched out to the range and taught how to fire the rifle in order to "qualify" with our M14s, which means to become proficient in the handling and firing of the weapon.

On our first day of marching to the range, Sgt. Wright got irritated with the platoon for being out of step and gave us a punishment we hadn't experienced before—the duck walk. We all had to place our rifles behind our knees, secure the weapon with our arms hooked around it at the elbows, and then march in a painful squat—quacking like a duck as we did so. It's not a sight that trainees would want to see on YouTube. We were usually ordered to duck walk when we were going down a hill. Since most of the hills at Fort Knox are quite steep, it didn't take long for someone to fall over and start a chain reaction. Duck walking was a source of amusement for the sergeants.

The most important lesson we learned during range week was to always keep the rifle pointed up and down range. The rifle barrel should always be pointed down range, toward the target, while the butt of the rifle is always pointed away from the target. It's a simple concept, but there were guys in our platoon who did not get the idea that every weapon must be treated as if it was loaded. One poor trainee made the mistake of turning around and accidentally pointing his rifle at a sergeant. The sergeant, reacting instantly, grabbed the guy's weapon and knocked him to the ground. The trainee then did scores of push-ups as various sergeants berated him for his blockhead mistake.

As we were coming off the range each day, we each had to report to our sergeant that we had no brass or ammo. Brass was the casing from a round that had been fired, and ammo was a live round. Anyone caught leaving the range with brass or ammo was severely punished. I had a lot of fun training on the rifle range, and most of the other guys did, too.

We were also taught how to use the bayonet. The bayonet, when attached to the barrel of the rifle, becomes a spear. You then have two weapons in one. Use of a bayonet implies hand-to-hand, life-or-death combat with an enemy and so requires the proper military mindset. To teach that mindset, the sergeant in charge stood on a wooden platform and told us that every time he asked, "What is the spirit of the bayonet?" we were to scream in reply: "KILL!"

We typically got to yell "Kill!" three or four times, then practiced various impaling movements with the bayonet attached to our rifles.

In our sixth week of training we got our long-awaited Christmas leave. From December 21 through the 28th, we were free to be civilians again. I went home and had an amazing reunion with my friends, my girlfriend, Gail, and of course with my whole family. It was just like old times. I was in the best shape of my life, and I felt proud about being in the army. It wasn't so much serving my country but doing what my dad and uncles had done before me. December 1964 would be my last Christmas at home for four years.

One evening a couple of days before Christmas, I was sitting at the kitchen table, having dinner with Mom, Dad, and Nancy. At one point, I said: "Pass the f***ing potatoes, please." My dad, who normally would have knocked me on my butt for cursing, picked up the bowl with a slight smile on his face and said, "Here's your potatoes, son." He'd emphasized the words "potatoes" and "son," and only then did I realize what I had done. The look of shock and horror on my mother's and sister's faces was a more obvious signal that I'd been crass. Seven weeks of military training with tough men, during which time cursing was the norm, had given me quite a mouth.

When we got back to Fort Knox, we had two final weeks of basic training before graduation. During that time, several of us were called to the battalion commander's office and given the opportunity to go to Infantry Officer Candidate School, or OCS. I jumped at the chance. I knew that my parents would be very proud if I could graduate from OCS. And I'd be proud of myself—I would have accomplished something great in my life. All those people at home who didn't think I'd amount to much would be so surprised. I changed my military occupational specialty (MOS) from personnel to infantry, a requirement for OCS. When basic training was over, I'd go to advanced infantry training at Fort Gordon, Georgia.

GRADUATION DAY

On Saturday, January 16, as I recall, my class marched into the Fort Knox auditorium in uniform. We were so proud! We had started basic training unable to do anything, knowing nothing. We weren't fit; we couldn't march; we couldn't do facing movements; we didn't know how to fire a rifle. We were just, as the military puts it, "raw recruits." But now we were soldiers!

We had all passed the final PT test, learned the code of conduct and everything in between. Some of the trainees got awards, such as best marksman, highest PT test score, and trainee of the cycle. I wasn't one of them. In the army every good soldier tries to be the best he can be. I certainly did—but for me, just graduating basic training was a huge accomplishment, both physically and mentally. I had not only learned to be a soldier, but also learned to get along with people from many different walks of life. I was so very proud.

FORT GORDON AND A GENERAL CENSURE

After graduation ceremonies, those of us leaving for OCS were given post privileges for a day or two. We turned in our equipment, packed our bags, and then were sent to a weeklong course at the Basic Leadership Academy at Fort Gordon, Georgia.

Fort Gordon, originally Camp Gordon, was named after John Brown Gordon, a Confederate major general, Georgia governor, U.S. senator, and businessman. Established in 1917, Fort Gordon is currently the home of the U.S. Army Signal Corps. The fort occupies more than fifty-six thousand acres of varied terrain near Augusta, Georgia (home of the Masters Golf Tournament), 139 miles from Atlanta. Every military post has peculiarities that add to the misery of training, and Fort Gordon was no different. I remember the red clay of Georgia getting into crevices in every piece of equipment that we had.

At the leadership academy, we were taught two basic principles on which all other leadership traits and principles are built. The first is "accomplish the mission." The second is "look out for the welfare of your men." We also learned additional practical skills, including map and compass reading, how to perform inspections, and how to be accountable not only for our men but for our equipment.

After wrapping up the leadership course, we graduated and were assigned to our advanced infantry training (AIT) units. Several of us were assigned to the same unit—Company C, 7th Battalion, 3rd Training Brigade (C-7-3). I was in 2nd Platoon as a squad leader.

Our platoon drill sergeant was a short, stocky white guy whose voice cracked occasionally. But God help the poor trainee who laughed when it did. We were back to being called trainees again. Like basic training, advanced infantry training was eight weeks long but involved more teambuilding drills. We weren't harassed as much as in basic training, and more was expected of us.

As a squad leader, I was responsible for twelve men—a role I'd had for a couple of weeks in basic training. I was expected to know where they were every minute of the day and to apply the skills I

 For me, just graduating basic training was a huge accomplishment, physically and mentally.

learned in leadership school. I was expected to know more than the men in my squad. I was expected to be a leader.

The squad leader position was an awful lot of work. I could barely keep track of myself much less twelve other men who were going on sick call, KP, and other details. I even had to keep track if they went to the latrine in the field. They were my responsibility. I stayed a squad leader for all of two weeks before I screwed up and lost the position. As happened in basic training, I lost my nice squad leader room and had to move out into the squad bay with the others.

At Fort Gordon, we were first assigned to World War I barracks commonly referred to as Tile City, because the buildings were made from glazed red tiles. The buildings also had housed German POWs during World War II. There were no bunk beds, just twelve single bunks on each side of the barracks. Two Franklin stoves for heating were in the middle of the barracks. Because there were two stoves, there had to be two fire guards whose responsibility it was to make sure the stoves stayed lit and that nothing caught on fire. Fire guard duty was a one-hour stint, rotated among everybody in the squad.

When we moved into Tile City, our first job was to "G.I. it." A G.I. party is when the trainees spend a full day cleaning every nook and cranny in their new barracks. We worked all day and into the night until the place passed inspection. Less than a week later we were moved into the World War II barracks, which were just like the barracks we'd had in basic training. We liked the new barracks because it was located across the street from the local PX and cafeteria. Once our duty day was over, we could go to the PX and enjoy 3.2 beer.

At Fort Gordon, our battalion commander and sergeant major had both served with Merrill's Marauders, a Special Forces–like unit that fought in the Pacific during World War II. The battalion commander was one of the ugliest men I ever saw. Yet he and his sergeant major made a tremendously positive impression on me. In the company, they were known as "smoke" and "thunder." They loved trainees but were brutal on officers and noncommissioned officers who didn't live up to their standards, and they had very high standards.

During advanced infantry training, we learned how to use new weapons including the M60 machine gun, .50-caliber machine gun, and explosives—specifically C4 and dynamite. We also practiced our hand-grenade throwing technique. We learned offensive tactics, such as how to assault an enemy position and "fire and maneuver," and defensive tactics such as digging a foxhole and "escape and evasion."

After eight weeks of training, we graduated. We had a formation in which each of us was told where he would be going next. Some men were headed to Germany and about five of the trainees went to Vietnam.

Several others and I were assigned as "permanent party" at Fort Gordon, while others were scattered around the country as permanent party at other forts. I was assigned to the committee group as a driver until my spot in OCS opened. I drove for the sergeant major of the committee group, which comprised officers and NCOs who ran special training such as rifle and machine-gun range, demolitions range, and escape and evasion.

I drove for the sergeant major from April 1965 until the end of August, and I enjoyed it. I was off almost every day at 1700 hours (5 p.m.). I had a nightly off-base pass, so I could go downtown to Augusta if I wished. Occasionally, I had to drive the sergeant major around at night, usually to check night firing or to observe escape and evasion simulations.

I got a humbling but important lesson with this assignment. It was my habit to read comic books while waiting for the sergeant major to finish monitoring a training session. On this particular day, as I was reading in the jeep, I noticed another jeep pull into the training area. There was a red flag with one star on the vehicle. I pretended not to notice the new arrival. Big mistake. I should have hopped out of my jeep, stood at attention, and saluted. But, for whatever reason, I just sat there reading my comic book. All of a sudden a general was standing right beside me. I jumped out of my jeep and snapped to attention. He saw the comic book and asked me if I liked reading the funnies, to which I replied. "Yes, sir, I do." He then gave me one of the best chewing outs I've ever had.

I say "best" because the general dressed me down in an atypical way. He never raised his voice, and he didn't cuss at me. He spoke rather quietly. He asked why I was reading a comic book when I should be improving my knowledge by reading a technical manual on the jeep I was driving. He told me that I reflected poorly on my sergeant major, since I was his responsibility, and I'd made him look bad by not getting out of the jeep and saluting. He told me that I should have been doing "BDA" on my jeep, not wasting time. BDA is army lingo for before, during, and after, meaning routine maintenance done before driving the jeep, during stops, and after the day's work is completed.

When the general was done with his firm but quiet criticism, I stood there feeling very small. He said, "That's all, now get to work." I rendered a salute, said, "Yes, sir," and pulled out the jeep's technical manual. After that embarrassing episode, I never sat around wasting time again, except during formal breaks. I should have learned that lesson after being fired from Tetco, but I'm a little slow sometimes.

A WINDOW ON RACISM

While I was still driving for the sergeant major, Mom, Dad, and Nancy came to visit me in Georgia. I was given a three-day weekend pass. We used the time to take a trip to the coast. I had been to Columbus, Georgia, several times after graduating from advanced infantry training, and had seen the signs on drinking fountains labeled "colored" and had noticed the segregation in the bus terminal. But on this trip, my eyes were to be opened to just how ridiculous southern segregation was.

We were taking back roads and at one point drove through a small town. I noticed an ice cream stand. We decided to stop. I got out of the car and offered to buy ice cream cones for the family. I went up to one of the windows, not noticing the word "colored" over the top of it. I stood there for a while and got a little angry when no one came to the window to take my order. I was the only customer.

Finally, the lady running the store said, "Honey, if you want me to serve you, you're going to have to come around to the front."

It was then that I noticed the "colored" sign over the window. I went to the front and gave her my order. As I was waiting, a young black girl went up to the colored window and ordered an ice cream. The proprietress took an ice cream cone out of the same package from which mine came and filled the girl's cone from the same scoop she used to fill my cones. She took the girl's money and deposited it in the same cash register in which she'd deposited my money. The only difference was the little girl was at the colored window.

I had never realized it before, but in the mid-1960s, the institutionalized discrimination in the South was not only offensive, it was absurd. I'll never forget that appalling little glimpse of racial prejudice in America. The rest of our trip was uneventful; we had a wonderful time, and on Sunday evening I gave my mom and dad and my sister a kiss goodbye and reported back for duty.

OFFICER CANDIDATE SCHOOL

In June, I took a two-week leave. I couldn't wait to get home and was happy to reconnect with Gail and my friends Jim, Paul, and Turk. About three days before I was to go back to Fort Gordon, my sister got very ill. She ran a high fever and was diagnosed with spinal meningitis and hospitalized. I called the Red Cross and was able to get my leave extended for a couple of weeks due to hardship. After a week or so in intensive care, Nancy began to recover. The danger to her life over, I returned to Fort Gordon to await orders for OCS, which finally came in early August.

On August 30, I reported to Officer Candidate School, 53rd Company, at Fort Benning, just outside Columbus. I did not do well in OCS. Even though I'd changed a lot for the better, thanks to four months of army training plus a leadership course, I was still in many respects the same insecure young guy I'd been before enlisting. I still had a low self-image and I still took everything very personally.

The training, advising, and counseling (TAC) officers at OCS were demanding, and I became anxious in a way that hadn't happened in basic and advanced infantry training. I'm not sure why, but I was again the little boy who thinks everybody is against him. It didn't help that I wasn't able to buy the proper uniforms because of

 I'm not sure why, but I was again the little boy who thinks everybody is against him.

a bureaucratic problem with my pay. I asked my parents to lend me the money so that I could buy what I needed, but they refused. That really affected my morale.

OCS was basic training and advanced infantry training on steroids. It was intense and relentless. There was an honor code— generally something like "I will not lie, cheat, or steal or tolerate anyone who does"—and, seemingly, 1,001 rules. Students were not to "quibble" (no hair splitting or half-truths), and your word was your bond. When we were outside, we had to either shuffle or run to our destinations. Before and after chow, TAC officers lay in wait around the mess hall, ready to gig us for any uniform violations, or to quiz us on the honor code or anything else they thought we should know. In the mess hall, we had to stand at our table until every place was filled and the last man to arrive said, "Take seats." We could only sit on the first five inches of the chair, with our backs straight. Officers checked.

There was even a prescribed way to eat—the "square meal" technique. It was a precise, mechanical way of using utensils. The fork, once filled, was to be raised straight up until it was level with the mouth, moved over to the mouth, and in. The fork then was to be moved away from the mouth on a flat plane until it was out over the plate, then brought straight down to the plate to gather another bite of food. Everything on the plate had to be eaten. Drinking was done the same way—glass straight up, then over to the mouth, and back again.

It was tedious but after a couple of days I got used to it, and it did promote good posture. When we left the table we had to say, "Excuse me, candidates." Sometimes, taking advantage of a tiny window for humor, we would say, "Excuse me, cantaloupes." A little levity to break up the day can do wonders for morale.

The TAC officers intentionally messed with our heads. For example, we were told that we could not have "pogey bait" (candy, Moon Pies, Hostess Twinkies, and other such goodies), yet the TAC officers encouraged us to sneak them into the barracks. We were told that we could not have pizza parties or soft drinks yet we were encouraged to have pizza parties and smuggle in soft drinks. This was supposed to help promote teambuilding and "outside the box" thinking. In reality, it was just part of the grand game that was being played during our six months of OCS.

One night, after training, we launched an elaborate plan for a pizza party. It was organized like an Army Ranger special operation, to the last detail. While a security detail watched for TAC officers, an assault team used improvised ropes and ladders to climb down the outside of the barracks, make their way onto the mess hall roof, then run across the roof without being seen. They climbed down to the ground and ran to the "pogey bait" truck to buy the pizzas and pop. (We often saw the pogey truck in or near the barracks or training area but could never patronize it.) Once our team had bought the pizzas, they returned to the barracks by the same route.

It was the perfect plan, perfectly executed, or so we thought. Moments after we got the food and drink into our quarters, while we were congratulating ourselves and getting ready to chow down, TAC officers came barging onto our floor like a herd of rhinoceroses, screaming and yelling at us. The whole platoon, fifty men, was ordered to take the cold pop and hot pizza to the bathroom and get into the shower. We crammed in, and the cold water was turned on. We were ordered to eat the pizza and drink the pop as fast as we could, while standing under a cold shower. It was miserable. All the while, the TAC officers screamed at us to eat and drink faster.

Once the food was gone, we were taken immediately outside to the airborne track, which was a mile long and went partway up a hill. The TAC officers ran us like wolves run deer: One would run alongside us, singing cadence, and as soon as he got tired another TAC officer took his place. Even though it was the airborne shuffle, our pace was fast. I don't know how many miles we ran over the next hour and a half, but I do know that many of us lost our pizza and pop along the way. Nobody dropped out; we knew better.

THE END OF MY ROPE

By the end of September 1965, one month after the start of OCS, I was starting to unravel—and I still had five more months to go! Spit shining the floor, spit shining our boots, the constant inspections, the running, the square meal, the harassment: It all wore on me. My nerves were frazzled. Not receiving my pay because of an administrative error compounded my frustration. I took it all personally. It was another case of "no matter where you go, there you are." I had grown a lot since basic training, but I was still immature. OCS was very hard, as it should be, so hard that one needed to laugh about it occasionally, to keep it in perspective, but I couldn't laugh at myself.

In fact, what should have been one of the funniest incidents in my life hastened my exit from OCS. It was my turn to smuggle pogey bait into the barracks. I bought the food and candy, put the stash at the bottom of two brown bags, and placed all the legitimate stuff that should have been in the sacks on top of the pogey bait. I was about twenty-five feet from the barracks door, and starting to breathe a sigh of relief, when a short TAC officer stopped me.

"Candidate! What's in the bags?"

Thinking quickly, I spoke slowly and said, "Sir! I have in the bag denatured alcohol."

To which the TAC officer responded, "And?"

"Sir, I have in the bag Brasso."

"And?"

"Sir, I have in the bag diapers." Diapers were used for spit shining the floor.

"And?"

"Sir, I have in the bag feminine hygiene products." We put them under our footlockers, wall lockers, and the feet of our bunks because they slid easily and did not mess up our spit-shined floors.

"And?"

"Sir, I have in the bag Kiwi boot polish."

"And?"

Finally, I had gone through all the legitimate items in the bags, and so replied, "Sir! I also have pogey bait."

The TAC officer turned a bright shade of red and screamed at me. "POGEY BAIT! Candidate, are you allowed to have pogey bait in the barracks?"

"No, sir," I replied.

He screamed: "I want a company formation right now!"

I ran into the barracks and had our candidate company commander fall out the company into formation. The TAC officer said, "Candidate Lynch thought you all needed a treat. So he went to the PX and bought you all some pogey bait. Candidate Lynch is now going to pass out a piece of pogey bait to each and every one of you. While he's doing that, he will sing to each of you, 'Here's some candy I bought for you.' You, the company, will reply, 'We thank you.' "

I passed out candy to each of about one hundred fifty men, and sang to each guy as I did so. By the end of it, I was in a state of rage. There I was, in the most ridiculous situation one could imagine, and instead of laughing it off I was furious.

I was standing there, trying to control my anger, when the TAC officer walked up to me. I'd failed to come to parade rest or attention and was just standing there with my hands at my sides. Not good. The officer heaped scorn on me, and told me to get to a position of attention. He must have seen how angry I was. He asked me if I'd like to take a little walk to the obstacle course, which was right down the road. I told him that I'd be happy to—and as we started to walk, he looked at me and said, "Why don't you just quit? This afternoon you could be drinking beer down at the local PX or be on your first pass. We're gonna cut you next week, anyway."

I knew he was right. I wasn't going to make it through the school. I told him I wanted out.

The next thing I knew, we were back at the company HQ and I was starting the process that would end my stay at Officer Candidate School. I signed all the papers, went up to my room, and packed all my stuff in a duffel bag. There was only one thing left to do—see the battalion commander. I was walked over to the battalion headquarters and was told to report to Lt. Col. Robert Nett, a World War II veteran and a recipient of the Medal of Honor. Col. Nett talked to me about staying in and starting over. I told him I was not officer material. He agreed and signed the papers. On September 30, 1965, I was no longer an officer candidate. I was back to the rank of Pfc., private first class.

I would see Col. Nett again, in 1973, at President Nixon's second inaugural. We chatted briefly and I told him how we had met before

 It confirmed, in my mind, all of my negatives. My self-image took a nosedive.

when I quit OCS. He told me he had retired but still liked to drop by Fort Benning to mentor young officer candidates. I would see him for many years at Medal of Honor conventions.

As soon as I processed out of OCS I was assigned to Headquarters Company at Fort Benning while I awaited orders. That night I got my first pass in many weeks. I took a bus to Columbus, found a great little bar, and had a few drinks. I thought about what I'd done, and what would happen now that I was no longer going to be an officer. I had mixed emotions about leaving the way I did. I went to OCS to make my parents and family proud. I'd failed. I was relieved to be done with it, yet deeply ashamed. It confirmed, in my mind, all of my negatives. My self-image took a nosedive.

The week after my OCS departure, several of my fellow candidates were cut from the class and assigned to my platoon. The night they arrived, we all went to a local bar, had several drinks, and reminisced about our time in the program. I was nineteen years old—underage for drinking—but they didn't card much in Georgia.

A few weeks later, November 3, I got orders for Germany. I took a two-week leave at home and then reported to Fort Dix, New Jersey, from where I'd be transported to Germany. The first phase of my army experience was over. A new phase was about to begin, one that would last a year and a half. During the time, I would reenlist, mature just a little more, be given responsibility as a platoon clerk, and earn two non-judicial company punishments commonly called an Article 15. And I would volunteer for duty in Vietnam.

CHAPTER 8

DUTY AND BOREDOM IN GERMANY

I TOOK A FIFTEEN-DAY LEAVE PLUS TRAVEL TIME BEFORE GOING TO Fort Dix and then on to Germany. I got home to Dolton around November 4, 1965, and left November 21 or 22nd. Mom was sad that I wouldn't be home for the holidays but made sure to cook all my favorites—pot roast, spaghetti and meatballs, lasagna, and, of course, chocolate chip cookies. I savored it all, knowing I wouldn't taste Mom's food again for upwards of two years.

I spent a lot of time with my former high school friends and with my girlfriend, Gail, who was three years younger than me and still in high school. We'd dated a little in 1964 and had seen each other when I came home on leave. Gail was seventeen, about five foot six, with dark brown hair, a beautiful face, and slender build. She was a good Catholic girl as I remember; I believe she even went to a Catholic high school. We hit it off. We liked many of the same things, including the same type of music. She was easy to be with. Mom once said that she had "personality plus." I didn't know what that meant, but my whole family fell in love with her. I thought sure I was in love with her, but looking back, I really don't think I was; I think I was in love with the idea of being in love. And it wasn't practical to get serious, given our circumstances: She was seventeen and I was in the army and preparing to go overseas. Still, I saw her as much as possible during my visits home.

Her parents placed some restrictions on her dating, and I was fine with that. They wanted her home by a certain hour, especially during the week, and wanted to know exactly where we were going when I picked her up. One night, we were parked in front of her house and taking a little time to say good night. All of a sudden, there was a knock on the window. Her mother had seen us drive up and evidently didn't like the way the windows were steaming up. They were a little concerned by the fact that I was older than Gail, and a soldier. I didn't mind: Her parents were very traditional, good people, much like my own family. Her dad had served in World War II and worked in a factory. Like most men of that generation he found ways to earn an extra dollar. He bought and sold cars. When I visited Gail, he would often be in his garage painting up one of his new buys, getting it ready for sale. I heard he later died of Alzheimer's. He had inhaled quite a lot of paint fumes and that affected his brain. I was sad to learn of his death; I always liked him. Gail had two older sisters who were protective of their little sister.

My mom and dad were members of a couple's social club for several years. It was made up of family and friends of the family. They usually got together once a month on a Saturday night to socialize and play games like charades. Sometimes the evenings were themed, such as a Halloween party with costumes. There were always adult beverages but the drinking was not excessive. It was more about enjoying the company of other adults and being away from the children. I used to make a lot of money from babysitting on those nights.

The club's November social was to be held a couple of days before my departure for Fort Dix. My parents decided to skip the social to spend more time with me. Their decision irritated one of my maternal aunts who belonged to the club with her husband. I saw her in passing on the Saturday of the social, and she was very cold to me. Mom told me later that day that her sister was upset that she and Dad were going to miss the club's Thanksgiving-themed get together.

She was easily offended and had gotten tetchy before. This time the situation felt different. I had always felt part of Mom's family, and yet never quite felt that I fit in with them. I knew they loved me, but I just don't know if they liked me. I always seemed to be a

 I knew they loved me, but I just don't know if they liked me.

little out of step with everyone else. I couldn't understand why anyone would begrudge parents spending extra time with a child who'd soon be leaving for a foreign country and be gone for two years. It didn't make any sense to me or to my parents. My aunt's reaction would have larger implications. It would permanently alter my relationship with her and the rest of the extended family, especially after Vietnam.

Near the end of my two-week visit, I found myself eager to leave and get on with my army life. I was excited about going to Germany and experiencing a new culture. But there was more to it: Anyone who's left their family and friends to create a new life in a different place knows that going home for visits can dredge up old issues and anxieties. That was the case with me. As much as you love being with family and friends, your new life subliminally clashes with your old life, and old tensions and insecurities resurface. My aunt's cold shoulder was one example. I'd gotten used to being independent, even if in the army it was a very constricted sort of independence. I'd been by myself, in some ways, for a long time—and rather liked it. I wanted to get back on my own.

GERMANY

I left for Fort Dix on a Sunday, and spent about a week at the base before my orders came to board a military air transport service (MATS) flight to Frankfurt. We took off in the evening and arrived the next morning. About thirty other soldiers and I then boarded buses for the reception center in Frankfurt where we would be assigned to units across Germany. I was assigned to C Company of the 1st Battalion, 48th Infantry (1/48 Infantry), located at Coleman Kaserne, Gelnhausen. Gelnhausen is a beautiful town about twenty-seven miles east of Frankfurt, situated between the Vogelsberg and Spessart mountain ranges. The Kinzig River ran south of the town and the base. My new home, Coleman Kaserne, was a moderate size U.S. base housing the 2/48 Infantry Battalion and some support units. Coleman Kaserne was just a short walk from the town of Gelnhausen and sat at the base of several hills overlooking a beautiful valley that reminded me of American farm country. The Nazis built the facility there originally to house Wehrmacht units. After World War II, the U.S. Army took it over and housed various divisions until the base was returned to Germany in 1992.

On the weekends, we'd often spend a few minutes watching a German ex-Luftwaffe fighter pilot fly his single-engine airplane through the valley. He performed loops, dives, and other maneuvers, and the story went that he would give a free ride to any G.I. who could accompany him and not "toss his cookies." I never took up the challenge.

C Company was already in the field when I arrived at Coleman Kaserne. I got checked in to my unit, got my bunk, footlocker, and wall locker, and was issued my field gear. Then I was taken by jeep to my new unit. It was training in a small town not far from the base. As a Pfc., that was all I needed to know. For the next three days, I learned quickly what it was like to be very cold. Much to my disappointment, I was not assigned to an infantry unit but to a weapons company, the 81-millimeter mortar section.

Because I'd been trained for infantry, not mortars, I faced a steep learning curve. My gun unit was fully functioning and had trained together for quite some time. I was the new guy who knew nothing. I spent the next three days becoming a mechanized infantry/mortar crewman. I learned the various parts of the mortar (baseplate, mortar tube, bipod, and sight). I also learned how to place aiming stakes, which are used to lay the gun on the proper azimuth to ensure that it fires in the right direction.

I learned all about sleeping in the field along with M113 armored personnel carriers (APCs). Sleeping in the wrong place could get you squished should an APC or tank decide to move. We often slept on the ground or if the weather was warm in the "track" (another term for APC). However, in the wintertime an APC was just a large freezer, as I soon found out. I also learned how to stand guard duty in the field and about passwords. Training exercises completed, we convoyed back to the barracks.

I was now part of a mechanized infantry battalion. We spent most of our time in one of two places—either in the track park, where all our APCs were stored, or in the field. It was our job to maintain the tracks, mortars, and anything else housed at the track park. Maintenance was easy duty as long as everybody worked as a team to get the tracks washed, cleaned, and ready for inspection and the next mission. There were probably twenty armored personnel carriers in the track park, with each squad responsible for its own track. We also did maintenance on our mortar, insuring that all parts were serviceable and properly oiled.

Once everything was clean and passed inspection, our workload lightened. Sometimes we were assigned to the track park when we had nothing better to do. We called it "mox nix" time—meaning there was no training scheduled and our officers didn't know what else to do with us. During these times we could sneak off to the cafeteria across from the track park for coffee and snacks.

In addition to maintenance and repair we attended classes. In one we learned to identify Russian military vehicles. If we saw one we were to report it to the nearest officer, MP, or higher authority, along with the exact location where it was sighted, what it was doing, how many people were in the vehicle, and their ranks (if we could see them).

We were required to learn the ranks of the Russian and East German military, and how to identify them. We learned how to spot weapons systems from various countries. In addition to the classes, lower-rank enlisted soldiers all had to pull various other duties, such as KP or CQ runner, who assisted the charge of quarters (a position filled by a staff sergeant or higher rank who basically had control of the company during off-duty hours). There was also kitchen detail (not KP), which was basically given to a soldier who displeased the first sergeant. All of this was interspersed with PT virtually every day. The 81mm mortar section took its guns out to a small training area and set them up over and over again, so when we got to the field for an exercise we could get a round in the air within seconds, not minutes.

Once the duty day ended, we could go on pass to Gelnhausen or even take the train to Frankfurt. In Germany, at that time, there was a military dress code for those on pass. We had to wear a suit or sport coat with a tie. The tie could be loosened but it had to be around the neck. Generally, soldiers would go to local G.I. bars. My first couple of times on pass, that's what I did, but I didn't care for the company. Many G.I.s could not handle their liquor, and fights would often break out over trifles.

As was my habit back in the states, I found a nice little bar where other G.I.s were scarce. During advanced infantry training, almost every time I had gotten a weekend pass I went out alone. I wasn't doing anything secret or special, just going to a bar off the beaten path. Several times my friends said they were going to follow me because they were curious about where I was going. I liked the freedom of being by myself and making my own decisions without the hassle of a group jawing about where to go. In the army, you are around your buddies constantly, so it was good to get some time alone. The bar I found in Gelnhausen was relatively quiet and relaxed, and once the employees and German regulars saw that I was not a troublemaker, they were happy to have me come in. I think they liked me being there.

One of my other favorite places to hang out was the Enlisted Men's Club, or EM Club, on the base. There was always entertainment of some type and they had slot machines that paid out money. I would go down there after duty hours, usually 1700, and have a few beers and occasionally dinner. When the club started to get crowded and crazy, I'd often withdraw to the barracks or to the Service Club, where soldiers could listen to music, play chess, read, and enjoy other pastimes at no cost. It wasn't as much fun as the EM Club, but it was less expensive and it had a snack bar.

During my first month in Germany, I found a bit of luck at the EM Club. About a week and a half before payday, I ran out of cash. I had one dollar left in my wallet. Just for the heck of it, I decided to put it in the nickel slot machine. I wasn't a gambler, but decided to give it a try. I'd put about fifty-five cents in the machine when I hit a jackpot. I won $37.50 and a free steak dinner. Dame Fortune had smiled at me, however briefly. I now had $37.50 in my pocket—a lot of money in those days for a Pfc.

Because of that unlikely jackpot, I got into the habit of playing the slot machines at the EM Club when I was down to my last dollar or two. Sometimes I won just ten dollars or so, and sometimes it was the jackpot (with the steak dinner). It was almost a fatalistic approach to living. I had only two dollars to my name. Two dollars wouldn't get me much. Why not take a chance and maybe win more? Sometimes it worked; sometimes it didn't. And when I had no money, I could eat in the mess hall and for my enjoyment go to the Service Club. Or just take a long walk.

In 1965 a Pfc., E3, earned a whopping $117.90 a month. A Sp4., E-4, earned between $165 and $216, depending upon time in grade. With such low pay, guys would regularly run low on cash. Enter the Coleman Kaserne loan sharks—guys in the company who lent money to cash-strapped buddies at exorbitant rates. A guy would lend you $3 but expect $5 in return; a loan of $5 meant a payback of $8; and if you got a tenner, you paid $15 for the privilege. Occasionally, someone wouldn't pay and there would be retribution by the lender. I decided never to borrow money.

BEER IN A BUNKER

One of the duties assigned to our battalion was supporting tank units at training sites. In March 1966, my company was assigned the job of pulling targets, as we called it, for tanks firing at the practice range in Grafenwöhr, Bavaria. The targets were on a pulley system: One rope was pulled to get a target out so tanks could fire at it, and another rope was pulled to bring the target in, so we could mark and repair it. We'd sit in a bunker all day and pull targets.

It was easy duty but very boring. G.I.s being G.I.s, we looked for ways to relieve the tedium. More than anything, we played a lot of poker. Then one morning, while trucking into the range, we noticed a German guesthouse where folks could buy lunch and a beer, and it had a store attached to it. The mental wheels started turning. Wouldn't it be nice, we thought, to have a little something extra in our bunker that day—perhaps some beer and sausage and, of course, German rye bread with some good German mustard? Yes, it would be nice, we agreed—and the guesthouse store was the place to get it. Besides, we were tired of the bland box lunches prepared by the mess hall. Those lunches contained sandwiches made with mushy white bread and little else. So something a bit more tasty would be really nice.

At the range, we worked for a while and then waited for a lull in the firing. When the action slowed, we made our move. Another soldier and I snuck out of our bunker and ran across the range field. We managed to get across it without being blown up by a tank shell or spotted by officers. We then dashed through woods and stopped at the road directly across from the guesthouse. We kept low in the woods and, as good soldiers with good infantry training, observed our objective. We stayed out of sight for several minutes and cased the joint to make sure there was no brass (officers or senior enlisted men) inside. When the coast was clear, my buddy and I ran across the road and into the store. We bought as much beer, sausage, bread, and mustard as we could with the money given to us, stuffed the contraband into our backpacks, and then ran back across the road and into the woods. We had to wait again for a lull in firing, at which point we hurried stealthily across the range and back to our bunker.

We were greeted like heroes—the group was exceedingly happy. We spent the next few hours happily drinking beer, playing poker, eating sausage, and, oh yeah, pulling tank targets. We were not discovered—and that meant, of course, that we repeated the escapade almost every time we were in our bunker for the day. We were sorry when our target-pulling duty was over.

FTX—FIELD TRAINING EXERCISE

We spent a lot of time engaged in field training exercises or FTX. Sometimes we'd be out in the field for a week, sometimes several weeks. I didn't mind. Often, when we got close to a town, we'd sneak into a store to get beer, food, and other things to improve our FTX quality of life. If caught, we could get an Article 15. That is a non-judicial punishment usually given out at company or battalion levels for insubordinate behavior or other rule infractions. An Article 15 can adversely affect your chances for promotion, and hence, was a serious thing.

After a couple of long, cold FTXs, I lost my enthusiasm for being in the field. One night, I made the mistake of climbing in a cold APC with some others of my platoon.

Then I learned the first rule of winter survival: When you get into a sleeping bag, undress and put your clothes in the bottom of the bag. That allows your body to heat up the sleeping bag, and your clothes will be nice and warm when you get up the next day. And never *ever* get into a sleeping bag with your boots on. Those boots kept our feet really warm as long as we were moving. But when not moving the boots can get very cold. After about three hours, I woke up and felt my feet burning from the cold. Both feet were mildly frostbitten. I thawed them by putting them as close to my underarms as possible. I rubbed one extremely cold foot to get blood circulating and then stuck it under my field jacket and winter fatigue shirt. As soon as I felt my foot getting a little warm I put on double socks and switched. It took a while for the burning to stop. Even today when it's cold outside my feet are the first things to start burning.

THREE MORE YEARS!

Every army battalion has a career counselor whose primary job is to persuade soldiers to reenlist. The army tries hard to retain its soldiers because it's efficient to do so. There is less pressure to find new recruits and the service maintains a well-trained force. So it was common for the counselor to swing by the barracks or even during an FTX when it was really cold or uncomfortable. The thought of a nice three-day pass and getting out of the field immediately is often a selling point.

One day, when we were back in the barracks, the career counselor came by and we started talking. He said if I reenlisted I'd get a financial bonus. It wouldn't be much because I had only been in the army a little less than a year and a half. But what sold me was the three-day pass and a promotion from Pfc. to Sp4. He also offered a thirty-day leave and a change of station—I could go to any U.S. Army base in Germany. Instead of getting out of the army in November 1967, I would get out three years from my new enlistment date. I'd only serve about another year and six months depending upon when I reenlisted.

I told him I'd think about it.

The army was very demanding about PT, FTXs, KP, and all the other details that I didn't like. Nevertheless, I was actually starting to like the army. I like being on my own, being responsible for only me. Frankly, I had no ambition for outside the army and sadly none for inside the army, but my whole life took an entirely different di-

rection when I reenlisted. And even with all the hardships, I had a
certain comfort level in the army. It is a career with security, if you
are competent (or better) and like the culture.

Beyond that, I was starting to make some extra money on the
side. I owned a Polaroid camera, and I'd learned to produce a variety of trick pictures. I was especially skilled at taking double negative shots—getting two images on one frame of film. As an example,
one would be of a soldier standing with his hand straight out to his
side. The second one on the same piece of film would be a picture

 **Even with all the hardships, I had a certain
comfort level in the army.**

of the jeep situated so that it was in his hand. I could show a soldier
holding up a tank by manipulating the camera's depth of field. Once
word got out about my trick pictures, I made a lot of money selling
them to guys at the base for five dollars each. That paid for my film
and put a profit in my pocket.

I had another skill that brought me extra cash. When I was a kid,
Mom had taught me how to sew (thank you, Mom). At the base, I
would do a bit of sewing for other guys—mostly sew stripes and unit
patches on uniforms for a fee. Mom also taught me to iron (thanks,
Mom), and I made money ironing uniforms for inspection. So I was
never without money. It wasn't an incentive to stay in the army, but
the idea that I could be entrepreneurial just like when I was in high
school made my choice just a little easier.

The counselor had mentioned one other incentive for reenlistment. He told me that in Berlin, no army unit did field training exercises lasting more than five days, and most were only two to three

days. We were about to go out for another weeklong exercise in the cold, so that was an enticing fact. I started to think seriously about reenlistment and the more I thought about it, the more I liked the idea. A three-day pass, a month-long leave, a promotion, a reenlistment bonus, and a new unit: It was a compelling package. I chose to reenlist.

On April 25, 1966, I reenlisted for three more years. I couldn't know, of course, what an epic decision that would prove to be—one that would radically change my life.

I took my three-day pass immediately and went to Lohr, a small town in Bavaria. I walked the town and enjoyed the local scenery. I ate in the restaurants and spent time in local bars/guesthouses. I spent two nights luxuriating in a bed and breakfast—what an experience! When I got back to the base, I was given my thirty-day leave and immediately set off for Frankfurt Main Airport. I was headed home—and sooner than I'd anticipated. I flew military standby to New York City, taxied to Grand Central Station, and took the train to Chicago. From Union Station in Chicago I took the Illinois Central to Riverdale, where my parents picked me up.

Life at home in Dolton was uneventful. I'd been gone for six months, but it felt like only a couple of weeks. Dad was working at Tetco, and my sister was going to St. Jude, a Catholic grade school. I don't remember what grade she was in, but she was doing fine. I had changed, but not much else had, seemingly.

In no time, I was back to my unit at Coleman Kaserne and getting ready to relocate. I cleared post in a couple of days, stuffed everything I owned in a duffel bag, and was off to Berlin. I took a train from Gelnhausen to Frankfurt. I stowed my gear in a terminal locker and decided to take a walk. Right outside the train station was a red-light district frequented by G.I.s. I started walking around aimlessly.

I had been to Frankfurt a few times over the last several months but didn't know the city very well. I walked around the block adjacent to the train station, then ambled over to the next block. After a while I noticed a woman who seemed to be following me. I kept walking, made a turn or two, and still she followed. Being from Chicago, I thought she might be trying to set me up for a mugging. I didn't linger to find out: I hoofed it back to the train station, got my duffel out of the locker, and sat down in the G.I. waiting area to wait for my Berlin-bound train.

I was reading a Mike Hammer mystery when I noticed four very shiny Corcoran jump boots in front of me. I looked up and saw two very tall MPs (military police).

There was no polite introduction. "Come with us," said one of them.

"What's this about?" I replied.

"Just get your stuff and come with us."

I followed them to an MP station. Once there I was taken to a small interview room. Memories of the Valparaiso incident, when I was caught shoplifting, flashed in my mind—except this time I'd done nothing wrong.

The room was something out of the 1930s. It had one table, two chairs on either side, and a light on the table with a dull bulb that gave off an eerie glow. I was told where to sit. Within a few minutes, a man in civilian clothes came in. He told me that I had been identified as a soldier who had raped a prostitute—the woman who had been following me. I felt the life drain out of my body. I told him that I'd never seen her before. He told me I had been positively identified.

I was in a state of shock and disbelief. I was innocent and yet she positively identified me. Then it came to me: "What day did she say she was raped?" I asked the investigator. He said it happened in early May. I laughed, not because anything was humorous but out of great relief. That irritated my interrogator, who asked what was so funny. I told him I was in Chicago in early May, on my reenlistment leave, which could be verified by my first sergeant as well as my family and friends.

About forty-five minutes later, I was back at the train station. They verified my story and let me go. Whew! An hour and a half after that, I was on my way to Berlin. I wrote my parents and told them what happened.

BERLIN GRAY

In Berlin I was assigned to Headquarters Company, 3rd Battalion, 6th Infantry. We were located at McNair Kaserne ("concern" in English). From the top of our barracks we could see into East Germany and watch the guards along the border fence. Once again, I was assigned to a unit in which I had absolutely no interest or training—a 4.2-inch mortar platoon. I was really angry. I wanted to do what I was trained to do—infantry. But I was informed that the needs of the army took precedence over my own wants. My platoon sergeant and platoon leader found out I could type quite well. My typing ability would end up being a blessing and a curse.

Our platoon sergeant and platoon leader were tasked, as were others within the battalion, with doing G2 (intelligence) patrols in East Berlin. The aim was to gather intelligence on Russian units stationed there. Whenever my platoon leader or sergeant went on one of those patrols, I was asked to type the report.

Soon, because I had an ability to organize and type, I was doing all the paperwork for the mortars and trucks assigned to our section. If one of the trucks had to go in for maintenance, I wrote it up. The platoon sergeant told me that though I was assigned to a gun as an ammo bearer, I was to be the platoon clerk. It was an unofficial job, but the unit needed a good clerk. I would be "exempt from duty," meaning no KP, guard duty, or CQ. The platoon sergeant even promised me a promotion. I would make sergeant, E-5, as soon as I was promotable—that is, once I had time in grade as a Sp4. All in all, at least initially, I was excited to be the platoon clerk. But that was not to last.

Even with all my clerical duties, I still had to become proficient with the mortar and be part of the team. My squad leader and I did not get along at all. He was upset that I was always exempt from duty because I had to take care of paperwork or do a report. He was constantly on my case and, looking back, I can't say that I blame him.

He rode me about not knowing how the gun worked or what my job was as an ammo bearer. I told him time and again that I was trained in infantry and not on mortars. Never once did he try to teach me about the gun or my job. I was frustrated and copped an attitude.

Then on October 12, 1966, at 1000 hours, I did—according to the language of my Article 15—"treat with contempt my superior Non-commissioned officer, Sgt. G., who was then in execution of his office, by using an extremely unnecessary amount of time in carrying out his lawful order to police the area. This is a violation of Article 91 UCMJ 1951. It has also been reported that you on or about 1400, 12 October 1966 were disrespectful in language to Sgt. G. by addressing him as a 'gutless MF' or words to that effect. This is a violation of Article 91 UCMJ 1951."

I was confined to the barracks for fifteen days, got fifteen days of extra duty, and lost a week's pay. What's more, I was given a "suspended bust" to Pfc E3. With the least infraction, I would lose a stripe/pay grade. I was livid but not with Sgt. G. With myself. I screwed up. Why, oh why, couldn't I keep my mouth shut?

Over the next couple of months, my relationship with the squad leader became very tense. I told my mom and dad in a letter what a jerk he was. But it's also true that I wasn't very mature at the time and probably gave him good reason to dislike me. There were times when I was a complete horse's butt. Had I been more mature or had a mentor, I might have handled the situation better.

Despite my problems, when I wasn't on extra duty and confined to the barracks, I enjoyed Berlin. I found a nice German bar near the concern, and went there every chance I got. All the locals hung

 I was livid but not with Sgt. G. With myself. Why, oh why, couldn't I keep my mouth shut?

out there, including a soccer team. I learned a little German—enough to order a beer and something to eat and, occasionally, to get my face slapped. After going to the bar for a couple of months, the regulars invited me to sit at their private table. They taught me a dice game called Chicago, which we always played for drinks. I got very good at it.

Our field training exercises in Berlin lasted only three to five days. The recruiter had been right. We trained in the Grunewald, a large forest right in the middle of Berlin. One beautiful day our unit was playing aggressor against the infantry. As we were setting up our machine guns, an old German man came walking over to us. He suggested that we set up the guns in a different spot. When we asked him how he knew where to set the machine guns, he said he'd done a lot of that during World War II, on the Eastern Front. A lot of Germans served on the Eastern Front. In fact, I never met a German who served on the Western Front my entire time in Germany. I imagine the Russians never met a German soldier who had served on the Eastern Front.

In August, we went for a two-week FTX in northern Bavaria. Early in the morning, we loaded our trucks and joined the battalion convoy headed through East Germany to Wildflecken training area. It was an all-day drive. At one point, we were stopped by East German military, who asked that all African Americans be moved to the back of our "deuce and a half" (a two-and-half-ton truck). That's what I was riding in.

I'll never forget the look on the face of the second lieutenant who had to go from truck to truck to inform African American soldiers that they had to move to the back of the vehicle. He made a point of saying that this was not U.S. Army policy but was demanded by the East Germans. I think he handled the situation quite well as there were no repercussions afterward. We were just starting to have some racial problems in Berlin. Some African Americans didn't like being drafted into the army, and Vietnam was just getting hot. The unrest of the antiwar movement and the civil rights movement was having an impact everywhere. There weren't a lot of problems, but there was some tension.

When we got to Wildflecken, we were assigned to a barracks and got ready to go out for training exercises the next day. After morning chow, we headed to the field. We set up on one of the ranges and within two minutes had fired our first rounds. During the day, we performed several displacements—a maneuver in which we would load the mortars on the back of a truck, move to another area, unload the guns, and see how fast we could get a shell in the air. Our best time was forty-five seconds—the time from when we pulled the baseplate off the truck to the time we got a round in the air. While we were at Wildflecken, I learned a lot more about mortars and being part of a mortar section. Finally, I was starting to become part of the team and I enjoyed our training.

One day during that Wildflecken FTX, we were doing an early morning fire mission in very foggy weather. We could hardly see the gun next to us. We had already put several rounds in the air when our section sergeant came running out of the FDC (the fire direction center that provided tactical and technical fire control) screaming, "Cease fire! Cease fire! Cease fire!" It seems one of our guns had been laid-in wrong and had been firing on a German's farm. Nobody was hurt, but a couple of cows and chickens were killed. Uncle Sam paid heavily to replace them.

After completing training at Wildflecken, it was customary to visit the monastery that sat on top of the hill overlooking the camp. The monastery was known for its beer. We didn't know what order the monks belonged to, nor did we care; it was beer we wanted and beer we got. The monks grew their own vegetables, made excellent rye bread, and brewed beer, and also cooked in the small restaurant. The beer had a very high alcohol content. After roughing it for two weeks, we looked forward to the monastery visit and were eager to drink its beer. We all got a bit of a buzz. The next day we headed back to Berlin.

A SECOND ARTICLE 15

By February 1967, I had been in Germany a year and four months. I had come a long way in my life but was not doing well as a soldier. I got in trouble again when I foolishly tried to help a friend. He was a bigoted guy from Georgia, and one day he received a letter from his mother telling him that his sister had been raped by a black man. It was a lie, and the same day the mother sent another letter admitting her lie—but the second letter arrived two days after the first. Too late, for my sake.

When my Georgia friend got the first letter, he blew his top and left the base. Before he disappeared, he'd made some very chilling statements about what he was going to do. Another soldier, who'd been in trouble before for going AWOL, and I were concerned and decided to find him before he did something stupid.

That was a stupid decision—well meaning but not smart. We went AWOL to find him and bring him back, so that he could contact the Red Cross and get emergency leave to go home to Georgia. We found him at a guesthouse I knew. As we sat with the guy, trying

 Chess taught me how to think and how to start controlling my life like I controlled the chessboard.

to convince him to come back with us, we all had a beer. Then we had a second beer. Then our lieutenant and platoon sergeant, an African American, came into the bar looking for us. Not good. My friend who'd received the letters said some very derogatory things to the black platoon sergeant. We were told to get back to the base immediately and to report to the first sergeant.

In my mind, trying to find my friend was the right thing to do. The first sergeant and lieutenant didn't see it that way, however. They recommended to the company commander that we each be given an Article 15. That's what happened—I got my second. This time wasn't as bad as I only got seven days' extra duty and seven days confined to the company area. I was fined forty-nine dollars and, last but not least, given a suspended bust to Pfc. I didn't lose rank, but I couldn't mess up again.

Meanwhile, the friend who'd fled the base produced the letter from his mother that had sparked the incident. The letter got him off the hook—no discipline! The next day the Red Cross confirmed that his sister had not been raped. The mother had made up the story to get some attention from her son, who'd not written home in a long time. I was mad at myself for screwing up yet again. But I felt kind of good because my heart was in the right place.

It was during the time of my second Article 15 that I honed my chess-playing skills at the Service Club. I'd made it a habit to go to the club on Sundays to listen to music and play chess. I had always loved the game, and at first I played it just to pass the time. The more I played, however, the better I got, and the more enjoyment I got from playing—winning is fun. There were several guys at the club who liked to play chess, too, and soon I was at the club practically every day after work, looking for a game.

One day I noticed a German playing chess with one of my friends. The German worked at the base's magazine and book stand. When the German won the game, I asked him if we could play. I found out that he had been the Berlin chess champion for three years running. The more I played with him, the better I became. Soon all the guys who used to beat me were falling to my vicious knight attacks. I started dreaming about chess matches when I slept. Chess taught me how to think, how to reason things out, how to think ahead, and how to start controlling my life like I controlled the chessboard.

But all things considered, I'd had enough of Berlin and Headquarters Company. Though I had some friends and some self-confidence for the first time in my life, I was still getting in trouble. I was still the platoon clerk, responsible for the platoon's paperwork and the G2 reports. I was stuck in the same position—being part of a gun crew without really being part of the team. I got more and more frustrated. To make matters worse I was taken off the exempt from duty roster and had to pull KP.

SIGNING UP FOR VIETNAM

In the meantime, the Vietnam War was heating up. It was the singular event of my generation, and I wanted to be part of it. Truth be told, I was not a garrison soldier—not a spit-and-polish guy. I wanted some real action, and having been bullied in junior high school and high school, wanted to find some way to prove myself. Serving in combat certainly offered that—and might erase the stench of cowardice I sensed about myself.

I had been thinking of going to Vietnam for a couple of months but had not worked up the nerve to do it. In 1966, there was still the feeling that we were fighting communism and defending our homeland. Years later, after my time in Vietnam, I would come to see the war far differently—as a geopolitical folly that wasted the lives of so many of my generation. But in February 1967, shortly after getting my Article 15 and having served at a base adjacent to East Berlin, I fully believed that we needed to fight communism.

I believe it was Thursday, February 16, that I put in a 1049 request for a transfer to the 1st Cavalry Division in Vietnam. I'll never forget my first sergeant's response when I handed him the 1049 form. "You know it's for real over there, Lynch, and unless you change your attitude you won't last a week....Good luck." About a two weeks later my transfer was approved. I had all of March to clear post—wrap up my duties in Berlin—and get home for a forty-five-day break.

I had always been good at dragging things out. Another guy had volunteered for Vietnam at the same time I had, and we could clear post at our leisure. We still had morning formation and physical training, but were otherwise exempt from duty and free to get to various offices to get our clearance papers signed. As soon as we were able, we turned in our TA 50 field gear, which ensured that we wouldn't be in the field should the company go on maneuvers.

After that, it was just a matter of getting out of Berlin and back to the States. My buddy and I shared the same flight to New York, where he lived. Once we landed I was off to Grand Central Station for the long train ride home. I had a forty-five-day "delay in route." I got home in early April 1967. I was surprised to see the remnants of a spring snowstorm in Dolton but was so happy to be able to spend time with my girlfriend, Gail, and my friends and my family. In many respects, it was like any other leave...except for one small thing.

I wanted to ask Gail to marry me.

My uncle Chester told me he knew someone who'd give me a good deal on an engagement ring. As soon as I got the ring, I asked Gail to marry me. She said yes. I went to her father and asked him for permission to marry his daughter. He said yes. I was thrilled, as was Gail. Our plan was to be married as soon as I got out of the army, in April 1969. That was two years away. Even so both families were very excited about the planned nuptials.

Gail and I spent a lot of time together during the few weeks I was home. About a week before the end of May, I was to leave for Fort Ord, California. My last night in town, Gail and I went out for one last date. We did a lot of talking, and I dropped her off at her home about 11 p.m. I headed for home, but I had one last thing to do.

In Dolton, as you travel south out of town on Lincoln Avenue, there is an S curve. I'd always wanted to take it going fast. I thought, "Well, this is my last night in town before I go to Vietnam. I want to take that curve as fast as I can." I drove quietly over to the start of the curve and then accelerated. I took that thing at eighty miles an hour—what a thrill!

As soon as I got past the curve, I slowed down. Too late. A police officer had set up on a side street in the middle of the curve. I no sooner slowed down than the red lights of his squad car came on. Soon I was at the Dolton jail. A police officer asked me why I had gone through the curve so fast. I told him I was on my way to Vietnam and this was my last night in town. I showed them my military ID card and a copy of my orders. They let me go. The next morning I was on a plane to Fort Ord.

I had learned a lot in Germany. I had matured. I had more confidence in myself. Still, I had a long way to go. But at the age of twenty-one I felt in charge of my life for the first time, even though I was in the army, had to follow orders, and was going to Vietnam.

Little did I know that Vietnam would push my personal development, rapidly, to a much higher level. I'd just have to go through hell before I got there.

CHAPTER 9

GOING TO WAR IN VIETNAM

I ARRIVED IN OAKLAND, CALIFORNIA, ON MAY 25, 1967, THE evening before I was to report to Fort Ord. Knowing it was my last chance for a good meal before my twelve-month tour of duty in Vietnam, I treated myself to some drinks and a steak dinner at a nice restaurant. Early the next morning, I reported to Fort Ord. Initially, I was assigned to the transit barracks for those of us going to Vietnam. Processing for Vietnam started immediately after reporting in to the barracks.

The next day, Saturday, the 27th, we finished processing. Following noon chow, we were told to get our gear; we were going to a new barracks. It turned out to be a warehouse, set up as makeshift housing for about three hundred of us. It was to be our quarters until we left. Bunks were stacked three high. There were no foot or wall lockers; we were basically living out of our duffel bags. There was a very small day room with a couple of pool tables, along with a latrine and showers.

A sergeant supervised us. A short man with a condescending attitude, he used a PA system to give us instructions—where to go, what to do, and when to do it. He constantly berated us about the dirty warehouse and daily conscripted several of us to clean it.

Though most of us would only be in the warehouse for two or three days, we quickly grew to loathe him. It wasn't so much what he said but the way he said it. Nobody likes being demeaned, especially just before going off to war. And for me there was another factor. I had volunteered to go to Vietnam, and in my naïveté, I thought I should be given more leeway at the base than those who were going involuntarily. That wasn't the case. We were all bossed around like a herd of cattle and that incensed me.

We marched to and from chow, then were left to our own devices throughout the day, as long as we stayed in the warehouse. On the second day, as we were sitting in the day room grousing, a few of us started talking about how great it would be to have just one last night in town before going to war. We were all in Class A uniforms and, therefore, could easily get off post. We started brainstorming and formulated a plan, but no one wanted to take a chance—except for me and another guy.

We didn't have much time, as we'd all be leaving in another twenty-four to forty-eight hours. Every day after morning chow, the NCOIC (noncommissioned officer in charge) would announce who was shipping out. Since our names had not been announced in the morning, our best chance to get away was that night. Roll call would be taken in formation right after evening chow, then we'd be marched back to the warehouse. There was no subsequent roll call until bed check at 2200 hours. The NCOIC always marched on the right side of the formation, close to the front. We figured that if we fell into formation on the left near the rear, we could disappear on the way back to the barracks without being noticed. Once the formation was out of sight we'd make our way to town. All we had to do was return to the base before bed check and find someone to let us in the barracks, as the doors were locked at night. One of our buddies volunteered for the job. We agreed to be at one of the doors leading to the shower room at 2130. He agreed to wait there between 2115 and 2150. If we were late, he said, we were on our own.

That evening after chow, we went outside and fell into formation, making sure that we were in the last rank for the march back. The sergeant took roll call and we started marching back to the warehouse. As we approached a dumpster, the two of us simply marched in place and let the formation move away. Then we hid behind the dumpster until the unit was out of sight.

We took a taxi to a nearby town. We had dinner and several drinks, hit a couple of bars, and then hurried back to Fort Ord. At 2145 hours, we arrived at the door to the warehouse, just in time for our buddy to let us in. We'd had our last night of freedom, a good time, and made it back in time for bed check. Nobody was the wiser. And that was our last night in the United States. The next morning, we fell in formation and our names were called along with several others. We were to leave that evening at 2100. We were taken to the Oakland Airport, military side, as I remember. We boarded a MATS (military air transportation service) flight, a civilian airliner contracted by the military to fly service members to Vietnam, around 2200. I remember feeling calm but anxious. At least a hundred soldiers were on the aircraft.

We spent the next fourteen or so hours traveling to Vietnam. Our first stop was Honolulu, Hawaii. We were allowed to deplane while the aircraft was being refueled, but the area to which we were directed was isolated and enclosed. MPs patrolled the area to prevent anybody from going AWOL. The second leg of the trip took us to Clark Air Force Base in the Philippines. We were again allowed to deplane, but there was nowhere to go except to a very small PX to buy some snack food or candy. After a short wait, we left Clark, bound for our last stop, Cam Ranh Bay, Vietnam. I noticed that a sergeant sitting a few rows behind me had somehow managed to sneak alcohol onto the plane.

'IN COUNTRY'

Cam Ranh Bay is located in Khanh Hoa Province, on the South China Sea. Cam Ranh Air Base was one of three main processing points for troop replacements and those leaving after their tour of duty. I came in at Cam Ranh Bay and left from Cam Ranh Bay.

The first thing we noticed after landing was the heat and humidity. It was stifling. Stepping outside in Cam Ranh Bay was like walking into a steam bath. When we got off the airplane, we were told to form four ranks. We fell in at attention, as we would in the States, but were quickly told to stand at ease. As it turned out, we would rarely stand at attention in Vietnam because it was just too damn hot. The sergeant who had been drinking on the plane crumpled to the tarmac shortly after falling into formation. Alcohol and oppressively hot weather are a bad mix.

Once we were formed up, we were put on buses and taken to our barracks. Security was paramount at Cam Ranh Bay, I realized, when I saw that every bus window was covered with wire fencing. It was to prevent hand grenades or other explosive devices from being thrown into the buses by Viet Cong or their sympathizers.

I expected to be immediately assigned to a unit, given a rifle, and sent off to fight. That didn't happen. First we had to acclimatize to the heat and humidity of South Vietnam. We were at Cam Ranh Air Base for two days and were given some basic information and the duty of filling sandbags. In Vietnam, I learned, filling sandbags was a near-constant duty, as they were widely used to protect bunkers and fortify bases. If there was nothing else to do, we filled sandbags and strengthened bunkers. Occasionally we carried sandbags in the field. We had to dig in every night and sandbags were a great way to protect the front of a foxhole.

Because of the heat, we were allowed to roll up our sleeves while on duty—a first. We were never allowed to do that in the States or in Germany, but Vietnam was a different story. What's more, we were told not to salute. It seems that snipers there, as in past wars, liked taking shots at officers, and saluting was an easy way to identify one. It wasn't easy to change the basic habits of military life—something that had been drummed into my brain for more than two years. But saluting just wasn't done. I can't remember saluting once while I was in Vietnam.

Our uniforms were also different. There were no white T-shirts, no shiny brass, no yellow stripes on our sleeves. We wore nothing that could be easily spotted by the enemy. Our rank was still worn on the sleeve, but it was olive drab, not gold. Our two dog tags (identity tags with name, service number, religion, and blood type) were taped together to keep them from clinking and making noise.

1ST CAVALRY

The morning of our third day at Cam Ranh Bay, we were assigned to our units. After morning chow, we were called down to a fenced-in area that looked like a cattle pen out of the Old West. Attached to the perimeter of the fence were all the division insignias. As our names were called and our assignments given, we were told to go over to the division patch and wait for the liaison to give us further instructions. I was assigned to the 1st Cavalry Division (Airmobile), the unit I had requested when I was in Germany.

I wanted to be in the 1st Cavalry for several reasons. I heard about them in 1965 while I was failing Officer Candidate School at

Fort Benning. About the time I was entering OCS, the 1st Cavalry was leaving for Vietnam. Throughout the rest of 1965 and throughout 1966 and 1967, their exploits had become legendary. I also liked that they were "airmobile"—the cutting edge of military tactics in the 1960s. All of it made me want to be a part of that unit.

The 1st Cavalry Division is closely associated with the Vietnam War, a fact of which I am proud. With the introduction of the versatile Bell UH-1 (Huey) helicopter, which was both a troop carrier and a gunship, the 1st Cavalry pioneered the airmobile concept that was a crucial element of the army's Vietnam strategy. Being airmobile meant that troops could be quickly deployed to an area of operation (AO) or redeployed as a ready-react force should another unit need assistance.

After getting our unit assignments, we were taken to the Cam Ranh Bay airstrip, where we boarded a C-130 transport plane and flew to Camp Radcliff in the Central Highlands. Headquarters of the 1st Calvary Division, Camp Radcliff was located on a flat expanse just north of An Khe. The base was named after the division's first casualty in Vietnam, Major Donald G. Radcliff, operations officer for the 1st Squadron, 9th Cavalry. The installation, one of two major base camps for the 1st Calvary Division, had at least four hundred helicopters, ranging from the UH-1 Iroquois to the CH-47 Chinook, a larger troop and supply transport.

The backbone of the division's airmobile capabilities, the Hueys and Chinooks ferried units to and from in-country missions, hauled supplies, and rescued the wounded. A modified Huey commonly called ARA (air rocket artillery) could attack the enemy with rockets and M60 machine guns. Even now, after almost fifty years, the sound of a helicopter brings back fond memories. If I hear a helicopter flying close I have to go outside to see it.

In addition to the 1st Cavalry Division, Camp Radcliff was home to the 173rd Airborne Brigade (Separate) and the 4th Infantry Division along with some other smaller units. I hoped to get an assignment with an infantry unit, which is what I'd wanted since going to Germany.

The forty-minute plane ride to Camp Radcliff was uneventful until we made our approach to the airfield. As we started our descent, we heard a strange pinging noise, as if something was hitting the wings and the fuselage. Suddenly the pilot pulled up into a

 I thought, "Just my luck. I'm not in Vietnam four days and I die in an airplane crash."

steep climb. He passed the word back to us to hang on tight. We had just been hit by small-arms fire and he was going to have to make a combat landing.

A combat landing is quite an experience. It is designed to minimize the time a plane is at low altitude within range of small-arms fire. The plane almost nosedived into the airfield, pulling up at the very last minute. It was a three-bounce landing. I don't recall being scared during the steep descent, but thought, "Just my luck. I'm not in Vietnam four days and I die in an airplane crash."

Shortly after landing we were met by the various unit representatives, including a Sp4. driving a "mule." The mule, a four-wheeled flatbed vehicle, could haul men, gear, and just about anything else just about anywhere. It was used a lot in Vietnam. We hopped on and were taken to battalion headquarters.

The ride from the airfield to headquarters was an eye-opener. The first thing I noticed were all the bunkers used for protection during mortar and rocket attacks. We also passed artillery emplacements. There were some permanent buildings, which surprised me. The roads, for the most part, were dirt and we made a small dust storm as we drove.

We passed the "golf course," where helicopters were stored between missions. It got its nickname in 1965, when the assistant division commander told his men that they were going to create an airbase "without the use of heavy machinery, because the earth-moving equipment would strip the scene of its natural vegetation, and with more than 400 helicopters on the way, the base would soon become a giant dust bowl or a huge muddy quagmire." Each helicopter was placed in an open-air, three-sided box made of corrugated steel reinforced with sandbags. The box provided some protection from mortars and rockets and yet allowed the crews quick access and a quick takeoff. When seen from above, the boxes scattered across the area looked like a giant golf course.

An Khe and Camp Radcliff sat on flat terrain, but what really impressed me was Hong Kong Mountain, which, though surrounded by jungle, was inside the perimeter of the base. It dominated the area and on its crest was the patch of the 1st Cavalry Division—the big golden patch with a black line slicing it diagonally and a black horse's head in the upper-right corner. On each side of the Cav patch were the patches of the 4th Infantry Division and the 173rd Airborne Brigade. The 1st Cav had established a radar site atop the mountain for counter-battery fire and communications.

MINES, MORTARS, AND PLASTIC EXPLOSIVE

A lot of things happened once we got to our battalion headquarters at Camp Radcliff on June 3. First, we were all assigned to our companies. I was assigned to Company D, consisting of about one hundred fifty men divided into four platoons. At last, I'd gotten my wish—infantry! We were taken to our company headquarters and assigned a barracks where we would spend the night. There we learned how to put up mosquito nets to protect us from the many strange bugs that thrived in the jungle, starting with the malaria-carrying mosquito. I hate bugs, especially flying ones, and I had an almost uncontrolled fear of bees, wasps, and hornets. Great! I'm now in the land of flying bugs.

After getting our company assignments, we spent four days at the 1st Cavalry Division's school, learning everything we needed to know about fighting in Vietnam. The school prepared us for being airmobile. We learned the intricacies of air assaults, and in particular how to get on and off a helicopter without killing or maiming ourselves. There was a special emphasis on staying clear of the helicopter rotor blades. We heard horror stories of soldiers who weren't paying attention, walked into rotor blades, and got cut to pieces.

We were taught how to use and maintain the new M16 rifle. The M16 is a gas-operated, shoulder-fired, magazine-fed, automatic, and semiautomatic weapon that fires a 5.56mm round. It was the weapon used by most infantry troops in Vietnam and is still in use today. The M16 rifle can fire 150 to 200 rounds a minute and is simple to use. That's the best thing about it. It is also very easy to clean; you could clean it while you were walking or, if necessary, in the middle of a firefight, and it took only a minute or so. The worst thing about the M16 was that it tended to jam. Sometimes after firing, a bullet's casing would not eject. That usually happened at the worst possible time, like during a firefight. But if you knew what to do and kept your head, you could get the rifle operating again in a few seconds.

Many pictures were taken of grunts in Vietnam with little bottles of mosquito repellent, commonly called bug juice, on their helmets.

We used bug juice not only to repel insects but also to lubricate bullets in the magazine. Rounds that were a little oily didn't jam as often. If there was a jam, we used rifle rods to knock the jammed rounds out of the firing chamber. We typically taped the rods to our weapons, and they made handy probes.

At the 1st Cavalry School, we also learned how to rappel. A sixty-four-foot tower was used for training. You first had to fashion a "Swiss seat" for support. A Swiss seat is made from rope, which goes around your waist, between your legs, then around both legs. You

 Being in the field was also called being "in country" or "in the bush."

had to be careful not to get your "equipment" caught up in the rope, as that made rappelling extremely painful. Luckily, I did my one rappel without any problems...or pain.

We were also taught how to set up a Claymore mine and how to booby-trap it. A Claymore is a green, convex piece of plastic with two layers inside. One layer contains about 750 1/8-inch steel balls. The BBs are propelled at a high rate of speed into whoever happens to be in front of it. The other layer, behind the steel balls, contains the high explosive C-4. The mine has three folding legs to allow directed placement. The Claymore can be fired by an M57 firing device commonly called the "clacker." The clacker sends an electric charge to the mine, detonating it. The Claymore can also be set off by a trip wire or other non-electrical means. We used Claymores offensively in ambushes and defensively to protect our night perimeter.

The plastic explosive C-4 was also used to blow up bunkers, add an extra lethal punch to a grenade, knock down trees, or even to make a quick cooking fire. Normally, we used "heat tabs" for cooking because they had a blue flame that was hard to see even at night. However, when we needed something heated quickly during the day, we'd light a bit of C-4, which burned at very high heat. The only down side was that, once lit, C-4 had to burn itself out. Trying to stamp it out like a normal fire could cause an explosion, sometimes costing an unwitting soldier his foot. C-4 also has highly toxic fumes. I used C-4 a lot to heat up coffee or ham and lima beans, commonly called ham and MFs.

In addition to rifles, mines, and plastic explosive, we learned how to set up trip flares. A trip flare illuminates an area at night when activated by an enemy soldier tripping a wire. They create an extremely bright light. When we were in a defensive position, the flares offered two benefits: They allowed us to see the enemy, and they momentarily blinded him. You had to be careful when setting up a trip flare, however. If one went off in your hand, you'd be severely burned. But out in the jungle, they were a lifesaver.

Our training ended with a patrol and a night bivouac in what we called "Indian country." (We were not politically correct at the time.) Being in the field was also called being "in country" or "in the bush." The school's cadre said that we were in enemy territory once we left the base, but we had no contact with the enemy during the patrol. We did come across a bamboo mortar used by the VC just a few nights before. It seems bamboo can be used to fire a mortar round. It makes for a neat improvised weapon. The patrol and bivouac were uneventful—except for one of the men opening fire on a bush that he thought he saw moving during the night. Truth be told, it was a mistake many of us would make. One of the things we were taught was not to look directly at anything at night. We were also warned about the "F**k you" lizard. When it hissed, the lizard sounded like it was saying "F**k you." There were more than a few times when an FNG (f**king new guy) would open fire because of that lizard.

The next day we went back to the division training area and were released to our units. We got one more night at Camp Radcliff. One of the best things that happened to me in Vietnam occurred that night.

'LIFE DEALS THE HAND, BUT WE PLAY THE CARDS'

There was a very small unit club in the battalion area close to our barracks. We had a couple of beers there before heading back to go to sleep. On the way, we passed one of the permanent buildings. A sergeant first class was sitting in front of it on a lawn chair. It was obvious that he'd been drinking. As we walked by, he stopped us and started telling us about his time in Vietnam. He said he'd been a part of a unit that had to march into Vietnam from Laos when the U.S. military was told to leave that country. He had spent several years fighting the communists in South Vietnam, both as an adviser and with major military units, including the 1st Cavalry Division. He was a day or two away from heading home.

As the conversation drew to an end, he said: "I have one piece of advice for you. It might be the most important advice you'll ever get while you're here. You may go home or you may die here. But you if you are going to die, you have the choice of how you're going to die. You can die like a man or you can die like a coward. You're here and what's going to happen to you is going to happen to you, but you have the choice of what you do with it."

I think those are close to his exact words. They affected me deeply and gave me an almost fatalistic attitude about being in Vietnam. I did not want to die a coward. One of the reasons I'd volunteered was to prove myself, and I did not want to fail, not this time. I knew

I couldn't change the possibility of dying, but I wanted to control how I acted when the bullets started flying. That's not to suggest that I was never scared. In fact, I don't recall a time in Vietnam when I wasn't afraid. But I learned how to deal with my fears and even control them...mostly.

LZ ENGLISH

Things happen quickly in the army. I had been in Vietnam less than two weeks. The morning after our talk with that sergeant first class, we boarded a Chinook helicopter carrying supplies to Landing Zone English (LZ English), about eighty miles by road from Camp Radcliff.

LZ English was one of two landing zones located outside Bong Son City. The other, LZ Two Bits, was located on the other side of the city. LZ English served as the 1st Cav's tactical command post from April to December 1967. It also served as a second headquarters for the unit. LZ English was what the army called a "forward fire base," from which men and armaments could be taken into the field and into battle. We would spend most of our time in the field or on an LZ.

LZ English was home to several artillery batteries that provided support for those of us in the field. English had an airfield, of course, including helicopter pad, and even a stage for the occasional USO show. I remember it being a dust bowl. There was a defensive perimeter dotted with bunkers to protect us from attacks. During my time in the field I would see LZ English six to eight times.

I remember LZ English as being a jumping-off point for operations in the Bong Son Plain and for movement to Kon Tum, Dak To, and other areas of operation. It was also used for short rest-and-recreation periods, commonly called "stand downs." That was the time to get a shower, grab new jungle fatigues and t-shirts, have our weapons serviced, and, if we were lucky, go into Bong Son City. We always took our weapons with us, but even so, we were able to get away from the war for a brief time. Needless to say, we looked forward to stand downs.

I remember getting to English for a couple of days after being in the bush for a month or so. It was an opportunity to get a real-

 Just to feel really clean after being in the bush for days or weeks—there is nothing like it.

ly good shower. Just to feel the water flow over you is amazing. To feel really clean after being in the bush for days or weeks—there is nothing like it.

Before we left Camp Radcliff for LZ English, we were told to pick whatever weapon we wanted to carry. Most of the men picked the M16. I, however, not being the sharpest pencil in the pack, picked the XM79. XM meant "experimental model." It was an M79 grenade launcher attached under an M16 rifle. It would become a new weapon in the infantry arsenal, called the M203 grenade launcher. It's a big weapon that gave me a whole lot of firepower, but I hadn't thought about humping it long distances in high heat and humidity.

I grabbed a pouch large enough to carry thirty-five high-explosive/fragmentation rounds plus a couple of white phosphorous rounds and two shotgun rounds—all for the M79. HE (high explosive) rounds were used like a small mortar. They can kill enemy soldiers with shrapnel and blow up stuff. Shotgun rounds were double-ought buckshot shells used for close-quarter combat. The white phosphorous rounds, commonly called "Willie Peter," were useful for marking a target with a thick white smoke, or for starting villages on fire. Because white phosphorous burns with intense heat it is also effective as an antipersonnel weapon. Chunks of white phosphorous are thrown out upon impact, and when they hit flesh just keep burning. They may not kill but will cause great pain.

I also selected thirty-five magazines for my M16; I did not want to run out of ammunition in the field. The rest of my gear included a poncho, poncho liner, and a new 35mm camera and film that I'd bought at the PX before leaving Camp Radcliff—plus some goodies for my platoon.

We got to LZ English in the late afternoon, but didn't stay long. Almost immediately, we were put on a Huey that was bringing hot chow and supplies to my new company, which was somewhere near the coast of the South China Sea. Such flights were called "log," or logistical, flights. In the field, we called them "log birds." As I got on the Huey I felt a tight knot in my stomach. I would feel that knot a lot over the next several months. I would not see LZ English for several weeks. Ours was a line company, so we spent our time in the field, only going to an LZ to get a short rest or to pull perimeter guard duty.

THE FOOD WE LOVED TO HATE

When we landed, the first sergeant assigned me to 2nd Platoon. S. Sgt. Gomez, a short tough Guamanian, was the platoon sergeant. He assigned me to second squad. I don't remember the squad leader's name, but he had been in some hard battles in country and was a serious man. There were four squads in my platoon, each consisting of twelve men at full strength, but that was rarely the case.

After chow, I was given one ammo can containing 150 rounds of machine-gun ammunition, which went into my pack. Two Claymore mines and four smoke grenades were strapped on the outside of my pack, and a variety of C-rations were put in my socks and tied to my pack straps. Altogether, we each carried 90 to 120 pounds or more.

C-rations were the food we loved to hate. They came in a case made up of 12 smaller boxes. The contents of each box varied, but might generally contain a can of meat or a "meat-like" substance, bread or crackers, a spread (typically cheese or peanut butter), and a dessert. There was also coffee with powdered cream and sugar, cigarettes, gum, and a packet containing toilet paper (though it was never enough to finish the job).

To be fair, our squad leader would open the case and mix up the small boxes, so nobody knew what exactly he was getting. Each of the smaller boxes was labeled: B-1-A, B-2, B-3, etc. The absolute worst box anyone could draw was the B-1-A meal, which contained "ham and eggs, chopped." It tasted as if someone had cooked ham and eggs, compressed it all into a very small jar, left it in the sun for ten years, and canned it. We tried it hot, cold, with Tabasco sauce (every trooper I knew carried a bottle of the sauce). No luck; it still tasted terrible. Those who drew ham and eggs just made do with the rest of the box. I never knew anyone who ate that canned crap.

There was no best box but the box with fruit cocktail was prized, as was the meal with pound cake. If you were lucky enough to get both fruit cocktail and pound cake, you could put them together and have a great dessert. We found many ways to make the C-rations palatable. I believe it was *Penthouse* magazine that came out with a G.I. cookbook for C-rations. It gave us ideas for turning boring C-rations into halfway decent meals.

I was told to remove my underwear to avoid suffering "crotch rot" and to remove my socks to avoid "trench foot." Our army jungle boots, designed especially for Vietnam, drained water quickly, and going without undershorts allowed the private areas to dry. Also, our jungle fatigues were made to dry quickly. So we wore boots with no socks and went "commando."

A 'ONE-KLICK' HUMP

Sgt. Gomez told us that the company was going on a short hump to the South China Sea. It was a "klick" away, and we'd bivouac for the night. A klick is army jargon for one kilometer, a little more than a half mile. Everybody in the platoon was excited to get to the coast. That meant swimming and relief from the heat. "Wow," I remember thinking. "My first night in the field and I get to go swimming." Vietnam's South China Sea coastline has some of the best beaches in the world.

It took us about an hour to get to the bivouac site, which was right on the beach. In Vietnam we didn't just walk. We walked and observed everything. It wasn't as if we were just walking a half-mile or so to the beach for fun and sun. We walked differently. I noticed that everyone in the platoon was constantly looking up into the trees, down to the right, out to the front, left, and back up. Everyone had a different way of observing but everyone was constantly looking for things that didn't fit, for hints that the enemy might be near. I didn't know what I was looking for, but I looked everywhere.

The short hump with a pack that weighed more than a hundred pounds had me sweating through my fatigues. I ached all over. As an FNG, I walked in the main body of troops. We were well dispersed, with about ten feet between us, so that one grenade or a burst from a machine gun wouldn't kill several men. Bunching up while on the move was not allowed.

When we got to the coast, we dug defensive positions in the sand. It was one of the few times when the digging was easy. As each platoon finished digging and established its perimeter, some of its troops hit the beach for a swim while others stood guard. We FNGs, also known as "cherries" because we'd not yet been tested in a firefight, had to stand guard with more experienced soldiers. We would not swim with the rest of the platoon—we'd not yet earned that right. One might think being called an FNG or cherry was demeaning, but it didn't bother me. Like the rest of the new guys, I was untested and capable of screwing up, and in combat a screw-up costs lives.

That night I stood my first guard in a combat zone. Thankfully, my position was along the beach and the moon was big and bright, so I could see a great distance. I was shown how to make coffee during guard duty using heat tabs. The trooper who stood watch with me showed me how to dig an indentation into the foxhole wall large enough for the heat tab and my canteen cup. Then I was told to take my poncho and cover the hole and myself as the blue fire heated up my coffee. The heat tabs gave off nasty fumes but the coffee tasted great—for C-ration coffee. I was taught how to light a cigarette the same way. I cupped the glowing tip of the cigarette with my hand—it could be seen from afar—and blew the smoke down into the foxhole to dissipate it. Those precautionary measures were taken seriously.

After my first watch, I stood subsequent hour-long watches alone. If anything caused me concern, all I had to do was reach behind me and wake up one of the "old" guys. The more experienced trooper would know what to do. It was standard operating procedure to put cherries with more experienced troopers until they could be trusted.

I was surprised at how cold it got at night. I was actually shivering at one point and had to use my poncho liner to get warm. The poncho liner is quilted nylon with a polyester fill and was excellent for keeping warm at night. I still have one and use it occasionally.

The next morning, first call came early, about an hour before dawn—not that I slept much. I would not sleep much at all during my time in Vietnam. There was guard duty every night, plus nightly ambush patrols and observation posts. The NVA and VC would often launch probing attacks at night, along with mortar and rocket attacks. We were all in a near-constant state of alertness and tension that made a good sleep, for even a few hours, almost impossible. As soldiers in the bush, we learned to sleep half awake—our senses attuned, even in a dream state, to sounds that didn't fit. We learned to function on little or no real sleep at all, except for brief naps.

After fifty years, I still sleep the same way. I can sleep soundly through a thunderstorm but leap out of bed at the slightest unfamiliar noise. My wife has learned to live with my odd sleep habits, though my constant need to get up and search the house after being awakened drives her mad.

During that first night at the South China Sea beach, I pulled three watches. In the morning before sunrise, we had eaten morning chow—for me ham and lima beans. Thankfully, I was able to use a heat tab to cook it. I had to be shown that in the field we didn't usually eat out of mess kits; we ate out of the can. I used my P-38 can opener to open the ham and MFs, bent the lid back, and put it over the blue flame. When it was warm enough, I drank it right out of the can. Ah, breakfast just like Mom use to make!

It wasn't long before the red-yellow sun edged over the horizon, and soon it was completely visible in all its heat and glory. The temperature climbed, and before 0900 hours we were all breaking another sweat. Then we got the order to move out. We would spend the morning searching villages in our AO (area of operation).

As we started to move, I noticed that along the beach were rows of punji stakes—shards of bamboo that the VC and NVA cut in the shape of a spear tip and sharpened to a razor edge. They are then soaked in human waste. A soldier who happens to fall on one, or somehow get stuck by one, not only has to deal with the wound but the terrible infection caused by the waste.

SEARCHING HOOCHES

We moved into our first village. I and one of the more experienced men searched a hooch, which is what we called any building in which people lived. It was very strange for me to enter someone else's home and search it. I was shown how to use my rifle rod to probe for tunnels. We were none too nice about searching; we moved everything and probed everything. One hooch done, we moved on to the next. As we came out of the second hooch I noticed a Vietnamese screaming into a bunker. "He's a Kit Carson scout," my partner said. "They're former VC who have 'chu hoied'—come over to our side. His wife and kid were killed by the VC." We walked over to the bunker just as he threw in a smoke grenade. Out came a male VC suspect (VCS) who was immediately taken under control by the scout and one of the officers.

As I stood there, watching, someone said, "Barry and Lynch, go into the bunker and search it." Heart in my throat, I went in. It was a family bunker, used for cover should the village be shelled. We took our rifle rods and probed for any sign of a tunnel. Nothing.

But I was learning how to search, and learning where the VC and NVA liked to hide stuff. I was told to always probe under the fire pit and under sleeping mats, and to move people if they were sitting. Often, they sat on contraband or tunnel entrances. After searching a couple more hooches, we moved out of the village. The VCS (Viet

Cong suspect) was put on a chopper and taken back to LZ English for interrogation.

As we moved across some dry rice paddies, I started to walk along a dike. The squad leader stopped me and told me the VC liked to booby-trap them. It was hot, and now that we were away from the coast, out on a flat plain, the sun just beat down on us. The dry rice paddies reflected the heat. In the village, we at least had some shade, but walking through the rice paddies, we were suffering. Finally, we came to a nice oasis—a little stand of coconut trees. We set up a perimeter and took a break for chow. More C-rations. It was a chance to cool down and relax a little.

 We were none too nice about searching; we moved everything and probed everything.

Generally, our mission was to search for VC and NVA, wherever they might be. We were to search villages for weapons, rice caches, and anything else that could serve the enemy. We'd move from village to village, searching. If there weren't any villages, we'd search any place we figured the enemy might hide supplies—or hide themselves.

As night approached, we selected a bivouac site. It had to be a good defensive location. We'd bivouac in a circle, just like in the Old West, to maximize security. First, we'd dig two-man foxholes. If we had sandbags we'd fill them with the dirt from the foxhole and place them in front for better protection. Once the foxholes were dug, the forward observer (FO) would call in defensive targets, or "delta tangos," the areas near the perimeter to be hit by artillery, air strikes, or naval gunfire should we be attacked. One FO was so good he could adjust delta tangos so that they'd be "danger close" to our perimeter, which was what you wanted when the enemy was in the vicinity. But "danger close" also involved the risk of being hit by friendly fire. One time the delta tangos were so close that we could hear shrapnel whistle over our heads. It was scary, but close-in artillery support was sometimes necessary. On those occasions, we were told to get low in the foxhole.

Every night the company set up observation posts (OPs). Each platoon was required to produce one OP, meaning the company would have four around the perimeter. Each OP had the platoon's radio—the "prick 25," which was short for the ANPRC-25. It was our basic radio and weighed about twenty pounds. I would learn all about the radio later when I became the platoon's RTO, or radiotelephone operator.

Depending upon the terrain, an OP could be anywhere from fifty to one hundred meters in front of the perimeter. After dark, the OP would quietly sneak out to a position that allowed a good field of vision. OPs were numbered by platoon and each was connected by radio to the company headquarters radio network—the "company net." Throughout the night, the headquarters, located in the center of the perimeter, would ask OPs for a SITREP (situation report). There was little or no talking on an OP. When contacted, the OP would check in by "breaking squelch," which meant simply pushing the push-to-talk button on the handset of the radio. One break of squelch meant everything was OK. When there was movement or the enemy was spotted, the OP would break squelch numerous times. This alerted the company radio watch. He would poll the OPs, starting at OP 1, and go on until he reached the one who saw movement. OP 1, when contacted, would be asked yes or no questions such as, "Do you have movement? Break squelch once for yes and twice for no." Then: "How many do you see? Break squelch for the number." Then: "Do you want to come in? Break squelch once for yes and twice for no." Then, depending upon the situation, the OP could come into the perimeter or stay in place.

OPs were called into the perimeter if contact with the enemy was made, and in the morning when their duty was done. Coming into the perimeter was very dangerous—you could get shot inadvertently by one of the men in the company. The word would be quietly passed down the line that OPs were coming in and not to fire. FNGs/cherries could be skittish and hence more likely to open fire if they saw men running toward the line. I learned very quickly that one had to listen carefully. If someone wasn't paying attention the results could be tragic.

Tending to personal needs could also be dangerous. We took care of business behind trees, bushes, and rice paddy dikes, and needed to inform unit members up and down the line of where we were headed. A trooper who wasn't paying attention could detect movement in a bush and fire on it. But when you got to go, you got to go, and you certainly didn't want to do it within the perimeter. So you made damn sure everyone knew where you were.

AMBUSH PATROLS AND A 'MAD MINUTE'

Missions for the night were the night ambush or "hunter-killer" teams. Once they were deployed, the company was set for the evening. Ambush patrols varied in size; some were platoon strength and some were as small as four or five men. Hunter-killer teams were made up of four or so men who'd silently roam the trails and villages in our AO. We'd quietly sneak through a village looking for VC or NVA, hoping to catch them unaware. We'd set up hasty ambushes along trails leading into a village. We had to be careful never to attack an enemy greater than we could handle.

Those who stayed in the perimeter usually spent the last of the daylight hours writing letters home, cooking C-Rations, playing cards, and quietly talking. One of the things that I and many others did was to memorize the terrain to our front, so that trees and bushes didn't turn into imaginary VC during the night. Sometimes we pulled radio watch. Usually one man from each platoon was assigned to the company command post, and every hour we'd contact the OPs for a SITREP. Those not assigned to the command post pulled guard duty in their foxholes.

First call was about an hour before dawn. The OPs would be called into the perimeter and after they were in we might have a "mad minute," depending upon terrain and the civilian population. During a mad minute, every man in the company fired his weapon. You can imagine the noise. It served two purposes. The enemy liked to attack around first light, when we were getting ready for the day and not fully organized. The OPs were back, we'd be eating, packing up our gear, and taking care of business, so their idea was to catch us off-guard. A mad minute would break up any attack preparation by the VC or NVA; it would also allow us to test our weapons.

Depending upon the mission, we might be allowed to heat up our C-rations, but usually we ate them cold. If we were quick enough we could make C-ration coffee, which we called "mud." Then we'd hump to another nearby village or be given a whole area to search. On one occasion, we had to search an area of hills and valleys just north of Bong Son Plain. Thankfully, we didn't carry our packs that day. Sometimes our "log birds" (logistical helicopters) would airlift our packs out and bring them back at night, making our day of searching much easier. Such was the case that day. As we started down a hill we had just searched, we came upon a stream rushing through large boulders. It was beautiful, yet we knew what boulders could hide. We couldn't let our guard down to enjoy the beauty.

The object of search-and-destroy missions was to find the enemy or his sympathizers, caches of weapons or rice, and destroy them. That's basically what we did day-to-day, with some variation. During my year in Vietnam, my platoon probably performed more than a hundred search-and-destroy missions. After a few weeks, they became very routine, yet we could never approach a mission that way. Getting complacent was a good way to get killed.

OPERATION DRAGNET

I didn't know it then, but our battalion was a part of Operation Dragnet in Binh Dinh Province, our AO. The goal of the operation was to destroy the Viet Cong underground. The South Vietnamese 816th National Police Field Force Battalion (PFF) gave us some help. The PFF was essentially a paramilitary group. They looked sharp in their tailored, tiger-striped, camouflage jungle fatigues, but most of them couldn't fight worth a damn. We called them "Ruff Puffs."

As part of Operation Dragnet, we did "snatch missions." We'd air assault an area close to a village, and then encircle the place, cutting off any escape routes. Once the village was secured, we'd call in the PFFs to do a search and to interrogate villagers, NVA, or Viet Cong suspects (VCS). The PFFs could be tough when questioning villagers suspected of being VC or having knowledge of VC whereabouts. They used some harsh methods that would make our waterboarding seem tame in comparison. Many times, our officers had to put a stop to their interrogations because they were getting way too violent.

I walked by a rice paddy on one such mission and saw our Kit Carson scout standing in the water smoking a cigarette. After a few seconds, he took a step back, bent down, and pulled a VCS up out of the muddy water. Rice paddies were fertilized with human waste, and the VCS's face had been planted in the muck. The scout said something to the VCS, and when he got no answer, he again stepped on the suspect's head. One of our officers saw what was happening and went nuts. He screamed at the scout, telling him to get the man back to dry ground and never to do that again. The lieutenant's M16 was raised and ready, and I thought he was going to kill the scout. I'd been shocked by the scout's harsh method of interrogation, but knowing the VC had killed his family helped me to understand.

If a snatch mission weren't feasible, we'd cordon a village. A cordon mission involved encircling a village on foot. Sometime late at night or very early in the morning, we'd quietly make our way to the village and surround it. Once in place, we would call in artillery illumination, which effectively turned night into day. We stopped anyone attempting to leave the village—and killed those who resisted. There was a curfew in effect at that time (mandated by the government of South Vietnam) and anybody found out of their hooch could be killed, no questions asked. If there was an enemy presence in the village there would be a firefight. After the firefight, the PFFs would be called in to conduct a search and interrogate the villagers.

My first experience with a cordon happened just two days after joining my unit. It was my first combat assault (CA), and the first time I saw an elephant in the wild. As our helicopter prepared to land on top of a modest-size mountain, I was amazed to see several very small elephants in the clearing. They lumbered into the jungle as soon as we made our approach. One experienced trooper told me that the Viet Cong used elephants to carry equipment.

After we landed and secured the LZ for the rest of the company, we formed up and started moving down the hill. We walked single file, with about ten feet between each soldier in the platoon. The company moved very quietly. It was hot and humid. Within minutes

I had sweated through my fatigues and my eyes were burning. The humidity made it hard to breathe. I was humping with a full field pack, including all my ammunition. We all wore "steel pots," our helmets, which actually consisted of two parts—a liner and the steel pot that fit over the liner. In addition to protecting our heads, the steel pot could be used for cooking, washing up, digging a foxhole, or even going to the bathroom if you were pinned down. It's funny but true, sometimes you just gotta go. Thankfully, I never had to make use of the steel pot that way.

As we moved down the mountain, we crossed a stream. A lot of the men took towels from around their necks and dipped them into the stream to cool off. My towel was in my pack and I was unable to get it until we took a break. Once we did, I soaked the towel in the stream and wrapped it around my neck. The effect was immediate, like standing under an air conditioner. I felt like a new man.

A LESSON IN COCONUT MILK

We made it down the mountain and onto the Bong Son Plain. Located in the northern part of Binh Dinh Province, the Bong Son Plain is bordered on the east by the South China Sea and surrounded by the hills of the Central Highlands. It is a flat expanse of land filled with rice paddies, dikes, and villages. During monsoon season, the plain floods, creating a vast lake with lots of little islands. It was summer, so the rice-paddy beds we walked through were mostly dry. We were always thirsty but we knew better than to drink the water.

We came out of the hills and onto the plain in the very late afternoon. We set up a company-size bivouac while we waited to move out for the cordon. Our platoon ended up on one of the many little islands that dotted the rice paddies.

It was there that I got my lesson in coconut milk. To pass the time some of the older guys knocked down some coconuts. They took Kool-Aid packets and shook them into the coconut milk, then passed it around for all of us to drink. It was refreshing. A lot of cherries, including a second lieutenant and me, eagerly drank the sweet, tasty liquid. Soon we'd drunk the milk of several coconuts. I remember being encouraged by some of the more seasoned soldiers to drink more.

Later in the evening, we moved out to take up positions around the village, which was about two klicks (a little more than a mile) away. That's when those of us who'd imbibed the coconut milk felt a sudden, very emergent urge. The column was stopped and one guy ran into the bushes. When he returned, I dashed into the bushes, followed by the second lieutenant. When he got back, the first guy again hurried into the bushes. I ran off a second time, as did the lieutenant. This went on for a short while before we were told to "pucker up and move on." We didn't find out until the next day that coconut milk is a laxative. That's when we realized we'd been had. The veterans enjoyed a big laugh at our expense. We laughed, too, and couldn't wait for the next cherries to arrive so we could play the same joke on them.

CHAPTER 10

FIRST COMBAT

W HEN WE REACHED THE VILLAGE ON THE BONG SON PLAIN that was the object of our cordon operation and my first combat assault, three other troopers and I set up a position on the top of a small berm. To our right front was a trail leading out of the village. Immediately to its right was a bamboo hedgerow. To our direct front was an open area with another hedgerow on the left. A third hedgerow was about one hundred meters directly in front of our position and ran perpendicular to the other two hedgerows. The hedges created a box with us at one end of it—two older troopers and two new ones. We dug a foxhole and camouflaged it with brush. We then set up our fields of fire. Sticks were pushed into the ground in front of our position to establish how far to the right and left we could fire without hitting friendly positions. Everything was done quickly and quietly.

About 0100 hours, illumination rounds started to light up the sky and the area around us. During one of the lulls, I noticed movement below and to my right front. Some Viet Cong were crawling along the trail, trying to sneak away from the village. I woke up one of the experienced troopers. He confirmed what I saw and very quietly woke up the other two guys. Once everyone was in position, we took the VC under fire, killing them all. It was the first time I'd fired my weapon in the field—and the first time I killed somebody. It all happened quickly. From the time I first spotted the movement to the time we killed the VC was maybe a minute, but it seemed like hours had passed.

Under the watchful eyes of our two foxhole mates, another trooper and I snuck down to search the bodies for anything that might offer intelligence on enemy movements or plans. The trooper asked me to help him move one of the bodies back to our position. We did so, though I'm not sure why—perhaps he just wanted to display a trophy and get a reaction from us cherries. I had no reaction. I didn't know what to think or what to feel. I had never shot anyone before. I had never seen a dead body before. Yet in the course of a few seconds, I had killed, searched dead bodies, and moved one.

In the movies, most heroes feel bad about killing the enemy. They sometimes even get sick. But I don't recall feeling any emotion. I didn't feel bad about killing Viet Cong. It was part of the job. Over the course of my life since Vietnam, I have wrestled with the indifference to death I felt at that moment. But I feel no guilt for anything I did as a soldier. Over the years, I've carried the memories of those I served with who were killed. I'm still haunted by the day when we loaded our dead brothers on helicopters for transport back to the rear and their final ride home. But we all had to adapt to the realities of war and combat. There was no avoiding the brutality.

Sometime around the end of June, we got a one-day stand down at LZ English. We had been ordered to Kon Tum Province near the Ho Chi Minh Trail, but were given a twenty-four-hour break before the new missions. After being in the field for about three weeks, I more than needed a brief period of relaxation. We all did.

After showers and hot food from the mess hall, we had our weapons serviced. Then, with our clean jungle fatigues, we got leave to go to Bong Son City to drink and—this will sound strange—to get our ears cleaned. The Vietnamese were very good at cleaning ears, if one trusted them. Some of our men even let Vietnamese barbers give them a shave with a straight razor. That took guts. I had my ears cleaned and couldn't believe the stuff that was pulled out of them. You get extremely dirty when you live in a jungle for weeks. And choppers kick up a lot of dirt. After the ear cleaning, we went to a local bar and drank and pursued other types of entertainment, as soldiers have done for centuries. Late that afternoon the squad met at a club just outside the perimeter. We drank some more and listened to the old guys tell war stories. The break was wonderful but over in a flash and we were on our way to Kon Tum.

THREE STRIKES AND YOU'RE OUT

On June 23, 1967, we were taken by Chinook helicopter to Kon Tum City. We spent the night there and the next day were airlifted into our new AO for search and destroy missions. I recall no enemy contact during our time in Kon Tum—but one incident there has troubled me for fifty years.

I began my tour as a replacement soldier with several other guys, one of whom became a good friend. Jerry was a small-town guy from Shullsburg, Wisconsin. He grew up on a farm and loved talking about it. He was a simple, generous soul. If the squad was nearly out of cigarettes, Jerry passed his last one around so we could all take a drag. If we ran low on C-rations, Jerry would share whatever food he had with us.

He often told the story of how as a boy, he had come close to death twice. He was struck by lightning while driving a tractor across the field during a thunderstorm, and on another occasion, was kicked by a skittish horse. Both incidents put him in a hospital.

He had a funny way of telling his near-death stories, and he'd always end by saying, "Three strikes and you're out," meaning that if anything happened to him in Vietnam, he'd probably die.

One day the entire company was on a search-and-destroy mission. We were the point platoon, which meant we walked out in front of the unit. Walking point was always risky—you'd be the first, usually, to be hit by an enemy ambush. We moved along a narrow trail and eventually reached a small clearing, where we stopped for chow. Jerry and I sat down overlooking a stream. Jerry said the spot and surrounding forest reminded him of Wisconsin. We talked about fishing and what we were going to do when we got back to the world (United States). We talked about getting together once we got home. It was a brief, peaceful interlude.

After about half an hour, we got the word to move out. The point man went first and got about fifty meters ahead of us. Then the rest of us took up our positions along the trail and started walking. We had gone about one hundred meters when the point man came back down the trail, signaling for the lieutenant to come forward. He'd seen movement ahead. Immediately, we found fighting positions. Jerry crouched behind a sizeable tree, and I got down behind a half-rotten log—the best I could do in a hurry. Our machine gunner, a guy I'll call Fred, found a place to set up his M60. He was a little behind Jerry and me, but seemed to have an open field of fire. After a couple of tense minutes, the lieutenant yelled, "Cease fire! Cease fire! Cease fire! They're friendly." Though we weren't shooting, he'd yelled "cease fire" because it carries more emphasis than "don't shoot." "Cease fire" is always yelled at least three times, so everyone hears and understands.

We were relieved. Turns out a U.S. Special Forces unit and CIDG (civilian irregular defense group) troops were patrolling the area, and we hadn't been informed. I stood up. Jerry stood up. Fred, inexplicably, pulled the trigger on his M60, shooting Jerry in the chest. Jerry went down like a rock.

We ran to him and did as much as we could. Everyone was screaming, "Medic!" We tried to stop the bleeding and protect the wound. The medic came up and took charge while some members of our platoon scouted an area that might serve as a landing zone for a medevac chopper. There wasn't enough space for a landing—too many trees—so we blew up several trees and tree stumps with C-4. We hoped the medevac would have enough room to land.

A few of us carried Jerry over to a spot close to the new LZ. We elevated his feet to prevent him from going into shock while the medic did his best to treat the wound. Jerry kept saying he was going to die, and we kept assuring him that he was going to be OK. "Three strikes, you're out," he mumbled over and over. "Three strikes, you're out." It was horrifying.

We soon heard the medevac overhead, its rotors thumping. Unfortunately, the LZ still was too tight; the chopper couldn't land. So the pilot brought the chopper straight down into the clearing and hovered while we loaded Jerry onboard. Because of the extra weight, one of the door gunners in the chopper had to jump out. He helped us put Jerry onboard, and we all watched the bird fly away, hoping Jerry could hang on long enough to make it to the field hospital. The door gunner had to hump with us the rest of the day until he could be picked up that night when the log bird came in to deliver supplies.

Fred was a wreck. As soon as the chopper took off, a few of us confronted him. I was far beyond anger. Fred kept apologizing, saying he didn't hear the cease-fire order, and that when Jerry stood up he'd been startled, panicked, and accidently fired his weapon. The machine gun had fired only one round and then jammed—but it only takes one round. We later learned that the weapon hadn't been cleaned in several days.

Fred had displayed a bad attitude since becoming a part of our unit. He was a know-it-all and had a smart-ass answer for everything. For whatever reason, he'd been made the assistant machine gunner and, on this mission, he was the platoon's only machine gunner because our primary gunner, Gandy, was out of the field for rest and recuperation (R&R).

 [The Montagnards] had great skill in tracking and moving quietly through the jungle.

I told Fred that if Jerry died, I was going to kill him in the next firefight. Then Sgt. Gomez chewed him out for having a dirty M60. Had our contact been with VC or NVA and not friendlies, we would have been in a terrible situation with an inoperable machine gun.

Before we left we talked with the Special Forces sergeant leading the patrol we had walked into. He explained that the CIDG patrol was made up of Montagnards, an indigenous, agricultural people who lived in the area (and still do). The Vietnamese look down on the Montagnards, and the Montagnards don't care much for the Vietnamese. They were some of the toughest people I've ever met, and were rabidly anti-communist. They worked with the Special Forces and were used to interdict the Ho Chi Minh Trail. They had great skill in tracking and moving quietly through the jungle.

We moved on to our next mission, which was to establish a perimeter around a crashed helicopter. As we humped to the site, I was told that Jerry was doing OK. The tension eased. I walked along thinking that Jerry would survive.

On the way, the platoon sergeant stopped us for a "leech check." You'd think that fighting a tenacious enemy in his country, in the jungle, in suffocating heat would be enough of a challenge. But there was an assortment of problems that could "just make your whole day," and one of them was leeches. Parasitic, bloodsucking worms, leeches are found in any place with damp jungle undergrowth or brackish water, and there's a lot of both in Vietnam. The leeches could be very small or very large, gray, and slimy. You don't realize that one has latched onto your warm skin until you examine your body. They can get underneath shirts or inside pants and shoes— and can make their way to your nether regions. One day a leech attached itself to the head of a guy's penis. Removing it was a painful experience for him, to say the least.

A leech check meant examining yourself and also getting real personal with your buddies. We had to examine one another's private areas, because leeches will crawl into places you cannot see. One time a modest soldier, whom I'll call Larry, refused to let anyone check his private areas. The sergeant ordered him to drop his pants. As soon as he did, he noticed a large leech on his inner thigh that was fat with blood. Larry passed out—fell right over.

We used salt, bug juice, or the tip of lit cigarettes to get rid of leeches. We decided to have little fun with Larry. One of the guys threw some water in his face to wake him up. He sat up and immediately spotted the leech on his leg. At that moment, another soldier sprayed bug juice on the leech, which immediately fell off Larry's leg and began belching his blood. He passed out again. From that day forward Larry was the first to drop trou and spread his cheeks whenever we had a leech check.

We finally made it to the helicopter crash site and set up camp. We would be there a couple of days, protecting it until a Sikorsky

Sky Crane could pick it up and haul it away. I had been told by Sgt. Gomez and the lieutenant that Jerry was doing fine. I heard that he was being taken to Japan. I heard that he was going home. Several squad members talked about what a great guy he was and shared their stories of him. I was happy that he was out of Vietnam.

Then one member of the company, who'd been on R&R, rejoined our platoon. I asked him if he'd had a chance to see Jerry. He looked at me with a blank stare and said, "Yeah, I had to identify his body before I went on R&R." Turns out Jerry had not even gotten to the hospital. He had died on the medevac. The lieutenant and Sgt. Gomez had decided to deceive me for a time, to keep me from doing something I'd regret.

I was shocked. I'd never suspected in the previous four days that Jerry was dead. I went off by myself and had a cigarette. I had to think. I can't remember who it was, but one of the guys came over and talked to me. He probably saved my life. He said if I killed Fred, I would wreck Jerry's memory, and I would destroy two more families—my own and Fred's. Three families would be devastated because of one tragic mistake. I sat for a while and thought about it. He was right.

Fred was scared. He knew that I knew Jerry was dead. I could see the fear in his eyes when I walked over to him. I told him that I wasn't going to kill him; he'd just have to live with what he did. I firmly believe that God gives us all a shot at redemption, no matter what we've done. It was true for Fred, the man who shot my friend. He had to earn his way back into our good graces. And he did. He became a good soldier and went on to become a sergeant. I think when I left Vietnam he was a squad leader. I'd like to believe that he went on to live a good, productive life, the life that Jerry didn't have a chance to live.

After Jerry's death, I found it very hard to get close to anyone. Something in the back of my mind told me that if I made another good friend, he'd probably be killed. Ever since Vietnam, I've found it very hard to have friends, to get close to anyone. It is something that I've had to work on most of my adult life. I have a lot of acquaintances but very few friends.

Shortly after we learned Jerry's fate, the Sikorsky arrived and hauled away the damaged helicopter. We returned to Bong Son on

 I told him I wasn't going to kill him; he'd just have to live with what he did.

July 25 and resumed our search-and-destroy missions (under Operation Pershing) along with our cordon and snatch missions (under Operation Dragnet). We also spent a week guarding bridges along Highway 19, outside of An Khe.

Guarding bridges was easy duty for the most part. We were responsible for preventing the VC and NVA from blowing them up. Each bridge had a bunker for defense. We were very alert at night because that's when the VC liked to attack. Days were a time for sleep, letter writing, and, occasionally, a quick visit to "Sin City" when we were near An Khe.

Sin City was a separate part of An Khe City. It had numerous bars and brothels and was a place to "relax." We would often go there to drink and to be entertained. Before I got there in 1967, the entertainment enclave was overseen by the army, which took measures to ensure that the area's "working girls" were healthy. Our medical corps checked them weekly. But the mommies and daddies of American servicemen were shocked to hear that their little boys might be doing sinful things and complained about it. So the medical evaluation and treatment of the working girls was stopped, which led to some unfortunate health issues for some soldiers.

One of the best things about An Khe was the bars that offered a steam shower and massage. Most of these steam showers were located just outside of Sin City. Unlike a shower on base, a steam shower will get all of the dirt out of your pores. There is nothing like a steam shower followed by a cold beer.

After the relaxing steam shower, you could get a massage, which was always amazing. I've never had a better one since leaving Vietnam. The masseuse, usually a young lady, would massage every muscle in your body and then walk on your back. Every joint was cracked, including the neck. Once she was done with the massage, other services were offered. After that, you could sit at the bar, have a few beers, listen to music, and escape the war for a few blissful hours.

Sometimes bridge detail could turn tragic. A young Vietnamese girl had a Coke stand right by our guard position. The "Coke girl," as we called her, was about twelve years old and cute. In some way, she reminded me of my sister, Nancy. Then one day a trooper broke one of her Coke bottles, and the cute little girl cussed him out with language that would make a hardened criminal blush. I never heard such filthy words come out of the mouth of a little kid. A day or two later, as we were waking up and checking the perimeter, we heard a loud explosion. We realized that the explosion was on a trail the Coke girl used daily to get to her stand. We sensed what had happened: She'd been too friendly with us, and the VC had decided to teach the locals a lesson.

We ran down the trail and soon found her lying on the ground, wounded and barely alive. The trail had been booby-trapped with an explosive device, which she had triggered. She was a mess, with blood all over. The medic did the best he could. When the medevac arrived, she was still alive, but barely. She was taken to one of our hospitals. We never found out what happened to her. I often think of her, and sometimes I can see her bloody little body just lying there on the ground, helpless.

A MISDIRECTED GAS ATTACK

One day we did a cordon of a village somewhere in Bong Son. We got into position around 2200 hours, nicely situated on top of a large berm overlooking the village. Just below us was a flat, dry rice paddy with a dike between it and the village. We had a tight, well-protected cordon. Should the VC or NVA try to break out, they had nowhere to go. We could easily take them under fire, and with a machine gun at our disposal, we were especially confident. We started getting fire from the village shortly after the first illumination round popped about 0300 hours. We returned fire and had sporadic firefights throughout the night. At first light, we moved our position down to the rice paddy dike and continued to return fire. After about an hour and a half we were told to return to the top of the berm.

Sometimes during a cordon mission, we used CS gas to flush out the enemy if they were dug in deep. CS gas, better known as tear gas, worked wonders. Using it depended on the direction of the wind, of course, and whether we'd been issued protective gas masks. After some inconclusive fighting with VC in the village, the company commander decided that artillery should shoot CS rounds into the village. What wasn't taken into consideration was the fact that the wind was blowing toward our position, and we had no protective masks. Talk about flashbacks to basic training. The gas that was supposed to flush out the Viet Cong had the opposite effect: It forced us out of our position very quickly.

As we "beat feet," we found a Vietnamese man trying to sneak away from the village. We caught him and saw that he had strap marks on his shoulders—an indication that he was an enemy soldier who had been carrying a heavy pack. We called it in, and he was picked up by the Ruff Puffs, the PFFs. Shortly after turning him over to the South Vietnamese, Sgt. Gomez got a call on the radio that the CS fire had been lifted and we returned to our positions.

Not long after, we resumed conventional artillery fire on the village, and what had begun as a simple cordon escalated into a major battle against a well dug-in enemy. Still, we were in absolute control of the area and doing a number on the Viet Cong. As the firefight intensified, we got additional support from two tanks and one hell of an artillery barrage. Then we assaulted the village. By that time, very little fire was coming out of it. Because it was a VC village and had been nearly leveled by artillery and tank fire, we destroyed the rest of it. The remaining population was relocated to a fortified hamlet. A fortified hamlet was one controlled by the government of South Vietnam and was meant to protect Vietnamese peasants. In later years, I would come to question their real purpose, but at the time, it seemed like a good way to protect civilians.

The PFFs interrogated the surviving villagers to ensure that no enemy was among them. We then swept the village ourselves, multiple times. The first time we removed all the civilians. The second time we searched for tunnels and contraband. The third time we used our Zippos to burn what was left. Sadly, we had to kill all the animals—water buffalo, pigs, whatever was left after the battle. We couldn't leave the livestock for the VC. One of the things I hated most about Vietnam was that we had to kill animals occasionally.

On one mission, we learned that the Viet Cong were using dogs to alert them to our movements. Consequently, as we went through an area we had to kill all the dogs. I felt bad about it, we all did. My dog, Duke, was my best friend when I was bullied in grade school. I really hated killing dogs, but not so much that I wanted to risk one of my friend's lives to a barking dog.

SPRAINED ANKLES

On August 2, on a search-and-destroy mission, we started taking fire from an island situated in the center of what I recall was the Song Lai Giang. It is the largest river in Binh Dinh Province and flows into the South China Sea. It was decided that we would air assault onto the island. Problem was, only one chopper could get to the landing zone at a time, and it wouldn't be able to land. We'd have to jump, about ten feet or more. You didn't jump out of a helicopter until the crew chief gave you the go-ahead. Usually, two soldiers jump at once—one from either side of the aircraft—so that the helicopter can maintain stability.

As we assaulted onto the island, the helicopter went into a hover mode. The first guy on each side made his jump. The guy in front of me was carrying an ammo box. When he hit the ground, he was supposed to take off running. He didn't, but the crew chief didn't see that and slapped my back to jump. I jumped and my feet hit his ammo box, spraining both of my ankles. Because I was wearing boots my ankles didn't swell, but they hurt like hell. I hobbled around the island as best I could until we were picked up later and taken back to the mainland.

Within a short time, we were taking part in another air assault. I'd told my squad leader that I had messed up my ankles on the first jump, but he thought I was faking. The next air assault was done by Chinook helicopter. As with all air assaults, regardless of the type of aircraft, once the helicopter hits the ground you've got to get off and seek cover quickly in case it's a hot LZ. My ankles hurt so bad I could only hobble away from the chopper. Thankfully, we were not under fire when we landed. But because I was moving so slowly, the squad leader decided to medevac me. It was embarrassing to be flown out because of sprained ankles. I ended up spending a week at the 18th Surgical Hospital in Pleiku, lying in a bed next to seriously wounded soldiers. I felt guilty, to say the least. But if you can't walk, you can't walk. After about a week, the swelling went down and I was released back to my unit.

I arrived back in An Khe and had a couple of days before I could leave to get to LZ English and my unit. I was assigned the "s**t burning" detail. Yep, that means exactly what it sounds like. It seems like a gross job, but it was an easy detail as long as I didn't breathe in the smoke. First, I had to pull the waste out from the outhouse. The waste was in the bottom and top quarter of cut fifty-gallon cans. There were four of them. I pulled out each can using a long pole with a hook on the end. Then I dragged them to the burning area, stirred in kerosene, and lit them on fire. Occasionally, I would have to stir the waste and add more kerosene. Once the waste was burned, I put them back in the outhouse. We always had one in place for use while burning the others.

R&R IN KUALA LUMPUR

A day or so later I was in the orderly room waiting to get back to my unit. Out of the blue, the company clerk told me that I could go on R&R if I wanted. He said that most people go on R&R once they hit six months in country. I hadn't reached that point yet, but he said I could go. I thought, "What the hell, I might as well do it. Why take the chance of being KIA before I get an R&R?" By then I'd become quite fatalistic.

I went on a four-day R&R to Kuala Lumpur, Malaysia. It was quite an experience. I did what most soldiers do on R&R and also learned about Malaysian peppers. I have always loved hot, spicy food; consequently, I know how to test the heat of a pepper. You put little bit of it on the tip of your tongue.

When I sat down at a local restaurant to await service, I saw a bowl of little, round green peppers. I grabbed a pair of chopsticks, picked up one of the peppers, and touched it to the tip of my tongue.

 "Why take the chance of being KIA before I get an R&R?" By then I'd become quite fatalistic.

Immediately, my face felt as if it had caught on fire: Heat surged through my eyes, nose, and mouth, down into my esophagus and all the way into my belly. I turned a bright shade of red and started to sweat profusely. I drank the water on the table, not caring what stomach-destroying microbes might be in it. I knew that water doesn't help and might even spread the heat, but I needed the cold from the ice. Several soldiers on R&R at the next table started laughing and offered me a beer. I drank it in one gulp, but it only exacerbated the burn. I then decided to wait it out and suffer in silence for several minutes. I learned an important lesson about peppers: They don't have to be big to light a giant fire in your mouth.

As soon as I got settled into a hotel room, I did three things. First, I filled the bathtub with hot water and soaked. Second, I drank a bit of whiskey while I soaked. Third, I called home. It was the first time I talked with my parents since leaving in May. I didn't know what time it was in Chicago, but I remember Mom and Dad sounding quite groggy. They were very happy to talk to me and to hear that I was OK. I thanked them for the several care packages they had sent. After about five minutes we hung up and I remained in the tub, soaking. There is nothing like a good soak in a deep hot tub to relieve stress. That and a good stiff drink.

I spent the rest of my Kuala Lumpur R&R eating, drinking a little too much, and enjoying other entertainments. But after two days of rest, I got bored. I walked around the city and saw a few tourist sites, but I was too much of a loner to do much else. Looking back, I wish I had enjoyed some of the Malaysian culture. But when you're young and stupid, you don't take advantage of opportunities. After four days, I was more than ready to head back to my unit. I landed in Saigon and wasn't able to catch a flight to Camp Radcliff, so I had to stay overnight. Just my luck, the base got mortared and I ended up spending much of the night in a bunker.

The next day I caught a flight to Camp Radcliff. I was back with D Company, 2nd Platoon, somewhere on the Bong Son Plain. We continued the search-and-destroy and snatch missions. We also conducted ambush patrols and four-man hunter-killer teams. I went out on a couple of them but never saw the enemy.

BACK TO WORK

Not long after I got back to the unit, we were sent on a search-and-destroy mission, but with a difference. There would be no resupply so we had to carry all of our food and ammunition. At one point after getting to our AO, we came out of some real heavy jungle and started following a stream down a long sloping hill. All along the stream were little pools of crystal-clear water—the spot was picture-postcard beautiful. At the time, each platoon was operating independently, so our platoon leader, Lt. Watkins, as I recall, decided that it was a good time to take a break. Security was sent out, and the rest of us plunged into the stream to cool off. We let the clear, cold water flow over our aching bodies. It was a little bit of heaven. After washing and cooling off, a few of us relieved those who'd been standing guard. After about two hours, we made our way on down the hill.

As we started to come out on the plain we noticed a cave. Caves were always searched, so another soldier and I entered it for a look. We were immediately overcome by the sickly sweet smell of rotting corpses. We hurried out and told the lieutenant that there were several bodies in the cave in various states of decomposition. He ordered us back into the cave to count the number of bodies. I can't recall how many there were, but I'll never forget the smell and the way they looked. Gruesome.

We made our way down to a valley floor, which like the Bong Son Plain was flat and dotted with villages and little islands. The rice paddies were all dry, so we set up our perimeter for the night on one of the islands. The next day we finished our mission and made our way to the coast.

It was about the middle of the afternoon when we finally made it to the South China Sea. We could see a navy destroyer about mile out at sea. The beach went on for miles to the north. To the south stood a small mountain with a sharp cliff on the side, facing the sea. On top of the mountain stood our destination, LZ Apache. It was a forward firebase housing an artillery battery. But before we made the trek up to the LZ, we were given a chance to swim. Security was posted and the rest of us went skinny-dipping. Many of us bodysurfed waves into shore. Funny thing about skinny-dipping and bodysurfing: Your skin is gently rubbed raw, but you don't know it until you get dry and start to sweat or wade back into salt water.

LZ Apache was a beautiful spot. We settled into our bunkers. I was lucky enough to get one overlooking the sea. I couldn't believe the beauty of this war-torn country. That night it was my turn to go on an ambush patrol. When it got dark five of us snuck down the mountain and started to work our way south. We wanted to find a good ambush site. To get where we wanted to go, we had to cross a saltwater inlet. The salt water irritated the areas of my crotch, stomach, and chest where the sand had abraded me while bodysurfing. We walked quietly along the coast, hiding in the tree lines until we reached the point where we were going to set up the ambush. We quietly waited for the enemy all night but made no contact. Early the next morning, we again waded across the saltwater inlet. I took a deep breath as the cold salt water chilled and stung me. When we got back to LZ Apache, we were allowed to catch some sleep during the day.

That night our first sergeant came in with the log bird. He brought with him several cases of beer and pop and containers of steak and chicken. We had a barbecue on Apache that night. After being in the field for a week, it was a wonderful to have a cold beer.

DAK TO

On November 11, our company was airlifted to an LZ in Dak To. Dak To is located in the mountainous southwestern province of Kon Tum, Central Highlands. It is close to the border of Laos and Cambodia. As soon as we landed, we went to our assigned area to spend the night. We were in the center of the camp so we didn't have guard duty and could relax. Shortly after we settled in, mortars and rockets started to hit the airfield just as two C-130 transport planes were trying to take off, one behind the other. The first one got hit and started burning. The second one was trying to get by it and take off. While that was happening, a Duster (armored track) and a Quad 50 truck (a truck with four .50-caliber machine guns mounted on it) came speeding by, headed toward the airfield. Soon both were spraying the hillside, where the attack had originated. It ended quickly.

On the morning of November 12, we were given a warning order. We were told that the 4th Infantry got their butts kicked and we were going in to relieve them. It would be a one-ship LZ (big enough for only one helicopter to land at a time), and the birds could only

 We were told that the 4th Infantry got their butts kicked and we were going in to relieve them.

carry four of us at a time. There would be enough birds to carry the two platoons, but we would have to get off them quickly. They would be doing a "touch and go," meaning they would barely touch ground before takeoff. There would be two flights, one carrying 1st and 2nd platoon and the second carrying 3rd and 4th platoon. The three days we spent on Hill 724 would be life changing.

The first sergeant of D Company, 3rd Battalion, 8th Infantry (3/8), came out to wave us in to the landing zone. Even from our helicopter, we could see the blank look in his eyes. It was as if he couldn't take in any more. As soon as we landed, we hopped from the bird as fast as we could and joined the defensive perimeter. As soon as the remnants of the 4th Infantry had left, we were given our assignments. I was assigned to a six-man bunker with others from my squad. While some of our men worked security on the perimeter, the rest of us started to search the hill for American bodies. The hill was littered with fallen trees. It looked like a giant hand had reached down and ripped up the land. It reminded me of a Wisconsin forest after a tornado, with trees piled everywhere.

Lying among the fallen trees was the body of an NVA soldier, his hands reaching up as if begging for something, his body twisted around the trunk of a tree. His head, though still attached, looked as if it wasn't; his eyes were open and staring. I found several like that. I thought I should feel something; I wanted to feel something; I knew I should feel something. But I didn't. They were just things. Yet after fifty years, I can't stop remembering them. You don't easily

 [Capt. Orsini] looked out for the welfare of his men and we would have followed him anywhere.

forget the sight of torn and twisted bodies. I remember taking pictures of them, which I still have. Why, I don't know.

It's one thing to see an enemy body, but it is entirely different to find one of your own. We took the bodies of our brothers in arms and very carefully got ready to load them on a helicopter. There was an unspoken reverence in how we handled them.

We stayed on Hill 724 from November 12 to the 14th—three very long days. During that time, we received mortar and rocket fire daily. There were also several probing attacks by the VC, but nothing prolonged or serious. Our company commander, a captain who was not well liked, was wounded during one mortar attack. Capt. "Hard Core" was a West Point graduate. He was rumored to have said, when he took over our company, that he was going to earn the Medal of Honor. He was one of those officers who could command but did not know how to lead. For example, while we would be humping with full field packs through rice paddies, he walked blithely atop the dikes, no pack on his back. There were several times we fantasized about him hitting a trip wire.

So we were not terribly saddened by the news that a single mortar round had wounded Capt. Hard Core when he was walking to a helicopter to mail a letter. There was a rumor that he had intended to send a twelve-man patrol off Hill 724 to make contact with any enemy in the area. That would have been a bad idea, most of us concluded: A twelve-man patrol is neither large enough to defend itself against a larger enemy force nor small enough to be unseen.

A few days after the captain's injury, Capt. Donald A. Orsini arrived to replace him as D Company commander. Capt. Orsini was the antithesis of Capt. Hard Core. He led by example. If we carried packs, he carried a pack. He looked out for the welfare of his men and we would have followed him anywhere.

In the mid 1990s, I visited with Orsini, who had retired a lieutenant colonel. I spent a wonderful weekend with him and his wife in Pittsburgh. He was suffering the effects of Agent Orange at the time and would die a few years later. I have only fond memories of my captain. I don't know how his fellow officers viewed him, but from my vantage point as a lower-ranked enlisted soldier, I believed that Capt. Orsini was an exceptional man.

A FATEFUL ORDER

We did a few more days of search-and-destroy missions, but had no contact with the enemy. On November 18, we were airlifted to LZ Becky, where we were assigned perimeter guard duty for an artillery unit. If I remember correctly, the entire battalion was on the perimeter. This was to be very good duty. We took over bunkers that had already been built. My platoon was on the bunker line at the base of a very large hill. We had clear fields of fire and concertina wire protecting our perimeter. For the most part, it was two or three days of uneventful guard duty.

On November 20, we were told to close down LZ Becky. Our company was the last to leave, and our platoon was the last unit in the company to leave. The only other remaining unit was a four-deuce (4.2-inch) mortar crew. They had several dud rounds that were very unstable and could not be fired. The crew wanted to booby-trap them for the Viet Cong to find. However, our new platoon leader, a second lieutenant who was the officer in charge, insisted that the mortar crew fire the rounds before leaving. The gunner and the assistant gunner both told him that doing so would be dangerous; the rounds could explode in the tube.

 I could step out on the skid of a Heuy and ride it into landing zones as well as anybody.

The lieutenant gave a direct order to fire the rounds. The gunner and the assistant gunner told us to step far away, which we did. The first round exploded about five hundred meters after leaving the tube. The second round exploded in the tube, killing the gunner. We all rushed to assist him, but the medic came in and said he was gone.

Our attention turned to the lieutenant, who we were ready to kill for essentially killing one of our own. It was unforgivable. Sgt. Gomez, with his usual coolness, suggested that we wait until the next firefight. Then he turned to the lieutenant and said, "Sir, I recommend that you figure some way to get out of the field."

We were airlifted out of LZ Becky into another area, where we had to hump a few klicks to our next position. As we were crossing a stream the lieutenant sprained his ankles. I was reminded of my recently sprained ankles and almost laughed. However, his sprained ankles must not have been too bad, as he managed to hump at least another klick or two without limping. When the log bird came in to deliver our supplies, he was medevaced out. I learned later that he'd been assigned to the battalion supply (S-4) shop.

By late November 1967, I had been in Vietnam fewer than six months. Even so, I was already an "old guy" by the standards of combat soldiers. I had arrived as just another FNG, naïve and unsure of myself, but within weeks had grown confident in my abilities as an infantryman. I had been on ambush patrols, hunter-killer teams, my share of observation posts, and more combat assaults than I could count. I could step out on the skid of a Huey and ride it into a landings zone as well as anybody. I could sit calmly as a Huey banked sharply and look straight down at the ground without fear of falling out. I could stay cool in hot situations. I could shoot and kill enemy soldiers.

I wasn't a great soldier but I was a competent one. And I was maturing on a personal level. I had wanted to be tested—that is why I volunteered for duty in Vietnam—and had been, several times. I had passed those tests.

But I would be tested again more than ever, in less than a month.

Here I am at age 5, having lunch at our apartment at W. 111th Place in Roseland.

ALBUM: A Hero's Life

With Dad and Mom in Roseland. I'm wearing my favorite cowboy shirt (left). Dad before being discharged from the U.S. Army Air Corps in 1946 9above).

My favorite vacation place on Lake Dorothy: a beach, boats, and the woods.

I graduate from kindergarten at age 6. My Grandmother Sytsma (right). Nancy, Dad, and I on vacation in Wisconsin (below).

Nancy and I with Mom at
Lake Eliza in 1957.

At our apartment in Dolton,
I'm getting ready to make
money shoveling snow.

Christmas 1961, with Dad,
Nancy, and me (left).
Me with my cousins Kathy
and Ricky (below).

Nancy with our dog, Duke.

My basic training picture, taken in early 1965, just before graduation. Nancy and I on vacation in Wisconsin, 1963 (right).

Inside our barracks in basic training, at Fort Knox, Kentucky.

Winter 1964: a cold, muddy day on the obstacle course. That night we ran it with machine guns firing overhead.

Waiting in the railroad station in Frankfurt, Germany.

On my weekend pass, Mom, Nancy, and I visit the Georgia coast in 1965.

Hacking our way through the jungle in the An Lao Valley, January 1968.

Montagnard villagers in Dak To, in the Central Highlands, with Staff Sergeant Gomez (center left) in late 1967.

Pedro Leos and me. We served together in the 2nd Platoon, Company D, 12th Cavalry, and we're still in contact.

My friend Gerald R. Brines, killed by "friendly fire," July 17, 1967.

Clearing an LZ for a helicopter in Kon Ttum, in the Central Highlands, July 1967.

Taking a break on maneuvers, in An Lao Valley in the Central Highlands.

Highway 2 near An Khe, view from our bridge-detail bunker, December 1967.

At Dak To, a VC mortar and rocket attack on the day before our
air assault on Hill 724 (top). U.S. Dusters moving up to fire on the
VC positions, November 1967 (bottom).

My unit, Company D, 12th Cavalry, at An Khe after I was pulled out of the field.

During our guard duty on Highway 19 near An Khe, this young "Coke girl" was grievously wounded by a VC booby trap.

Me with my gear at Dak To (above). My friend Bill, leaning on a 4.2 mortar (left).

New arrival at Dak To: HH-43 combat rescue helicopter.

A night position on Hill 724 (above).
Darrel Shelly, a well-liked young trooper
in my unit, killed in a firefight with NVA,
February 1968 (left).

On Hill 724 shortly after we relieved elements of the 4th Infantry Division on
November 12, 1967, and began searching for American bodies.

Our six-man bunker on Hill 724, after we had improved it during our stay.

The view from our bunker on Hill 724 during an air strike. VC rocket and mortar attacks happened daily.

The day after my "Welcome Home" arrival (top). Guest of honor at Dolton's Fourth of July parade, 1970 (below).

Me wearing the "hat" I earned on promotion to drill sergeant.

Susie and I on our wedding day in April 1970, with Reverend William Sheppard at the Ivanhoe United Methodist Church in Riverdale.

President Nixon awarding my Medal of Honor, with Susie, Mom, and Dad.

After the MOH ceremony on May 14, 1970, with family and local dignitaries.

Me inspecting naval cadets on Memorial Day 1970 in Dolton,
shortly after receiving the MOH.

Susan, son Eric at 5 months, and me.   At one of Brian's high school games.

Wearing my Medal, in full U.S. Army uniform.

At the 100th anniversary of the 1st Battalion, 12th Cavalry Regiment, 1st Cavalry Division, with former commander Capt. Kent (in tuxedo) and me.

Event with a Chicago high school Army ROTC class where I presented them with my challenge coin (above). Granddaughter Cailinn and me at her favorite restaurant (right).

Frankfort, Illinois, late 90s. One of the many middle school classes I spoke to.

In my office at the Illinois Attorney General's office, where I led
the Veterans Rights Bureau for twenty years.

CHAPTER 11

MOMENT OF TRUTH AT TAM QUAN

E VERYONE WHO FOUGHT IN VIETNAM HAD AT LEAST ONE MOment of truth—one situation in which your life was put in the hands of the Fates, or God; one challenge of courage and fortitude; one battle where there was the strong possibility of defeat and death; one random accident or incident that could alter your life. Many have said that combat is long stretches of boredom punctuated by moments of terror. It is those moments of terror that you hope to survive.

A lot of people who served in Vietnam had many such moments—they were engaged in multiple firefights, piloted helicopters taking enemy fire, went on night patrols. In those moments, your life effectively becomes a ball rolling on a roulette wheel with many landing boxes marked "death." That was a fact of which every soldier, including me, was acutely aware but tried not to think about. Because thinking about it could paralyze you with fear.

Actual engagements with the enemy, when bullets and shells are coming at you, were hardly the only risk. In Vietnam, it felt like there were 101 ways to die. That was the nature of the place. As one 1st Cavalry Division veteran put it: "Death followed us everywhere, and sometimes we followed it. On every helicopter air assault, it lurked. At every river crossing, at every bend in the trail, behind every bush, in every village." You could trip an improvised explosive device and be dead in a second; you could be riding in a helicopter that gets shot down; you could be sitting in a bar in Saigon on what seemed a quiet night when a VC throws in a grenade. We train to beat the odds and survive, but nothing defines the random nature of life like combat.

MY MOMENT OF TRUTH ARRIVED ON DECEMBER 15, 1967, IN THE last major firefight in the Battle of Tam Quan, a tough, on-and-off, two-week fight whose significance would not be fully recognized until later in the war. It took place at a hamlet named My An (2), part of a collection of hamlets making up the village of My An. The My An battle was a sort of crescendo—the climactic and most violent of a series of clashes between U.S. troops and the NVA.

On our side was the 1st Brigade, 1st Cavalry Division. First Brigade comprised 1st Battalion, 12th Cavalry (1/12); 1st Battalion, 8th Cavalry (1/8); 2nd Battalion, 8th Cavalry (2/8); 1st Battalion, 9th Cavalry (1/9); 1st Battalion, 50th Infantry (Mechanized) (1/50 Mech); and the 40th ARVN Regiment. Various artillery batteries and tactical air squadrons also pitched in, thankfully. On the enemy side were major elements of the NVA's 22nd Regiment, 3rd (Sao Vang) Division. The NVA was estimated to have had about 1,200 men involved in the engagement; we had 650.

The 1/50 (Mech) had only been formed three months earlier, in September 1967. It was a unit with a lot of armored firepower, and its role was to join with other major army units that needed more heavy weaponry. It was attached to the 1st Cavalry, and we were happy to have the extra punch provided by APCs sporting recoilless rifles and armed with .50-caliber machine guns, two M60 machine guns, and flamethrowers. We felt a lot more secure with the 1/50 (Mech) tracks nearby, plus artillery batteries and tactical air support. Tam Quan was not one of Vietnam's classic battles, but it was significant, something of a grudge match for the 1st Cavalry. I was not aware at the time, but the previous Christmas, the 22nd Regiment broke a Christmas truce when it attacked C Company, 1/12. Apparently, some 1st Cav officers had not forgotten that event.

Tam Quan is a village in the northern end of Binh Dinh Province. The larger area around Tam Quan, known as Bong Son Plain, is a mostly flat expanse of land with rice paddies, lots of coconut and mangrove trees, thick hedgerows, and numerous hamlets near the coast. The area is about three hundred miles north of Ho Chi Minh City (then called Saigon). Bong Son was the tactical responsibility of the 1st Brigade of the 1st Cavalry Division.

We were in Dak To when the first engagements with the NVA's 22nd Regiment occurred at Tam Quan. We'd heard that the situation in Bong Son was getting sketchy. From the last week of November to the first part of December, our intelligence units were a hive of activity. Between December 1 and December 5, aerial reconnaissance was initiated across the Bong Son Plain. It was reported that the regimental headquarters of the 22nd had moved from somewhere in the mountains surrounding Bong Son into the area around Tam Quan. It became clear that the North Vietnamese were engaged in a major buildup of their forces, and we readied ourselves to find and confront them. As it turned out, the NVA and VC were preparing for the Tet Offensive, which would commence a month later in January 1968 and involve attacks on U.S. and South Vietnamese forces in major district capitals in South Vietnam.

According to research on the Tam Quan campaign prepared by Lt. Tom Kjos, platoon leader of 3rd Platoon, D Company, 1/12, and Rigo Ordaz, a soldier with the 1/50 (Mech), based on after-action reports, battalion daily staff journals, and other sources, the fighting started in early December with planned attacks by elements of the NVA's 22nd Regiment. On December 1 and 4, the NVA conducted probing attacks on bridges and installations along Highway 1, between Bong Son and Tam Quan, some of which were manned by ARVN units and some by our troops. In addition, the NVA hit the ARVN's subdistrict headquarters and their base at LZ Tom with ground attacks on December 4.[1]

FIRST ENGAGEMENT: SPOTTING AN ANTENNA

During the last week of November and the first week of December, intelligence reports noted that the 22nd NVA Regimental Headquarters had relocated to about fifteen hundred meters south of LZ Tom. In response to those reports 1st Brigade increased aerial and ground surveillance of the Bong Son Plain, with particular attention to the area around LZ Tom, ARVN installations, and the bridges along Highway 1. LZ Tom was north of the Bong Son River and just east of Highway 1 and the village of Tam Quan.[2]

Late in the afternoon of December 6, A Troop [3],1/9, spotted a radio antenna and immediately started to receive small-arms fire—an indication of a large concentration of enemy soldiers. They quickly air assaulted a platoon of infantry into the area, which immediately got pinned down. The Battle of Tam Quan had begun.[4]

Weapons platoon from D Troop, 1/9, was inserted to reinforce A Troop's platoon, and it too came under intense automatic and small-arms fire from NVA bunkers and trenches. Two additional platoons, one from B Troop, 1/8, and a platoon from A Company, 1/50 (Mech), Armored Cavalry, were inserted to assist the beleaguered 1/9 platoons. The NVA were well hidden in thick undergrowth. The relieving units from A, 1/50 (Mech), and B, 1/8, extracted the two pinned-down platoons. They then established a night peri-meter. A pair of flare ships, named *Moonshine* and *Spooky*[5], along with artillery units from various forward firebases[6] provided addi-tional support.

The next morning, December 7, at 0725, a time-on-target (TOT)[7] artillery barrage, complete with air rocket artillery (ARA)[8] and CS (tear) gas, hit the enemy's entrenchments. A Company, 1/8, then made a combat assault into the area. At 0730, the U.S. units hit the NVA positions, supported by ARA and CS gas. By 0815 the bat-tle had been joined by A Company, 1/8, another platoon from 1/50 (Mech), and two Dusters.[9] By 0915 Companies B and C, 2/8, had combat assaulted into the battle area as a blocking force to stop the NVA's escape to the east. An ARVN company from 1st Battalion, 40th Regiment, and one APC troop were to act as a blocking force to the north, between the South China Sea and Highway 1. The 4th Battalion and one company of the ARVN 3rd Battalion, 40th Regi-ment, also set up to the south.

The 1/8 met heavy resistance to the east and pulled back to allow artillery batteries and tactical aircraft to pound NVA positions.[10] At 1406 A and B companies, 1/8, and flamethrower APCs, commonly called "Zippo Tracks,"[11] hit the NVA again and broke their line. Two bulldozers were brought in to destroy the bunkers and trenches. The two companies of the 2/8 had only minimal contact as they pushed west. The NVA's 22nd Regiment hadn't gone away, however, and at 1645 the headquarters of C Company, 2/8, was pinned down as they crossed a rice paddy. By 1900 they were extracted and joined the rest of C Company in their night bivouac.

On December 8, C Company, 1/8, made an air assault to relieve B Company, 1/8. Artillery and air strikes and CS gas hit the NVA positions again. Ordaz notes in his recollection of the day:

The wind shifted and the CS cloud hit us as we were poised to attack. The problem was that there were not enough gas masks to go around. Some of the troops were choking and coughing. Even with the gas mask on, the CS was so concentrated that all our body was stinging with the gas. Most of the ARVNs didn't have gas masks and were seen running toward a ravine for protection.[12]

The after-action report for that day states that the CS gas drove the NVA from their positions into a TOT artillery barrage, killing about twenty-three. At 0845 D Company, 1/50 (Mech), started a reconnaissance in force. Artillery and CS gas were again used in preparation for another attack. Company D, 1/50 (Mech), and A and C companies, 1/8, coordinated an attack to the east and north. They found destroyed bunkers and trenches and several enemy killed by the artillery and air strikes.[13] The three companies then swept through the area around the hamlet of Dai Dong (2). "Some of the guys in the mortar platoon loaded dead NVA on to their APCs...and took them to a designated area," Ordaz writes.[14]

DELTA COMPANY JOINS THE FIGHT

On December 9, my unit, D Company, 1/12, was transported from Dak To to LZ English. We got to the base at 0900[15] and at 1545 we hopped on Chinooks and were air assaulted into the Tam Quan AO.[16] According to the daily staff journal, our "foxhole strength" at the end of the day was 101 men. We were put under the operational control of Task Force Dolphin. Along with B Company, 1/8, and B Company, 1/50 Mech, we set up blocking positions in a beach area adjacent to the village of My An. At roughly the same time, just north of our position, the NVA's 8th Battalion, 22nd Regiment, attacked the ARVN 40th Regiment. "The attack was repulsed," writes

Ordaz, "but they had sporadic to heavy contact continued during the day…five klicks north of My An (1)."

There was heavier fighting the next day, December 10. At 0500, the NVA 8th Battalion, 22nd Regiment, again attacked 3rd and 4th battalions of the ARVN's 40th regiment and an APC troop. The attack was repelled by the ARVN with the help of ARA, artillery, and *Spooky*. At 0900, civilians were seen running from the village of Truong Lam, near the coast. Nearly two hours later, B Company,

 At the end of the day, the foxhole strength of D Company was ninety-four men.

1/50 (Mech), and B Company, 1/12, approached the village. They did not know that an NVA force of unknown size had dug bunkers under some of the hooches and was lying in wait. The NVA hit the 1/50 (Mech) with a fusillade of heavy automatic and small-arms fire. According to Ordaz's report, "Apparently, B 1-50 Mech company had been split up by a big ditch and part of the company came under intense enemy fire. The other part of the company could not cross the ditch to come to the aid of the beleaguered troops. The company lost 10 soldiers in that encounter." The daily staff journal records that B, 1/50 (Mech), lost seven KIA, eighteen WIA, and five MIA; B, 1/12, had one KIA and one WIA (friendly fire).

In the afternoon, B Company, 1/50 (Mech), supported by B and C companies, 1/12, attacked enemy positions near Troung Lam after intense artillery preparation. C Company hit the left flank of the NVA position while B Company hit the right. At 1545, D Company, 1/50 (Mech), arrived with armored tracks and joined the ARVN's last assault on the NVA position. They pulled back at 1850 to establish night defensive positions. Flare ships provided illumination for artillery to pound the NVA throughout the night. B, 1/50 (Mech), suffered eight KIA, twenty-two WIA, and one MIA. B, 1/12, lost one KIA and four WIA.[17] It was a bad day.

That same day, my company continued search-and-destroy missions along the South China Sea southeast of LZ Tom. We had light contact with the enemy, according to records. We were looking for elements of the 7th Battalion, 22nd NVA Regiment, which was believed to be withdrawing into our area.[18] Our battalion, the 1/12, had a little over four hundred fifty troops in the field.

We were hit by small-arms fire. About 1420, a grenade was thrown into a bunker, killing one VC and setting off a huge secondary explosion. Our 3rd Platoon captured a wounded NVA soldier and engaged several enemy troops who were escaping artillery fire. About 1740, we engaged another enemy bunker and suffered one KIA and three WIA. One NVA was killed. At the end of the day, the foxhole strength of D Company was ninety-four men. Our sister units—a few kilometers away—were also finding NVA KIAs, weapons, and other items. There were numerous small firefights throughout the area of operation.

There wasn't much action during the next two days. On the morning of December 12, my company and B, 1/50 (Mech), linked up to sweep an area east of Dai Dong (1). Around 1030, we took small-arms and automatic-weapons fire. Working with the 1/50 APCs, we came on line—meaning we infantry troops positioned ourselves between the armored tracks and moved forward.[19] It was just as I had practiced in Germany months earlier during field training exercises. Forward observers called in artillery and ARA. After a 20-minute engagement, everything went quiet. We continued our "find 'em" mission until December 13, with little or no contact reported. Our foxhole strength was ninety-three men.

December 14 started normally. We got up and searched for the NVA. In the morning, we found some booby traps and punji pits and destroyed them. In the early afternoon, we were told we'd be going to LZ English for a stand down. After being in the field for several weeks, we were very happy to get a break for showers, fresh fatigues, and a big hot meal. Thanks to our company commander Capt. Orsini, there was also plenty of beer and ice cream. After chow, we drank some more beer and then settled in to watch *One Million Years B.C.*, starring Raquel Welch.

At some point during the show, there was an announcement asking all officers and senior enlisted men to report to company headquarters. Shortly after that, everyone in D Company was told to report to headquarters. When we got there, Capt. Orsini gave us unwelcome news: We'd been ordered to air assault back into the Tam Quan area, near the village of My An (2), at 0730. Some break! Intelligence reports had noted one or two NVA platoons in the area, but as Orsini later recounted in his journal, an officer at the brigade command post told him that "he didn't trust the reports. He thought the [NVA] force was much larger—at least a reinforced company, or maybe even a battalion size." Orsini passed that warning along to various officers.[20] Either way, our brief stand down was over.

RADIOTELEPHONE OPERATOR

A few days earlier while we were in the field, I had been made 2nd Platoon's radiotelephone operator (RTO). That meant I carried the platoon's ANPRC-25 radio, which we called the prick 25. It was a roughly twenty-two-pound, battery-powered radio that was the link between our platoon (or any small combat unit) and headquarters. I carried it on my back along with my regular pack, which meant that when we humped with packs I was probably carrying 125 to 150 pounds. It was common knowledge that the enemy targeted the RTO, knowing his key communications role. I didn't worry about it. When the company RTO, William Gorges, asked me if I wanted to be platoon RTO, he warned me about being a walking target. But he also said the RTO hears orders coming through and knows what is going on. That was appealing to me—and it was true: For the few days I was RTO I knew when we were getting hot chow, when and where the company was moving, and other details. I liked being in the know. I also had to prepare maps for my lieutenant by covering them with acetate. In a sense, being an RTO was like being a personal aide to the commanding officer.

The RTO's basic job is to stay close to the platoon leader. Instead of merely looking out for myself and following orders, as I had done since arriving in Vietnam, I had to be with my platoon leader at all times and be his voice should he need to relay a message. The RTO and the platoon leader must develop a relationship of absolute trust, which is not accomplished overnight.

When I was made RTO, 2nd Platoon had no leader, but we got a new one just before our air assault into the My An area. First Lt. Roy Edward Southerland was attached to brigade headquarters but wanted to get into the field. When he learned D Company was short a platoon leader, he asked Capt. Orsini for the job. This was on the night of December 14, only hours before we'd be boarding the choppers. Orsini was hesitant and suggested that Southerland wait until after the air assault and get to know his troops better before taking over. But Southerland persisted. He'd already packed his bag. Orsini relented and informed brigade command that he'd accepted Southerland as a platoon leader. They, too, were reluctant and said they'd release Southerland after our air assault the next day.

Again, Southerland pressed to start immediately. Brigade agreed and Southerland got 2nd Platoon.[21]

HAMMER AND ANVIL

Brigade conceived a plan to flush out and destroy the NVA with B, C, and D companies, along with the 1/50 (Mech), if needed. According to Capt. Orsini, this would be a "hammer and anvil" operation, with D and C companies functioning as the anvil and B as the hammer. The plan was for D and C companies to establish blocking positions east of My An (2), near the coast. D Company would hold down the left flank with C Company on our right flank. B Company would swing two kilometers west of D Company, move north, engage the enemy, and force him back toward D and C companies. But until we established our "anvil" position we were in "march to contact" mode—meaning we had a pretty solid read on where the NVA was and we were looking to destroy what was left of the 22nd Regiment.[22]

But as happens in war, no plan ever survives contact with the enemy. It's Murphy's Law of combat: What can go wrong, will go wrong. Our units found the 22nd NVA regiment, and the plan for D and C companies to function as an anvil was lost.

Our foxhole strength at 1800 hours on December 14 was, according to the daily staff journal: A Company, 109 men; B Company, 104 men; C Company, 115 men; and D Company, 94 men. That was a total of 422 men for the battalion; total strength for the three companies involved in our operation (B, C, and D) was 313 men.

The U.S. Army Table of Organization and Equipment (TOE) shows the rifle company strength in the Vietnam era to be 165 men, organized into four platoons plus a headquarters element. The maximum foxhole strength was 155 men. But we never had anywhere close to that many men. No company did. Why the shortage of man-power? Attrition was a main factor. Some soldiers were killed or wounded in combat. Some caught malaria or got injured, and we always had one or two guys on R&R. Replacement soldiers did not arrive fast enough to maintain ideal troop strength.

It is a truism of war that you send units into areas where the enemy is positioned or might be discovered—but often you don't know how big the enemy force might be. Likewise, the enemy does not know how big your force is. This is why units that come in con-tact with the enemy tend to pull back. They initiate probing attacks or reconnaissance by fire, or rely on air assets to assess the strength of the enemy. It is also a truism that you never want to attack a large, well dug-in enemy with a smaller force. But sometimes you can't avoid it. As we were soon to discover on this day, the NVA had the larger force.

MY AN

Lt. Southerland and I met early on the morning of December 15, before we boarded the choppers. On his first day as 2nd Platoon leader, Southerland was twenty-two years old and from Morris-town, Tenn. I wish I could say more about him, but we did not have much of a chance to get to know each other. For now, wherever Lt. Southerland went, I went, and we were heading into what we ex-pected to be a hot LZ.

According to the after-action report for December 15, we made a combat assault at 0703 from LZ English to an area east of the village of My An (2). My memories of exactly what happened the rest of the day are hazy. Combat is intensely stressful and chaotic. It is hard to remember what happened thirty minutes after a battle—and it has now been fifty years. My memories are mostly like the fragmented dreams that run through your head during a heavy sleep. You never remember the full dream, only bits and pieces. What's more, what I do recall is sometimes at odds with other written accounts of the action. That's not unusual. Fortunately, my company commander, Capt. Orsini, wrote a detailed account, which, while probably not completely accurate, is surely more reliable than my memory. Orsini's journal, the official records, and the research and recollections of 3rd Platoon leader Tom Kjos have all helped me piece together what I think is a fairly accurate account of what happened. Where there is a discrepancy between military reports and Orsini's journal, I note the difference. However, the purpose here is not to write a detailed account of the battle but to give a sense of my experience of the events of the day.

After air assaulting into the area, we moved a short distance to one of the My An hamlets. We searched it and were taking a break when a small observation helicopter, an H-13, landed. We called the H-13s "Winchester whites." Why, I don't know. We just did—probably for the same odd reason we called hot chow "hot green grass."

The observer hopped out of the aircraft, shaking like a leaf in a windstorm. They had spotted two radio antennas, and when they flew down to investigate, they were hit by heavy ground fire. A round had come through the floor of the helicopter, passed between his legs, and hit the top of his combat vehicle crewman's helmet. The guy was slightly wounded and so jittery he couldn't light a cigarette; it had to be lit for him. He kept saying, "I came that close to losing the family jewels." After he calmed down the chopper took off and headed back to LZ English. "Radio antennas," as Capt. Orsini wrote in his journal, "were a sure indicator of a large force, probably a battalion."[23] Around 0805, we found and detained several VCS, and the captain requested an interpreter.

During this time, and without our knowledge, a squad from C Company had moved south and west of our position. That is not where C Company was supposed to be. Why and how they ended up out of position is not entirely clear. The staff journal reflects that at 0810 C Company reported small-arms fire from the west and returned fire. Two troopers were wounded and had to be medevaced.[24] According to Orsini's journal, however, C Company's commander was going to send another squad to assist the squad in contact.

Orsini recorded that his D Company command post was monitoring C Company's radio network when it heard an outbreak of heavy gunfire. The RTO for C Company's 4th Platoon, 1st Squad, "was screaming for help over the radio." The squad was being hit by intense enemy fire and was in trouble. This was approximately 0810 hours. "What the hell were [C Company] men doing west of me?" recalled Orsini. "Who had they made contact with and where were they now?"[25] Then at 0905, C Company again reported receiving heavy small-arms and automatic-weapons fire from the trees. In the meantime, B Company, which was just about a klick north and east of My An (2), started to receive sniper fire and automatic-weapons fire. Meanwhile, C Company reported capturing two NVA soldiers at 0930, and that one of the company's men had to be medevaced with a head wound.

At 0938, we—the 1/12 Cav—had our area of operation changed. We took over the 40th ARVN Regiment's AO. Battalion commander Lt. Col. Daniel W. French ordered us to relieve C Company immediately. We moved out and within minutes made visual contact with C Company troops, who were hunkered down in a depression. The NVA were positioned in a tree line about fifty meters north. French radioed Orsini again and gave him new instructions: We were to move south half a kilometer, then proceed west until we were beyond C Company's position. From there, we were to move north until we were abreast of C Company. Finally, we were to make a sweep northeast, across C Company's front, thus relieving pressure on that beleaguered unit.[26]

Orsini was incredulous. "If I took that route, I would run head-on into whatever had C Company pinned down, and with machine guns and antennas, it was at least a battalion in size," he wrote in his journal. "And I would be making contact with them in extremely dense bush." He objected, telling French that we'd be stuck between C Company and the NVA with our rear and flank exposed. He suggested pulling back the infantry units and hitting the NVA with artillery and air strikes. French wouldn't have it; he insisted that we proceed with his plan.[27]

We didn't know it then, but the enemy was waiting for us with two rifle battalions, a heavy weapons company, and support units—including a signal company and headquarters personnel—from the NVA 22nd Regiment. The number of NVA in the field that day has been estimated at about six hundred. They outnumbered us by roughly two to one. Their weapons included, in addition to standard rifles, heavy and light machine guns and recoilless rifles. Recoilless rifles fire small shells and function as both antitank and antipersonnel weapons. They were well supplied and dug in, and had picked the terrain on which to fight. It is never good to let the enemy pick the battlefield. My An village was surrounded by rice paddies and thick bamboo hedgerows that severely limited visibility. NVA morale was said to be high.

As I remember it, we moved out and walked about 800 meters, taking some sniper fire as we did so. Around 1100, we continued our advance and took up positions on a road just short of the area that we were to sweep. We were in a loose square, or diamond, formation. My platoon (2nd) took the front and left flank and led the way forward. First Platoon was right-front while 3rd and 4th platoons were tail gun—back left and back right, respectively. The command post and attached engineers were in the middle of the formation and would function as a reserve force if needed.

We moved forward for about another twenty minutes as the sniper fire intensified. Suddenly all hell broke loose: We were taking heavy fire from NVA positions in and around the hamlet just north of us. We had found the 22nd Regiment and they had found us. I remember a row of bushes and small trees to our right, and I saw

 They were well supplied and dug in, and had picked the terrain on which to fight.

a hooch as we moved to the front of the platoon. To our left some distance away, were more hooches and another row of small trees and brush. To our front was a small line of bushes, then a clearing, a dirt road, a ditch—with which I would become very familiar—and a very thick bamboo hedgerow running along the far side of the ditch.

When we came under assault, everyone took cover except Lt. Southerland and me, his RTO. He ran toward the front of the platoon to assess the situation. I wasn't sure if he was brave or crazy, but I surprised myself by staying right with him. As we ran forward, he stopped just short of the road and took the radio to call in our situation. He was calm and deliberate. His calmness settled me, even as bullets were whizzing past us. We were doing a job. Looking back at that day from a distance of fifty years, it seems weird that I can remember some things damn clearly and yet other moments are wrapped in fog.

PINNED DOWN IN A TRENCH

Lt. Southerland gave his report and returned the radio handset to me. I relayed messages from Southerland to Capt. Orsini. Moments later our point man, Sgt. Irving Wilhelms, who had been walking point with Sgt. Javier Casares from 1st Platoon, came running toward us. Everyone called Wilhelms "Duck." When he was maybe twenty-five meters from us, he got shot in the shoulder. Without thinking, I ran out to him, calling for the medic as I ran. The medic reached Duck with me, and the two of us pulled him back to a spot where Lt. Southerland had taken cover. While Duck was being worked on by the medic, he said that Casares had been wounded in both legs and couldn't move. He asked me to go get him.

I remember telling Lt. Southerland that I was going to get Casares and would be right back. I dropped my radio, took my M16, and dashed across an open area—about fifty meters, according to my citation. I saw Casares lying in a long trench, and I wasted no time diving into it myself. We would spend a lot of time in this three-foot-deep ditch. I can't recall if I fired my weapon while running up to the trench, but I was being fired at. (It's a funny thing: I remember reloading my rifle in various firefights but not firing, though I certainly did.) Along the trench ran a very thick bamboo hedgerow, behind which we could hear NVA troops talking. That was scary. The rate of fire increased greatly after I tumbled into the trench. I don't know whether it was the VC/NVA trying to kill me or just our guys giving covering fire. Staying low, I tried to figure out how to get us back to our line with both our weapons.

Then our situation got even more complicated: I peered out of the trench and saw Pfc. Joe Esparsa, who I think was also in 1st Platoon, running in our direction. He got about halfway to us and then fell to the ground hard, as if he'd been hit by a linebacker. He, too, had been shot in the leg. Before I knew it, I ran out and grabbed Esparsa and dragged him toward the trench. Esparsa would later tell me that he was trying to get to his squad leader, Sgt. Casares, when he got hit.

Once in the trench, the three of us kept low. I did what first aid I could on Casares and Esparsa. Under pressure, everything is done instinctively; there is no time to really think, just to act. I used Casares' first aid bandage on one leg then mine on the other. As I remember, Esparsa wasn't bleeding much. Then he got shot again, this time in the arm. Both men's wounds were serious but not life threatening.

NVA troops were just two or three feet away on the other side of the bamboo hedgerow. They were trying to set up a firing position. It was clear they were unaware of our presence as they chattered excitedly in Vietnamese. When they talked, we stuck our rifles over the lip of the trench and fired into the hedgerow. It was impossible to see, but the talking suddenly stopped. Some time passed and we heard more chattering from behind the bamboo hedge. Again, we fired and the talking stopped. More time passed, and then there was more chattering, so we fired again. We were credited with killing a bunch of NVA troops, and I'm sure we did, but I don't know how many.

We were stuck in no-man's land between the NVA and our troops. There was no chance of my getting out of the trench and back to safety with two seriously wounded men. We would have been cut down quickly. We knew our situation was bad. All we could do is fire at the voices on the other side of the hedgerow and reload our magazines. We talked in very low voices or communicated with hand signals. I remember Casares motioning that he was going to throw a grenade over the hedgerow. I saw the grenade go up and hit the top of the bamboo and come right back down in our trench. We knew it was over, but the grenade was a dud! I think one of us

241

picked it up and tossed it down the trench. It still didn't go off. One of my friends told me several days later that we were "in God's pocket." I tend to agree.

We didn't know it at the time, but while we were in the trench, hoping not to get our asses waxed, our company was catching hell, especially 1st and 2nd platoons. They were under tremendous pres-

 I wanted to leave the wounded and get back to friendly lines. But I didn't.

sure from all sides. At several points during the firefight, the company was almost overrun. Still, various troopers tried to get to us. As I recall, one of the men in my platoon started yelling, asking how many of us were in the trench. I shouted back, amid a multitude of retorts, that there were three of us and two were wounded. Not long after that, the firing became sporadic.

Someone in my company yelled at me again, telling me to leave the wounded and get back to our lines. He said they'd figure out how to rescue the wounded men. I remember yelling, "F**k you." Lord knows, I wanted to get the hell out of that trench. I wanted with every fiber of my body to run. I wanted to leave the wounded and get back to friendly lines.

But I didn't.

Over the years, I've been asked why. I believe that under extreme pressure, we become our real selves. My parents, grandparents, family members, drill sergeants, priests, and others shaped the man I'd become, and when tested, as I was tested in that trench that day, my decisions and reactions reflected the collective values of those who raised, taught, and trained me.

By this time, we'd been in the trench for perhaps two or three hours. At some point, the intensity of the NVA fire coming from our front, our flanks, and the trees—just about everywhere—increased a lot. Then we had no contact with our troops. They had pulled back. Nobody could reach us. We were on our own.

Back in D Company, Capt. Orsini and three volunteers—Sgt. William E. Gorges, Sgt. Rudolf H. Ford, and Sp4. Leonard Ferreira—decided to move forward to try and help extract 2nd Platoon, which was getting hammered by machine-gun and rocket fire and in danger of being overrun. They were right where I'd left them, directly to our west. Orsini later quoted Ferreira as saying, "The men were in a state of shock, confused and didn't know how to get out of the mess they were in." The captain added: "He was right. The poor bastards were in a world of hurt." There were concerns about the 2nd Platoon's security squad, which had been isolated early on and was nowhere to be seen.[28]

With Lt. Southerland providing machine-gun cover, Orsini and the three others moved forward. They immediately came under heavy fire from a hooch about twenty meters in front of them. Gorges and Orsini fired several rifle bursts into the hut and two NVA toppled out. Orsini described the scene:

As we moved closer, more fire came from the hooch, plus eight to ten NVA popped out of nowhere about ten meters to our left. We all opened fire and, since they were in the open, killed most of them. We got close enough to the hooch to lob in several grenades. We waited a few minutes, then moved forward toward the hooch. We didn't see any movement, but I told Ford to toss in a few more grenades, just to make sure. When we went in, we found 12 NVA dead. We came out and moved to the other side. We found our

security squad. They were all dead, and all were shot in the back:
Hicks, Rosa, Lebron and O'Neil.[29]

The guys from the 2nd Platoon security/flank squad had been at the front when the NVA opened fire on us. Orsini reckoned that they returned fire, unaware of the enemy hiding in the hooch behind them. That would explain why they were shot in the back. Cpl. James Tierno, who'd also been with the flank squad, was missing. His body would be found a day or so later. Orsini's group scrambled back to the perimeter. There, the captain had some tense conversations with Battalion Commander French.

A RESCUE ATTEMPT

Capt. Orsini then turned his attention to our situation. He aimed to pull us out, if possible, and hoped that Tierno was with us. He figured that the only reason Esparsa, Casares, and I had not been killed was that the NVA viewed us as bait. The enemy knew that our men would try to reach us, and "maybe he could get a few more of us."[30]

I doubt that was the case, since I don't think the NVA were really aware of us in the trench—or if they were, they had more important concerns. Orsini again called for volunteers. Again, Sgt. Ford, who was lugging the radio, and Sgt. Gorges stepped forward. Orsini also picked Sp4. Richard T. Scott to go with him. Lt. Southerland volunteered as well. Orsini told Southerland that he was needed with the rest of the platoon, but Southerland was nothing if not determined to do his part. Orsini told him to come along.

The five men crawled to the edge of the perimeter, where there were bushes for cover. There was a large stretch of open terrain ahead, then another clump of bushes. The two wounded men and I were only a few meters from those bushes. How to get to us without getting shot—that was the problem. The men started leap-frogging forward and got about halfway across the gap when the enemy opened fire. "We were receiving heavy fire from three sides," wrote Orsini, "and I don't know how the hell they missed us."

The men made it to a trail not far from the clump of bushes. Ferreira, who was with the covering force, radioed Ford and said he was going to saturate the area with fire from M79s—shoulder-fired grenades. After several dozen rounds, the enemy fire eased up. Orsini yelled to me for a status report and wanted to know if Tierno was with us. I told him Esparsa and Casares were wounded and that I didn't have Tierno. I was OK. Orsini described what happened next:

I told Southerland to cover our left flank, and to move down the trail about 5 meters. Ford would cover our right flank and Gorges, Scott and I would try to reach Lynch's position. Scott went first and after crawling several feet, Charlie opened up again. Scott yelled back that there was a large trench running right in front of the bushes, and that he could hear NVA voices in that trench. Ford and I, with our heads buried in the dirt, rolled several grenades into the trench and the firing stopped. We threw some more grenades into the trench and, when the smoke cleared, Scott said he could see a bunch of dead Charlies. While he was talking, a spider hole door opened no more than two feet from Scott. A rifle barrel was pushed out and fired, point blank, at Scott. Christ, it happened so fast, we didn't have time to react! Scott was moaning and the three of us moved to his position. The trap door hadn't closed flush to the ground and it was easy to detect. I took a grenade, pulled the pin and popped it inside the spider hole.[31]

Ford and Orsini dragged Scott, who'd been shot in the arm, back to the trail. Gorges tended to Scott while Ford and Orsini moved forward again to try to reach us. But they started taking fire in their right flank, and Ferreira radioed a warning that a bunch of NVA were moving into a trench about fifty meters away. He told them to get the hell out of there, as more were on the way. "Against that many, we didn't have a snowball's chance in hell of survival," wrote Orsini. He had to abandon his rescue attempt. "So close and yet so goddamn far away! I yelled to Southerland and told him to close back in on us."[32]

The men hurled two of their last four grenades at the trench filling with NVA and started pulling back. Southerland, meantime, had not moved. Orsini thought the lieutenant might have frozen in fear. Both he and Gorges crawled over to him; Gorges got there first and discovered that Southerland was dead. He'd been shot in the head—killed on his very first day of combat. I never got to know the guy; nobody did, but he had courage and died as part of an effort to save me and two other men.

Orsini and Gorges crawled back through the brush to Scott and Ford. Ford threw their last two grenades at the NVA, and with that as a momentary diversion, Orsini slung Scott over his shoulder and ran with the other two men back to the company perimeter. "How the hell we made it, I'll never know," wrote Orsini later. "It felt as if the Earth had come alive with all the bullets kicking at our heels." Scott and the other wounded would be medevaced out in the evening.

It's weird but one can halfway adjust to life-or-death situations. Lying in the ditch, pinned down by the North Vietnamese, I needed a smoke. We had just gotten our sundry packs, so we all had cigarettes, but none of us had a lighter. We only had C-ration matches, and Casares had bled on mine. C-ration matches supposedly will light when wet, but they didn't. My mind went back to the cowboy movies in which nobody dies until he sees the sun rise one more time or gets a last cigarette. While I coped with my nicotine fit, artillery shells were landing nearby. I was trying to think of our next move when a spent piece of hot shrapnel landed on my leg. It burned, but I let the metal cool and then picked it up, hoping it still had enough hit to light my cigarette. No such luck.

SECOND RESCUE ATTEMPT

By then it was late afternoon, and we'd probably been in the trench for three or four hours. Battalion Commander French had ordered the commander of the 1/50 (Mech) to detach three of his APCs from other duties—C Company was still engaged with the NVA east of us, and B Company was fighting as well—and send them to D Company. Orsini told Ford that the tracks gave them another chance to get back up to us, though it meant the possibility of more casualties. When the tracks arrived, the three heroes—Orsini, Ford, and Gorges, plus a medic—moved out again under supporting fire.

With the APCs unloading on the NVA positions, the men got up to us and made contact. Esparsa, Casares, and I were elated. I saw that one of the APCs was backing up toward the ditch with the ramp down, so that the two wounded men could be loaded into the back of it. I was beside myself. I knew if we could just get into the APC, we'd be OK. Orsini described what happened next:

> *They were still alive. I told them to hug the ground, and that we would be coming in just left of their positions, and we would be firing as we advanced. We moved [forward] with the three tracks and just as we reached the point where Southerland got killed, there was this deafening explosion. I felt as though I was*

floating. There was a bitter taste in my mouth and my nostrils were burning. Then I felt a sharp pain in my shoulder and neck and I must have passed out.[33]

The NVA in a nearby trench had 75mm recoilless rifles and B40 antitank rocket launchers, both powerful weapons. They'd blasted one of our APCs with a recoilless rifle from a short distance. "I stared at Gorges," wrote Orsini, "who said we must have run smack into the whole goddamn regiment. And he was right! We'd been fighting steadily for about five to six hours and with all the shit they have thrown at us, it couldn't be any smaller!"

All we heard was a big bang. Then all hell broke loose again.

The captain was lucky to be alive. He'd taken a bullet in his right arm and been thrown about fifteen feet by the explosion. He had three large pieces of shrapnel in his neck, chest, and shoulder, but was still lucid. His injuries were not life threatening. That was good news, but the latest and most promising rescue attempt would have to be aborted. With the company commander seriously injured and the NVA possessing rocket launchers and recoilless rifles, Battalion ordered the men and APCs back to the perimeter. Moments later, the tracks began to pull away. They were so close to us. So close.

We were crushed. I couldn't talk. I knew if I did, I'd lose it. There we were again, all alone. Orsini later wrote about the situation at that moment:

In fact, with the firepower Charlie had, if the platoon didn't extract itself ASAP, we would be surrounded and would lose the entire platoon. Nobody wanted to leave; those guys out there were their buddies. If I would have asked, the whole damn pla-

toon would have volunteered to make another try. But, hell, there weren't that many left in the platoon. I was shot up pretty badly, Scott was wounded, Southerland was dead, we'd lost the entire flank security element, plus a few others. Our only hope was to pull back, regroup with main body, then try again.[34]

It took an hour for the men and APCs to fight their way back to the perimeter. A chopper was called in to retrieve Orsini. Meanwhile, calls went out to hit the NVA with artillery and air strikes. For most of the day, D Company had been fighting with little artillery or air support, because the two sides were too close—the area too confined. Anything that hit the NVA would likely have hit us, too. But D Company was pulling back, and Orsini had pinpointed our position on the map as a spot for artillery batteries to avoid. It was hoped that an artillery barrage and air strikes would persuade the NVA regiment to retreat. "With accuracy on our part, and a helluva lot of luck on their part," wrote Orsini, "[Lynch, Esparsa, and Casares] just might make it."[35]

ENDGAME

Before long, artillery was pounding the NVA 22nd Regiment's positions. I was told later that artillery batteries at four different landing zones were firing at the enemy. All I know is that my ears still ring. The shells exploded so close to us that we could feel the ground shake. The artillery fire surely saved our lives. When it stopped, ARA gunships peppered the NVA with rockets, and a U.S. Air Force F-100 Super Sabre pelted the enemy as well. There were heavy explosions all around us. There was one right on the other side of the hedgerow from which NVA soldiers had been shooting at us hours earlier. It was nerve-racking.

Sometime very late in the afternoon, a jet came roaring toward us at low altitude. It couldn't have been more than four hundred feet above us, not far above the treetops. We saw it coming down the trench line. The trail that ran beside our trench was pockmarked with bullet strikes from strafing by other U.S. aircraft. When the pilot was almost directly above us, he dropped napalm. He let it go right over our heads. It scared the piss out of us.

Had I done well in math in school, I would've known the napalm was not going to hit us. The speed of the jet and the height from which the napalm was dropped made the bomb fall at an angle away from us—not that far away, but far enough. I estimate, roughly and through the haze of time, that it exploded at least one hundred meters away. We felt the burst of heat from the napalm and we could smell it too—a toxic smell.

I would learn later that continuous artillery fire had been called in, along with the air strikes and ARA. The barrage went on for what seemed a lifetime. After the napalm strike, the scene got very, very quiet. After hours of mayhem, the battleground was like a graveyard after midnight. There was no more shooting, no more explosions, no more noise at all. It was as if all life had gone.

It was time to act.

I waited a little longer, to be sure. There was no movement, no noise, and no NVA were visible. I told the guys that I was going to recon the area and would be back shortly. I got out of the trench, ran to the nearby hooches, and checked them for NVA. I was surprisingly calm. I don't remember being fearful, just calm. I knew I had to check the area, make sure there was no enemy, and then go back and get Esparsa and Casares. As I was searching the area, I came across the body of Lt. Southerland. Seconds later I saw a Viet Cong suspect we'd captured earlier that day. He was squatting on the ground, still tied up and blindfolded. He had been sitting smack in the middle of all of the fighting—machine guns, artillery, airstrikes—and didn't have a scratch on him! My first impulse was to shoot him, but I reconsidered: If he'd made it through all of that, maybe he should live. He wasn't hurting anybody; he couldn't. So I left him alone.

I went back for Casares and moved him to an open area, so it was easy to see him. Then I went back for Esparsa. He was very weak and when he tried to follow, he fell on the trail that ran alongside the ditch. I managed to get him over next to Casares. I told them I was going to find our company and started a slow trot around the area. I figured that if I didn't find my guys in the vicinity, I'd go back and move the men to a better-protected spot, and then go out again in search of D Company.

Thankfully, I had not gone far when I heard someone yelling. I'd found the company. I ran over to them, pointed in the direction of Casares and Esparsa, and said they needed medical attention. Our ordeal was over.

THE NEXT THING I REMEMBER IS BEING MEDEVACED OUT WITH Casares and Esparsa. When we landed at LZ English, they were taken into one section of a medical tent for treatment while I went into another section. I was given a little white pill—probably a sedative—and a little while later I was drinking whiskey in the company's rear command post. I was surprisingly calm, no doubt due to the little white pill and the whiskey. I slept, and the next day wanted nothing more than to get back to my company.

The Battle of Tam Quan wound down over the next few days. There were more troop movements, more search-and-destroy missions, more pursuits of the NVA, but the subsequent combat contact was light. The Battle of Tam Quan officially ended at midnight,

December 20, after a final battle involving the 2/8 and the 1/50 (Mech) near the village of An Nghiep.[36]

In the end, Sgt. Wilhelms, Sgt. Casares, and Pfc. Esparsa all survived, though Esparsa would lose an arm from his bullet wound. I never saw any of those three men again. I know that Esparsa went on to become a rehabilitation specialist. We talked in the mid '90s and exchanged emails periodically, but eventually we lost contact. Cpl. James Tierno's body was recovered on December 16. Lt. Roy Southerland, our heroic platoon leader, was posthumously awarded the Silver Star. Capt. Donald A. Orsini, who was brave and popular with all the men in D Company, received the Distinguished Service Cross for his valor. He retired a lieutenant colonel.

WHILE I WAS LUCKY TO SURVIVE, MANY OTHERS WEREN'T. IN ALL, 58 Americans lost their lives in the two-week Tam Quan campaign, and 250 men were wounded. Nearly half the fatalities, 26, died during the fighting on December 15 around the village of My An or from wounds suffered that day. Two of them were medics—killed while trying to save the lives of wounded soldiers. The ARVN lost 30 men and had 70 wounded in action over the two weeks. The 1st Brigade's after-action report estimated that 650 soldiers from the NVA 22nd Regiment were killed.[37]

The 1/12 Cavalry had 21 men killed in action and suffered 22 wounded in action during the Tam Quan campaign. A Company, 1/50 (Mech), which had been attached to us, lost 1 killed and 12 wounded.[38] Company D started December 15 with a foxhole strength of 94 and ended the day at 72 (plus 44 attached).[39]

The commanding general of the 1st Cavalry Division, Maj. Gen. John Jarvis Tolson III, later explained the importance of the Tam Quan campaign:

[It] had a much greater significance than we realized at the time. In that area, it pre-empted the enemy's Tet offensive even though the full impact wasn't then realized. As a result, that part of Binh Dinh was the least affected of any part of South Vietnam during Tet.

All those who survive a battle and a war, all those who make it home, carry within themselves forever a certain amount of survivor's guilt and grief for their buddies, their brothers in arms, who were killed or seriously wounded in action. I certainly have.

BACK TO MY PLATOON

I needed to get back to my platoon and company, but was told at LZ English that they had taken up base security at LZ Two Bits on the other side of Bong Son City. I was released from English the next day and driven to LZ Two Bits. As I walked into the company area, several soldiers came up to me and told me I had been put in for the Medal of Honor. I didn't believe it. After all, anyone in our company would have done what I did. I just happened to be in a position to do it.

In any case, I was back to being a squad member. I was no longer a radiotelephone operator. I was glad to be just a rifleman again. Then I found out that Capt. Orsini, Sgt. Rudolph Ford, Sgt. Barry Brewery, Sgt. William E. Gorges, D Brewer, Sp4. Marvin Sims, and Lt. Col. Daniel W. French had indeed put me in for the Medal. I didn't think, and don't think, I deserved it. Lt. Southerland died, as did Sgt. Flores. Capt. Orsini was wounded trying to rescue me and the others, as was Sp4. Richard Scott, Sgt. Leonard Ferreira, and others. I've tried to live a life of gratitude to those men and all others who served, giving back what I can. I have a deep sense of regard for the sacrifice others made so we might continue living. It is a debt I cannot ever repay.

We provided base security at Two Bits for a few days and ran some ambushes. It was easy duty. Then my company was airlifted to LZ Laramie in the An Lo Valley. The An Lo Valley was a "free fire zone," meaning no civilians were supposed to be there. We were bivouacked outside the LZ but things were quiet. We even had a USO show. Gen. William Westmoreland, commander of U.S. forces in Vietnam, was there and presented. awards for heroism to some of our men. I didn't get one, didn't really expect one. I found out years later my paperwork got lost. We were told there would be a Christmas truce and rested somewhat easier, but we were still on guard. We knew the VC and the NVA would break it if they felt there was an advantage in doing so.

The truce lasted from Christmas Eve until 0001 December 26. Neither side violated it, but at one minute past midnight on the 26th, our M42 Dusters and Quad 50s opened fire on suspected NVA/VC locations. Our unit was just letting the enemy know that we were still around. The war was back on. At the time the firing started, I was sleeping in a makeshift hooch—we buttoned ponchos together to make a pup tent–like structure. The sudden noise startled me; I almost tore the hooch down in my rush to get out. I thought we were being hit.

Over the next couple of weeks, we did our usual search-and-destroy missions. One night we were bivouacked and put out booby-trapped Claymore mines. We also put out grenade traps: We put a little bug juice on the grenade pins to make them slippery, so if the trip wire was even nudged, the pin would fall and the grenade would go off. Of course, that meant we had to be very careful the next morning when we retrieved the grenades.

The next morning, one of my platoon mates retrieved his grenade. He pushed the pin all the way in, but he forgot to bend it, as we were trained to do, so that the pin would not slip out. As we were making our way through some very heavy underbrush, he started whispering my name frantically. I turned around and saw him holding his grenade with both hands, his M16 on the ground. The grenade pin was almost completely out of its slot—an explosion waiting to happen. I laughed, pushed the pin back in, and bent it to keep it securely in place. Disaster averted. He got ribbed pretty seriously the next time we stopped for a break.

I BECOME AN REMF

In January 1968, D Company was airlifted to An Khe for perimeter security and bridge detail. I was promoted to sergeant and given a fire team and a bridge to protect. It was my first time leading a unit and it felt good. We had two bunkers on each side of the bridge. We were very close to an ARVN base camp. During the day, we could take it easy; officers came by only once or twice. At night, a couple of troopers stood guard duty, but we had to stay vigilant. I managed to get some beer and other refreshments. I thought as long as we did our job, what's the harm with a little cold beer? We had earned it.

A day or two after being on the bridge, I was standing on top of the bunker closest to the road when our new platoon leader came by in a jeep. He stopped at our bridge just long enough to call my name. "Yes, sir!" I yelled down from the top of the bunker. He replied, "Get your sh**t packed and be ready to leave when I get back." He offered no explanation. I had just made sergeant and thought, "Well, damn, I only lasted a week." I thought I was in trouble—why else would he relieve me?—but had no idea why.

He came back, and I threw my stuff in the back of the jeep. "I just got my ass chewed out by the regimental commander because of you!" the platoon leader said.

I thought, "Holy crap, what in the hell did I do?"

"You were supposed to be taken out of the field weeks ago. Everyone put in for the Medal of Honor has to be taken out of combat. You're going to spend the rest of your time in the rear with the gear."

I was happy and disappointed at the same time. No grunt liked men who worked in the rear, away from combat. We called them REMFs (Rear Echelon Motherf**ks), and now I was going to be one. I wanted to be with my company, my platoon. We in the field, in harm's way, had a bond that was deeper than family. We trusted each other, looked out for each other, and now I would no longer be a part of the platoon. I was an REMF.

I was assigned to permanent charge of quarters (CQ) at battalion HQ. I had radio watch all night. I had to report any incidents that occurred while I was on CQ and relay messages from higher headquarters to the appropriate person. I occasionally supervised Vietnamese who were brought on base for various work details. The nice part was, as a sergeant, I didn't have to do manual labor.

Shortly after I was assigned to the rear, the battalion was ordered north to help the marines in I Corps. But prior to moving out, the battalion, including my old company, returned to An Khe for a few days. I could already feel the separation between us. They were friendly, but it was what wasn't said that told me I was no longer one of them.

A few weeks later, D Company got hit hard and lost some good men. One of those killed was Darrell A. Shellie, an African American kid who was a good man. We were friendly but, as I recall, in different platoons. Everyone liked him and then he was gone. I hated my new assignment, so I went to brigade headquarters and asked to be reassigned to my old unit. They laughed. I was in limbo. I was still in Vietnam, and in the war, but not really. I simply had to wait for May 31, when I would be rotated home.

Life in the rear was boring except for occasional mortar and rocket attacks by the enemy. During the Tet Offensive, things did get a little interesting. We had infiltrators at Camp Radcliff. The VC snuck in and did some damage to the ammo dump. There were several areas where the VC could hide and hit us when we were not alert. To make sure there no more threats, I led a patrol within our battalion area. We found no VC, just other American units patrolling for the same reason. Thank God, we called out before firing!

As the Tet Offensive ended, at least in Camp Radcliff, things got back to normal. We still had the usual mortar and rocket attacks. But those were mostly directed at the golf course, where the choppers were housed. I resigned myself to being an REMF. We had movies most every night. There was always plenty of beer and other adult beverages to pass the time and the food was really good (compared to cold C-rations). Life was good and I fully understood why we had hated the REMF so much. War for us was just an inconvenience, a disruption to our easy living. I couldn't wait to get short.

CHAPTER 12

COMING HOME

O N February 23, 1968, I became "a double-digit midget."
I had just ninety-nine days to go in Vietnam. I was a short timer!
I had a short timer's calendar with ninety-nine segments on it, each
representing one day. After each of the segments was colored in, I
would be on the "freedom bird" back to the world.

Just about the same time, I found a small puppy. I named him
Fred N Guy (FNG), Fred for short. He was so small he could fit into
the pocket of my fatigues. He was my buddy and I took him everywhere. I even got him into the mess hall a few times. For the most
part, I was alone. I had friends but not family like the one I served
with in combat. In a way, Fred filled that part of me that was missing. Dogs are God's gift to lonely and broken people.

But as my time to leave drew closer I was afraid for him. I had
heard that the Vietnamese ate dogs, and I didn't want him to become
someone's dinner. One of my buddies said he'd take good care of him.
On my last day in An Khe I gave him Fred. It broke my heart. It was
like when my childhood friend, Duke, died. I haven't had a dog since.

Short timers constantly made jokes about how short we were:
"I'm so short I have to look up to see down; I'm so short I sleep in a
matchbox; I'm so short I can walk under a dime" and so on. We had

a short timer's attitude and got vocal about being short: "No problem, sir, just 60 more days!" This irritated some officers and senior
NCOs, especially if they weren't short. As our time wound down to
a month or less, the "this is the last time I'll…" started, as in "This is
the last time I'll pull guard duty." At the end of every day I filled in
the appropriate segment of my short timer's calendar. It was a ritu-
al. Then I would say something like "80 days and a wake up," meaning that I had eighty full days left and on the last day I'd wake up
and get on the freedom bird. But there was also a bitterness about
being short. We felt we were leaving the job undone, leaving our
buddies—men we had entrusted our lives to and who had entrusted
their lives to us. We were going back to the world while our military
family was still in hell. Behind the joy of leaving we felt miserable
about feeling so damn good.

About a month before leaving Vietnam I started sending short
timer letters to my parents. The letters told them that I had only
thirty days before I'd be home, then twenty days, then fifteen days.
The last letter I sent said, "I'm leaving tomorrow. I'll probably be
home before this letter," and I was.

The shorter I became the more paranoid I got. I stopped going
off base when I had two months to go. I would take different routes
to the mess hall and return by a different route. Making my paranoia worse were the stories about being shot as the freedom bird
took off for the States. There were stories of soldiers making it all
the way home only to be hit by a car or shot in the airport by a de-
ranged parent whose son had been killed. Or the story of the soldier
who tried to sneak into his parents' home late at night to surprise
them only to be shot by his father who thought he was a burglar.
All these stories were just urban legends, but they were plausible
enough to add to my paranoia.

Finally, the great day came. Just as in Germany I had to clear post, which meant I had to turn in all my gear including my M16. Then came time to board the C-130 to Cam Ranh Bay. I must admit I was a little scared flying out of An Khe. But we took off without incident and landed at Cam Ranh Bay late that morning. I went to the transit area for a short orientation about what was to happen over the next day or so. I was scheduled to leave within forty-eight hours.

There were mandatory things I had to do first. I had to see the VA benefits counselor who would explain my benefits. I didn't know it at the time but the counselor was Richard E. Bush, who had earned a Medal of Honor on Iwo Jima during World War II. I would later work with him at the Naval Hospital at Great Lakes, Illinois, from 1971 to late 1972, assisting Vietnam returnees in filing their claims. He gave a very quick briefing. Then I got a briefing from the transit personnel about contraband. If contraband was found during a duffel bag search, leaving could be delayed by days or even weeks. I wasn't worried about that, but some guys very quickly got rid of dirty pictures, pot, weapons, and plunder. After evening chow, the flight manifest for the next day was posted and my name was on it! So I would leave Vietnam May 1, 1968, exactly 365 days after my arrival.

The next day I boarded the flight that would take us home. The plane was very quiet as we took off. It was obvious that I wasn't the only one who'd heard about freedom birds being shot at during takeoff. About ten minutes into the flight, the stewardess came on the PA system and told us we were now over international waters. A deafening cheer went up. Finally, we were really on our way home.

The flight from Cam Ranh Bay to Fort Ord, California, was uneventful. We got off the plane, collected our duffel bags, and were waved through customs. Then we boarded buses for out-processing and a steak dinner. Later that afternoon at Oakland airport I boarded a plane to Chicago. As soon as my flight was confirmed I called my mom and dad and told them when I would be arriving at O'Hare and where I would meet them. On the plane I got a little plastic bottle of whiskey and slowly drank it and just looked out the window.

It was dark when I landed in Chicago. I got my duffel bag and found a quiet place to wait for my mom and dad close to one of the large windows that runs along the sidewalk on the lower level of O'Hare. Surprisingly, the area was all but empty. I was the only one in uniform, so I thought I'd be easy to spot. Suddenly I heard "There

 We didn't talk about Vietnam or what I did, nor did we talk about the Medal.

he is!" I looked up to see Dad, Mom, and Nancy running toward me. I was hugged and kissed as if I had just come back from the war. We were soon in the car heading towards Dolton. I would have forty-five days' leave and then go to Fort Hood, Texas, for my last nine months in the army. But at that moment I was just looking forward to reconnecting with my family and friends.

We pulled up to the house where a big red, white, and blue sign over the front door read "Welcome Home Allen." As I walked toward the front door I noticed a small red, white, and blue flag hanging in the window with a star in the middle, which let everyone know that this family had a soldier serving in Vietnam. I was very happy to take it down. Many of my aunts and uncles were there, as was Gail and my friends Jim, Paul, and Turk. I got my second steak dinner with cold beer. It was a low-key welcome home. We didn't talk about Vietnam or what I did, nor did we talk about the Medal. The two-thousand-pound elephant in the room was silent and unseen.

Around 9 or 10 p.m. everyone left and it was just Mom, Dad, Nancy, and me alone. Mom went into the kitchen and brought me out a great big glass of ice-cold milk and a whole plate of chocolate chip cookies. Throughout my time in Vietnam Mom, Nancy, Gail, and my aunts had sent packages filled with homemade goodies. My sister made the best cinnamon rollups, my very favorite. Funny thing about milk: When you've gone a year without it, drinking a lot of it at once has disastrous results. I don't know how many cookies I ate. I don't know how many glasses of cold milk I guzzled down. But shortly after I drank my last glass, there was a rumbling deep in my stomach. I made it to the bathroom before the gusher hit. Let's just say the nice clean bathroom was decorated with milk and cookies. I was so embarrassed, but Mom told me not to worry and she cleaned up the mess.

I was home about two days when Dad told me he had a surprise for me. He was going to take me to Wisconsin for a long weekend. He thought it would be a good idea just for him and me to get away by ourselves so I could decompress. Dad rented a small cabin on the lake. It was quiet and we fished, ate, drank, and talked. It really helped me, at least initially, to put things behind me. When we got home I still had several weeks to hang out with my friends and to reconnect with Gail, my fiancée.

Gail and I went out several times over the next couple of weeks. But things were not the same. I had changed. She was still sweet and innocent. I had killed. She had just graduated high school. I had just returned from war, no longer naïve. She still viewed the world through innocent eyes.

One night after dinner, I told her I couldn't marry her. I tried to explain. I desperately wanted her to know that she deserved better. But I screwed it up. She had been worried about me while I was gone, wrote me letters, sent me goody boxes, and I showed my appreciation by breaking her heart. My family had fallen in love with her while I was gone. Dad even took her to the senior prom as my stand-in. When I told them I had broken up with her, they were shocked. But I think that on some level they understood. They were starting to see the change in me.

I was already starting to feel different and out of place. Once when I was at the home of one of my high school friends, we were sitting in the family room having a beer when his mother walked in and welcomed me home with "How many people did you kill?" I just sat there with a blank look. My friend scolded her but the damage was done. Her question was like a slap across the face. I knew she didn't really mean anything by it and was probably just curious, but I took it to heart.

I was feeling more and more disconnected and started to plan my drive to Fort Hood. I bought a used convertible. I don't remember the make but it was light green with a white top. It was exactly what I wanted, and the price was right. I was planning to take three days to drive it to Texas. It was going to be my time away from everyone. But Mom and Dad had a different idea. They were going to visit my Uncle Jack in Tulsa, Oklahoma, and thought it would be nice if I took Nancy with me. Their plan was that I would drive her to Tulsa and spend a day or so with Jack and his wife, Pat, then leave Nancy and head to Fort Hood.

As the time came close for me to leave I was feeling more and more out of touch and angry. I don't know why I was angry, but I was. It culminated one night when I was out with Jim and Paul. We went down to a local club to listen to a band and have a few drinks. I was sitting there having a beer and I noticed all the people were dancing and enjoying themselves without a care in the world.

I turned to one of my friends and I said something like, "My friends are being killed in Vietnam and I'm here. My friends are being wounded and I'm here. My friends are fighting for our country and I'm here and nobody cares about what they're doing." I needed to leave, to get away, and get back to my world, the army.

Finally, the day for Nancy and me to leave for Tulsa arrived. As was traditional with the Lynch family, we started our drive before dawn. We were having fun driving along with the top down and visiting. We made it most of the way through Missouri before my car broke down. We sat in a diner drinking coffee and eating some not-so-good food, and after a three-hour delay we got back on our way.

We spent two days with Uncle Jack and his family. We went waterskiing and swimming, and grilled out on the patio. The night before I left he grilled steaks and after everyone else had gone to bed he and I spent some time alone. The conversation went different directions but at one point we talked about coming home. After being away from his family when he was in the navy, Jack had the same feelings that I was having. I realized that trying to go back home as if it was the same as when I left it is like trying to put your foot in the same river twice. It may look the same but it isn't. Both the river and the foot have changed.

BACK HOME IN THE ARMY

Early the next morning after breakfast, I said goodbye to Nancy and Uncle Jack and his family and left for Fort Hood. I was assigned to A Company, 2nd Battalion, 41st Infantry, 2nd Armored Division. I was more mature than when I'd left for Vietnam. I was a better soldier. My uniform was always clean and starched, my boots shined. Being an NCO, I had responsibilities for my men. I was now a leader. I shared a room with one other sergeant, also a Vietnam veteran.

I was again in a mechanized unit but this time with no mortars. I was infantry.

Most of us in A Company were Vietnam returnees just biding our time until our enlistments were up. Some of the officers, especially the new ones, were interested in learning how to survive Vietnam. On one occasion, a second lieutenant was giving us a class on ambush. About ten minutes into his presentation, he looked around the room and saw that almost all of us had a CIB (combat infantry badge). He said, "I'm probably going where you all have just been. Now, I must teach this class. So if someone comes in the room, I'm going to take charge. But until then, please tell me what I need to know." So we gave him an impromptu class on combat in Vietnam.

I was fire team leader for several months and really enjoyed it. We went to the field on FTXs, but it was like a bunch of guys going camping. The night before going on the FTX, we made sure we got to the local liquor store. When the day's problem was over and we settled in for the night, we'd have a few drinks and tell war stories around an open fire.

In early August, we got an extra duty: riot control. Hours were spent forming into a V formation, and armed with M16s with bayonets we "step jabbed" across the drill field. Great! We spend a year in Vietnam only to have our days taken up learning to control antiwar protesters. Even those of us who were not happy with the war were highly pissed off about the assignment. To make matters worse whenever President Johnson went to his ranch outside Austin, we would be restricted to the base and put on alert, just in case. We grew to really intensely dislike Johnson.

Then came the riots in Chicago, the "days of rage." We were put on alert and told we'd probably be going north. I think it was a good thing that we didn't go there. We were in no mood to deal with rioters. Shortly after the riots were over, the president's visits to his ranch became less of a hassle. Ready react units that move at a moment's notice were put on rotation. I think we pulled ranch duty only twice more before Johnson was out of office.

We were starting to question what was happening in our country. In addition to the Chicago riots, there were demonstrations in every city and many of us were angry at the punks who were protesting. Hell, we didn't like the war any more than they did, but they hadn't seen what the VC and NVA could do to people. We were also

 I was searching for answers and wasn't finding them politically or religiously.

very aware that Johnson was not interested in winning the war. In Vietnam, we had started to use the term "wasted" when referring to a KIA. Wasted because our country wasn't interested in winning, just in stalemating. Our government was wasting our lives.

Personally, I was in turmoil. I was raised a Democrat but it was a Democratic president who'd lied about keeping us out of Vietnam. It was a Democratic president who'd stopped bombing North Vietnam, allowing more ammunition and troops to come unmolested to the South. It was a Democrat and his Congress who'd voted to continue the war, then voted not to. This after thousands of good young men and women had given their lives.

Then I discovered that the Catholic Church, my church, the church that I was told was unchanging, had changed! All during my tour in Vietnam I wore a St. Christopher's medal and a rosary around my neck. I prayed the rosary regularly. I had a small Bible that I carried in the pocket over my heart, which I read most days.

Helping to bolster my faith was Father Lucid, who came out to the field after every firefight. He'd give general absolution, say mass, and give communion, then spend time with us. But when I got back home and went to mass everything had changed. Mass was said in English, the altar had changed, and St. Christopher was no longer a saint! I had a vision of the saints suddenly being kicked out of the lounge up in heaven because they got demoted.

Still I found comfort in the Bible and read it quite a bit. I was also quite fond of *Playboy* and *Penthouse* magazines. Having only a footlocker and wall locker in which to store my personal gear, I put my Bible on top of the *Playboy* and *Penthouse* magazines on one side of the top tray of my footlocker. During one inspection I thought my platoon leader was going to lose his mind. I was standing at attention beside the bunk when he started to inspect our room. When he got to my footlocker he stopped cold. "What the hell! Sergeant Lynch, you have the Holy Bible on top of these filthy books. What the hell is wrong with you?" I told him I liked to read both of them. He just shook his head and moved on. I was searching for answers and wasn't finding them politically or religiously. But I kept looking. Something had to make sense to me.

Most nights I'd walk to the nearby town of Killeen. I've always loved walking to settle myself and think. On my way to Killeen I'd cross a huge athletic field on a gently sloping hill. One night on my way back to my room I was feeling particularly down and stopped on the hill to rest. As I sat there I had an overwhelming need to talk to God. There was no one around to hear me so I had a whole conversation with him. I held nothing back and it gave me a sense of peace. Over the next several weeks every time I walked back from Killeen, I'd stop at that field and talk to God. I found no answers there, but it helped.

In January, I was called to battalion headquarters by the sergeant major. He saw that I had been recommended for the Medal of Honor and wanted me to become the battalion career counselor, the guy who tries to talk his fellow soldiers into reenlisting. I told him that I was very interested in making the army a career and was looking forward to reenlisting myself sometime in March or April. So I became the battalion career counselor and I was very good at it. For three consecutive months, I had the highest reenlistments in the brigade. For that I got a three-day pass for three consecutive months, January, February, and March.

HOW I QUIT SMOKING

When I made battalion career counselor, I was moved to Headquarters Company. It was on the other side of the same building, and I got a private room. I was in heaven. I worked hard at my job and did quite well. Once a week I gave a presentation on reenlisting to soldiers coming back from Vietnam and newly assigned to the battalion. I would visit the troops in the field, especially if the weather was bad, and talk of the benefits of reenlistment. Things were going well for me. After duty hours, I could go on pass or go to the NCO Club for a good, cheap dinner.

When it was time for bed, I would read a little, have a cigarette, crush it out in the ashtray, and go to sleep. When I woke up, the first thing I would do is light up and think about the day. I was smoking three packs a day at that time. My favorite cigarettes were after a meal, before bed, after waking up, and when I was at the NCO Club or drinking. Then one morning I got a real wake-up call. I started to cough, a lot, and after a few minutes, I coughed up a hunk of black phlegm. I had already developed a smoker's cough but this was different. The next day the same thing happened before I could even light up. It happened again a couple of times throughout the day. It scared me.

I decided to quit smoking. But I didn't want to waste the four packs left in my carton. Even at thirty-five cents a pack, I didn't want to waste money. So I decided to just cut down and smoke only half as much. That didn't work and I was still coughing a lot. When I finished the four packs I quit. I lasted three hours then started to bum cigarettes. I bought another pack and was determined it would be my last, but it wasn't. I was still coughing a lot.

I was at my favorite little greasy spoon in Killeen. I finished my hamburger and was getting ready to leave. As usual, I took one of their huge toothpicks and stuck it in my mouth. That gave me an idea. I asked if I could buy a box of the large toothpicks. A couple of bucks later I had the box in my pocket next to my pack of cigarettes. The next time I wanted a cigarette I took a toothpick. It was large enough for me to hold between my fingers like a cigarette. I could put it in my mouth like a cigarette. In fact, I could do all the things with a toothpick that I could do with a cigarette, except light it and inhale.

Over the next couple of days, I smoked the remaining cigarettes in my pack, occasionally substituting a toothpick. The last few cigarettes lasted a couple of days and when they were gone I never bought another pack. I did, however, go through several packs of restaurant toothpicks. Over the next several weeks whenever I wanted a cigarette I took a toothpick. I often joked that I would die of Dutch elm disease but not cancer. Within a month, I had kicked cigarettes.

My biggest trial came when I was up for soldier of the quarter. Soldier of the quarter was a competition for the best soldier and noncommissioned officer below the rank of sergeant first class in a given quarter. It was meant to be a morale booster. Becoming soldier of the quarter came with some perks, the biggest of which was a three-day pass. There were three finalists, and as I sat waiting for my interview, the other two lit up. I was tempted to bum a cigarette, but something told me that if I smoked now, I would never quit. I kept my mouth shut.

I dearly loved to smoke. Thankfully, after I'd quit for a few weeks, I started to realize that I was a slave to the weed. I didn't want anything to control me. The last challenge during the soldier of the quarter interview was the last time I ever craved a cigarette. I haven't smoked in over fifty years except for an occasional cigar usually with a bourbon or brandy.

FAMILY COMES FIRST

In March, I decided that I was going to stay in the army. I called home, talked to Mom, and told her I was going reenlist. She told me that Dad had been sick while I was in Vietnam and had taken several months off work. They thought he might have multiple sclerosis and though he was doing well now, he still wasn't at his best. She said I was really needed at home.

I got angry because they hadn't told me about Dad even after I came home on leave. She said they didn't want to worry me. I had found a home in the army and dearly wanted to stay. Yet my family needed me. I was disappointed but decided that I would not reenlist. After my time was up, I would go home.

Still, I was doing an excellent job as a career counselor. When people asked me if I was going to reenlist I told them no and why not. I never lied to those whom I was counseling, and I think my honesty helped me meet my quota. I remained a career counselor until April 1 when I started to process out. By April 25, I had cleared post, said goodbye to the army, and headed home to Dolton.

HOME AGAIN

It was with mixed emotions that I walked into my mom and dad's house. I wanted to stay on active duty. It was something I knew. I had grown up in the army. But I was needed at home. It was time to put the army behind me.

Dad converted part of the living/dining room into a room for me. It was a nice room, just big enough for sleeping. It had a door, bed, dresser, and shelving. But as I started to settle in, it became clear that the room was temporary. The furnishings did not give the feeling of permanence. As for the walls, Dad was proud of the fact it only took him three hours to put them up, including painting. I knew then that I needed to accomplish two things in short order: I had to get a decent job and I had to find my own place to live.

I went back to my last civilian job at Libby, McNeil & Libby on the southwest side of Chicago but they weren't hiring so I looked elsewhere. I ended up getting a job at United Parcel Service as a route driver.

After working with a trained driver, I was given my own route in Chicago. Most of my route ran through some very bad neighborhoods. But I had spent a year in Vietnam and being in the ghetto didn't scare me. I treated my customers with respect and never had a problem—except with my supervisor. He constantly harped that I wasn't doing my route fast enough and that I should be at a certain location by a certain time. I got frustrated and tried again to get a job at Libby's, but no luck. Then I went back to UPS and tried to make the best of it. Dad had always taught me never quit one job before you have another. I took his advice.

I had been at UPS for about a month when I was notified I would be getting the Distinguished Service Cross for the action at Tam Quan on December 15, 1967. UPS gave me the day off and sent a photographer to take pictures for the company magazine. The ceremony took place on the parade ground at Fort Sheridan. Mom, Dad, and Nancy attended the ceremony. They were very proud. But I felt nothing, no pride, no sense of satisfaction. I did what anyone in my company would have done. I don't recall even looking at the citation. "Now, I can really get on with my life," I thought. There was nothing hanging over from my time in the military. The next day I went back to work.

About two weeks after the award ceremony I was on my route and having a dreadful day. The supervisor was again driving me nuts and had given me extra pickups. I was not happy; I just wanted to get the day over with. Then I hit a curb. All my neatly sorted packages on the shelves in the truck came crashing to the floor. I would need to re-sort them before moving to my next stop. That was it. I let out a string of curse words at the top of my lungs, drove back to the hub, and quit.

The next day I went to Libby's. A different personnel clerk, a cute blonde, told me they had no openings but to fill out an application. I did, and this time attached a copy of my discharge form to it. One of the questions was had I worked there before. I answered yes. I handed her the application. She smiled and said, "Take a seat. I'll give your application to Mr. Gala." Ten minutes later I was in his office being interviewed. He told me they had to rehire me because I was a veteran. I would start in shipping the next Monday, doing the exact same thing I did before going into the army a little over four and a half years ago.

It didn't take me long to get into the swing of things. My shift was 7:00 a.m. to 3:30 p.m. We were given two fifteen-minute breaks, which could easily turn into twenty-five minutes. But everyone worked on a bonus system. There was no need to motivate workers.

Work hard, do your job, do it fast, and reap the rewards on payday.

I loved my job. I was making good money. I made some new friends and occasionally after work went out, shot pool, and drank beer with them. There was one other thing that made my job interesting. I kept running into the cute blonde personnel clerk. Once or twice a day she'd show up somewhere I was working. Or we'd meet as she would be cutting through the large cooler where I, too, was taking a shortcut. I'd always say hi or something like "we have to stop meeting like this." She was always pleasant, but that's as far as it went. Just short pleasantries. Still, I kept running into her.

PRETTY WOMAN WALKING ...

Get up, go to work, come home, go out with the guys. Rinse and repeat until something changes. Before I knew it, it was September. I kept running into the cute personnel clerk but never thought to ask her out. I was in a rut. Then fate took a hand: I met her in the cooler one day, and before I could stop myself I said, "Hi, I keep seeing you and don't even know your name." "Susan," she said with a smile. A few days later I saw her again and asked her out.

We were to go out that Friday, just dinner and perhaps a movie. I was nervous. I hadn't dated since Gail. That afternoon, as I was walking past personnel on my way to the parking lot, Susan stopped me. "I must break our date," she said. "I forgot I already have one." My heart sank. Then she said, "But how about next Friday?" I told her that would be fine. I didn't know how to feel. Was she playing hard to get or had she really forgotten?

We went out for dinner to a Mexican restaurant in Frankfort. It would become our favorite. We ate a great meal, listened to the mariachi band, drank some wine, and talked for a long time. Then I drove her home to Riverdale.

Susan and I started dating. We went out a lot during September and into October and really hit it off. We liked the same things. We loved movies and Mexican food. But more important, we enjoyed each other's company. Finally, the time came for me to introduce her to Mom and Dad. I was a little nervous, as was Susan. I picked her up at her home in Riverdale, just down the block from Tetco, the place I worked as a kid.

 **In a sense, life had come full-circle.
Yet I was apprehensive about the holidays.**

I opened the front door to our house, and Mom and Dad met us almost as soon as we walked in. I introduced Susan and Dad said something appropriate but Mom, who lost her filters when she was nervous, said, "Did you know Allen was arrested for rape?" Susan got a look of panic on her face and I wanted to sink into the shag carpet. "Mom!" "Vi!" Dad and I said in unison. "Oh, he didn't do it but it's a funny story." Mom was referring to my arrest in Germany when I was falsely accused. It is a funny story, especially when you are introducing your girlfriend to your parents. Except for those first few minutes, the evening went well. They liked Susan and she liked them. I tried to apologize for my mother's remark when I took Susan home, but she would have none of it. "She was just nervous." That was that. I was falling in love.

In late October, Susie said, "Are you seeing anyone else?" I told her no, to which she replied, "I'm not either. I think we should be exclusive. What do you think?" I agreed. Things were getting serious.

One day Susan invited me to attend her church. I had for all intents and purposes left the Catholic Church when I got back from

Vietnam. I agreed to attend services with Susan and her mother, Mary, at Ivanhoe United Methodist Church in Riverdale. After church, we went for brunch and spent the rest of the day together.

NO PLACE LIKE HOME FOR THE HOLIDAYS?

Thanksgiving 1969 was my first at home since 1963, the year before I went into the army. I had not been home for Christmas since 1964, just after I joined the army. I was excited to be home. In a sense, life had come full circle. Yet I was apprehensive about the holidays.

I had a new girlfriend and we were getting very serious. When Thanksgiving came, I felt a little relief. We had the traditional Thanksgiving dinner, though the whole extended family did not get together. There was the usual visiting, but now I had a car and other places to be. Thanksgiving was when Susan and her family celebrated her birthday, November 27, and I spent more time with her than with my family.

Christmas approached and again I started to feel apprehensive. The traditions I grew up with were gone. There was no midnight mass, no Christmas Eve family gathering. During my years in the army, I thought of those idealized family times every holiday season.

Susie and I spent the holidays at each other's homes. Though our holiday traditions were markedly different, we enjoyed them. Both our families thought we made a "cute couple." The holiday season ended with my family's New Year's Eve party. It was a great time with Uncle Dick, Aunt Laurie, and Dad knocking out some beautiful harmony as usual. Great food and drink and no drama!

NEW YEAR, NEW DECADE, NEW LIFE

Then it was January 1970, a year and decade that would change my life and Susan's forever. We were in love and starting to make plans.

I was not happy being home. I felt manipulated. There had been no need for me to come back to Dolton; it had become quite clear that Dad wasn't physically ill. His drinking had become more of an issue, but he wasn't at death's door. And yet, if I had stayed in the army, I would not have met Susan.

In early January, Susan and I were driving to our favorite Mexican restaurant and we were at a stoplight. We had talked about marriage at length over the holidays. But I had never acted upon it. Somehow, as we were sitting at the stoplight, the time just seemed right. I turned to her and said, "Well, what do you think? Should we get married?" Not exactly romantic.

Surprisingly she said, "Yes." We kissed and went on to dinner where we discussed possible dates. I suggested April 18. She wanted to wait. As a joke, I suggested April 25, the day I got out of the army. She agreed. April 25 it was. We would be married one year to the day after I left the army. Susan wanted a small wedding out of respect for her father, who had passed away less than a year before. I had never wanted a large wedding, so small was good. When we told our parents, they were excited and happy for us.

Over the next three and a half months we did all the things engaged couples are supposed to do. Our families met. We found an apartment, a nice one-bedroom just three blocks west of Susan's house. We got our marriage license and decided to have the reception at Susan's church immediately following the wedding ceremony, which would be performed by the Methodist minister, Pastor Sheppard. We arranged for the women's group at church to cook. Paul, her brother, would be my best man and Nancy, my sister, would be Susan's maid of honor. We planned our honeymoon, a week in Gatlinburg, Tenn. Everything was settled. Easy-peasy, simplicity itself.

'I'M GETTING MARRIED IN THE ...'

On Friday, April 24, one day before our wedding, I was headed home from work to get ready for the rehearsal dinner that evening. I got an idea on the way home. It had worked when I was going to Vietnam, so why not do it again but not as fast? I made a short detour to the S-curve on Indiana Boulevard in Dolton. If things were clear, I could take the curve fast and then immediately slow down. I did a route recon to make sure there were no speed traps. Then I went to the stop sign just before the curve and took off. I hit the curve at about fifty-five miles an hour then hit the brakes. No cops, no fuss, no muss.

I started to drive home, self-satisfied. I hadn't gone a half-mile when I noticed a squad car following me. Damn! I thought I had gotten away with it. But he didn't turn on his flashing lights. Maybe I did get away with it. I kept driving at the speed limit, of course. The police officer followed me. I turned down Woodlawn Avenue toward my house. When I pulled into the driveway, he followed right behind me. Damn!

I got out of the car. The officer got out of the squad car. "Is your name Allen Lynch?" he asked.

"Yes."

"Is your social security number so and so?"

When I answered yes, he walked over and handed me a piece of paper. "Call this number." He turned and got back into his squad car.

"Wait a minute, what is this?" I asked.

"Just call the number. Don't worry, it's a good thing." Then I noticed his squad car was from Alsip, a town way to the west of Dolton.

I entered the house. No one was home, and I made the call. An army colonel answered and asked the same questions. When I confirmed, he said, "I have the honor to inform you that on Armed Forces Day, May 14, the president will present you with the Medal of Honor."

I was in shock. "But I'm getting married tomorrow!" I said.

"Well, you can still get married if you want to. Just please keep this between you and your immediate family until the president makes the announcement."

"Yes, sir, will do," I said. And that was all the conversation.

I told Mom, Dad, and Nancy when they got home, then called Susan and told her, Mary, and Paul. I wanted no one else to know. The 25th was our special day and I wanted nothing to overshadow it, not even the Medal of Honor. But as soon as our wedding rehearsal was over the talk revolved not around the wedding, but the Medal. Both Susan and I were a little unhappy. I didn't know what to think or expect. But Saturday morning was coming and I had lots to do.

Making matters even more tense, my car broke down that night after dropping Susie off at her house. I frantically looked for a mechanic who could fix it before the wedding. It was a long morning. We were going to be married at 1:00 and I needed the car by 11:30. I told the mechanic my dilemma. He promised to get it done if possible. I was very nervous.

We wanted a simple wedding. We thought it was so simple that nothing could go wrong. Then we heard about the Medal, and the car broke. All I wanted to do was get married and go on our honeymoon. I got the car to the mechanic at 8:00 a.m. Plan B was to have Dad drive me to the church. But I wanted my car so we could have some control after the reception. Over the last several months, I'd found that being in control was very important to me. The mechanic called at 11:20. He'd replaced the starter and the car was ready. Dad drove me to the shop, I paid the mechanic, and made it to the church by 11:40. Now I could relax, or try to.

The ceremony went off without a hitch. As I stood at the altar looking out at family and friends, I thought about how lucky Susie and I were. It seemed as if everything pushed both of us to this very moment. Had I stayed in the army, we'd never have met. Had I been happy at UPS, we'd never have met. Had I taken the first and second no at Libby's as final and not gone back the third time, we'd never have met. Had I not kept running into her in the plant, we'd never have gone out. So many things pointed us to this one day.

Then there she was, beautiful in her wedding dress, walking down the aisle with her Uncle Jack, with her cute, unique smile that gave—and gives—me such joy. Before I knew it, the ceremony was over and we were being introduced as Mr. and Mrs. Lynch. We walked back down the aisle into our new life together.

As we were taking pictures, our family and friends made their way to the upstairs fellowship hall. The reception went well, the food was good, and the talk was quiet, just as we wanted it. Soon it was over and we went back to Susan's house to look at our wedding presents and pack the car. By 2:30, we were on our way to Gatlinburg.

Our honeymoon was exactly what we hoped it would be, a time away by ourselves. I called home a couple of times during the week. Each time I was told that the press wanted to interview me. I kept telling Mom and Dad not to let them know where we were; you only get one honeymoon and this was our time. Susie and I enjoyed our honeymoon. We talked a lot and enjoyed getting to know each other. Then it was over, and we headed back to our new apartment in Riverdale.

We were excited and apprehensive about what was going to happen next. Little did we know how much our world was going to change in the next year. It started simply enough with pictures at Fort Sheridan, where just over a year before I had received the Distinguish Service Cross. It was about fifty miles from our apartment in Riverdale. But I had a military escort pick me up at home and drive me to Fort Sheridan where I was given VIP treatment, fitted for a uniform, had my picture taken, given lunch, and then driven back to our apartment. The next day I went to work. There was little more to do before flying to Washington, D.C., on May 13, 1970.

About 7:30 that morning, Susie and I were picked up in an army staff car. We convoyed to my parents' house to pick them and Nancy up, then it was on to Midway Airport for our flight to Washington National Airport. Susie and I flew first class. We had never flown first class before and it was quite an experience. Mom, Dad, Nancy, and my military entourage flew coach. It hit me that I was, at least for today, a big deal. I mean, flying first class!

We landed in Washington and were whisked to our hotel. Susie and I were overwhelmed by our accommodations. We had a suite, a very large bedroom, sitting room, a bathroom, couch, and a big round table. Mom, Dad, and Nancy were in much smaller rooms. Our military liaison saw to our every need. We checked in, then rushed off to a briefing. We were told what was going to happen on the 14th and were given several options for dinner. We chose to see Lou Rawls at a dinner show. It was a late night and we were wined and dined like royalty.

The next day we were up and out early to breakfast. Then it was off to the White House for the ceremonies. Twelve of us got the Medal that day: enlisted men and officers from the Army, Navy, Marine Corps, and Air Force. President Nixon stood before each of us and, as the citation was read, he placed the Medal around our necks. He then asked us a couple of questions like "Where are you from?"

When the ceremony was over, we were taken to a VIP room in the White House. I think it was in the East Wing. We met Gen. Westmoreland, Defense Secretary Melvin Laird, and other national leaders. Julie Nixon was the hostess. She seemed nice. We were taken on a special tour of the White House and were awed by what we saw. Then it was back to the hotel and some sightseeing. The most impressive site, to me, was the Tomb of the Unknown Soldier. It was awe-inspiring to see the behind-the-scenes training of the soldiers who stood guard there. All too soon, it was over and we headed home to Riverdale.

Reality smacked me in the face as soon as I opened the door to our apartment. We'd had fish for dinner the night before we left and

 It hit me that I was, a least for today, a big deal. I mean, flying first class!

I forgot to take out the garbage. Susie was not happy. The apartment stank. I looked around for my military aides, but they had gone. I was no longer a big deal, so I took the garbage out while Susie started to Lysol the kitchen to kill the fish odor.

Our time in the spotlight had not quite ended with our coming home. I was recognized at the Riverdale Memorial Day parade. Then the towns of Dolton and Riverdale named June 14 Allen J. Lynch Day. There was a testimonial dinner that night. And on the 4th of July I was recognized in the Dolton parade and invited to attend a reception with Governor Richard Ogilvie. There were several articles in local newspapers about Susie and me.

Our lives were forever changed, in ways neither of us could have imagined.

CHAPTER 13

MY FAMILY
AND MY PTSD

SHORTLY AFTER I RECEIVED THE MEDAL OF HONOR, THE DI-rector of the Chicago VA regional office asked me to take a position there as a veterans benefits counselor. I would be responsible for assisting my fellow veterans with applying for federal benefits. The job required that I learn a lot. It was hard at first. I had to have a firm grasp of all the federal benefits available, know the requirements for each, and then be able to assist vets in obtaining the benefits. I had to learn how to help them file appeals if claims were denied. Once I learned what I needed and settled into the position, I became good at my job. I spent the first several months at the regional office's contact division, 2030 West Taylor Street in Chicago. I assisted veterans who came to the regional office, and also spent time with the telephone unit, handling calls about benefits.

My new career was exciting. I got to interact with veterans from all eras and services. After I had been with the VA about nine months, I was asked if I would like to take a new position assisting Vietnam returnees at Great Lakes Naval Hospital in North Chicago. I told them nothing would please me more. The next week I reported for work in Building 82H, Great Lakes Naval Base, Hospital Side. There I met my colleague Richard E. Bush, the Medal of Honor recipient whom I had met in 1968 at Cam Ranh Bay. Together, Bush and I assisted hundreds of veterans returning from the war. We'd see every returnee who came to the hospital from Vietnam. Mostly they were service members from the upper Midwest. We would visit them on the hospital ward and file their claims for disability benefits and educational benefits, and advise them on military retirement pay and severance pay. We worked together for about a year and a half and took great pride in assisting the veterans. He became a great friend.

In April 1971, Susie and I moved to Hoffman Estates, a suburb about twenty miles west of Chicago and closer to Great Lakes. The move meant that Susie had to quit her job at Libby, McNeil & Libby, but she found a new job with Sears, Roebuck in Schaumburg. Except for the new location, our routines didn't dramatically change. We worked during the week and visited with our families on the weekends. On Saturdays, typically, we either drove to my parents' home for dinner or they drove to Hoffman Estates for dinner with us. We usually spent Sunday with Susan's mom, Mary, a great lady who was lots of fun, and my brother-in-law, Paul. If it was football season, we spent the day watching the Bears.

We didn't want to start a family just yet. Our parents made it very clear that they wanted grandchildren, but we held our ground. Then, later in the year, we decided it was time, and Susie quickly became pregnant. We told the family in November and they were ecstatic.

In Hoffman Estates, we were somewhat removed from family problems—particularly my dad's drinking—but there was no escaping them entirely. Dad had a different kind of alcohol problem: He never missed a day's work, and he didn't binge drink. His problem was that after very few drinks, usually beer, his personality changed. The alcohol lowered his inhibitions. We all have things we'd sometimes like to say but don't because they are hurtful or petty. But after just a few drinks Dad would say such things. His problem was getting worse and becoming disruptive to the family. Dad and my sister weren't getting along then. She planned to get married soon and, with my moving farther away, he was just not handling life's changes well.

BIBLE LESSONS

In late January 1972, Dad called me with surprising news: He had "found the Lord." Dad had spent several months seeking God. He read the Bible a lot but didn't know what he was looking for; he just knew that the church he was attending wasn't it. Then one day, as he explained it, "I was watching a salesman named John, who was pitching Nancy on pots and pans. I was just pretending to read and just wanted to make sure Nancy wasn't getting taken. He saw me sitting there reading the Bible." After he completed his sales pitch, John and Dad started talking. After a few minutes, John took Dad down what Christians call the "Roman Road."[1] When he finished, Dad said, "I want that!" John led Dad in praying the "sinner's prayer," a prayer for one who wants to turn from their "I"-centered life and live a life for Jesus, accepting him as Savior and Lord.[2] After praying, Dad told me he had a deeply spiritual feeling that he couldn't explain. Mom had a similar experience a week or so later. They left the Catholic Church and started to attend a conservative Bible church, which had no liturgy and relied on preaching directly from the Bible.

Over their next several visits with us, they talked at length about the Bible. As with everything that sparked his interest, Dad dove into Bible study and soon became a self-proclaimed expert on the Good Book, seldom missing an opportunity to pontificate. Unfortunately, Bible study did not significantly change his behavior. He kept saying that God had forgiven him, but he continued to drink and cause problems. Dad was trying to change, to be a stronger and less volatile person, but it was a struggle. He failed many times, but never quit trying to be the man he believed God wanted him to be.

I was miffed about my dad's conversion experience. I was jealous. I had been reading my Bible for years. Susie and I had been attending church since before we were married. I listened to religious radio programming for two years while driving to and from work. I had even started praying an hour a night. Yet he had had this "big bang" epiphany and I had not. I'd had one experience while praying; I felt a welling up inside and felt compelled to say "Abba,"[3] which means "father" in Greek. But that moment was more frightening than enlightening, and I stopped praying because of it. I think what scared me was that it was so unexpected and uncontrolled. It was a deeply spiritual moment for me. It let me know in no uncertain terms that God exists. Through my darkest years, that one experience kept coming back to me. It was like a life preserver. Every time I thought I was done, that I just couldn't go on feeling depressed and angry, that experience would come into my mind and remind me that I wasn't alone.

In any case, Dad's conversion prompted me to intensify my Bible study—not for faith reasons, but so I could hold my own with him when he started reciting chapter and verse. He was fascinated with the "end times" and often held forth on the subject. My motivation for Bible study then was cynical and totally wrong, yet I learned a lot from it about living, faith, and what salvation really means. That knowledge would benefit me in later years when I taught Sunday school, led a men's Bible study, was part of a group that did Bible study at the Lake County jail, and occasionally delivered sermons at various churches.

NEW JOB...AND A BABY!

In July 1972, in the last stages of Susie's pregnancy, I got a new government position. I was moved from Great Lakes Naval Base to the Drug Rehabilitation House at Downey VA Hospital (now called Lovell Federal Health Care Center). Today it serves as both a VA and military hospital. In the 1970s, it was the largest psychiatric VA hospital in the country. My title was changed from veterans benefits counselor to veterans assistance counselor. In addition to assisting veterans with their benefits and helping them obtain employment, I was given an entirely new role: I became part of the therapeutic community and started taking part in group therapy sessions as a co-therapist.

It was a serious assignment for someone who had only a high school diploma. I loved the job, but it showed me that I needed a better education. I started attending the College of Lake County in Grayslake, Illinois, working on an associate of arts degree. I attended half time, which gave me VA educational benefits. Essentially, I got paid to go to college, a benefit that really helped us financially.

On August 25, 1972, Susie went to see the doctor for her normal appointment. We were starting to get very concerned because our baby was a month overdue. The doctor told her it would be another six weeks. She was very depressed. When I got home from work that evening, we decided to go shopping and see a new movie, *The Godfather*. As we were shopping Susie started to have stomach cramps. We thought nothing of it. After all, the doctor said she had another six weeks. We finished shopping and headed home to our apartment on Huntington Avenue, in the Hill Dale apartment complex in Hoffman Estates.

It started to rain—hard—a rainstorm of biblical proportions. My Honda Civic didn't like rain and, as usual in bad weather, was sputtering a lot by the time we got home. Moments later, Susie called out from the bathroom, "My water broke!" Realizing that her cramps were contractions, we called the doctor, who said, "Get her to the hospital, I'll meet you there."

The car barely started. I had the choke pulled out and kept my foot on the gas; thank God, it was a stick shift. I kept the engine revved up at every red light—we caught them all, not one damn green light! After a harrowing fifteen-minute drive that seemed like

 It was a serious assignment for someone who only had a high school diploma.

three hours, I pulled up to the Northwestern Community Hospital's emergency entrance. I rushed in and told them Susie was in labor. A wheelchair was brought out quickly and away she went. I parked the car. It was 8:00 p.m.

I got to the admissions area, filled out some papers, and made it up to her room. I wasn't there ten minutes before they wheeled her into the birthing room. I paced. At 9:50 p.m., I got the word: "Mr. Lynch, you are the father of a 9-pound, 5-ounce baby boy. You can see your wife just as soon as we get her and the baby back to the room." There I was allowed to kiss Susie and to hold our new baby for the first time. Susie told me she checked that he had ten toes and ten fingers. I breathed a sigh of relief. I was happy. I was excited. I was terrified. I needed a drink.

We felt that we were ready to become parents. We'd had over nine months to get prepared. The baby's room was all set up. We'd had baby showers for Susie and had a whole lot of baby clothes and cloth diapers. We had a diaper service lined up. We even had names picked out: Eric, because it was a strong name and spoke to Susie's Scandinavian heritage, or Carolyn, if the baby was girl. But when our first child was actually born, I got nervous. Was I really prepared to raise another human being? It was too late for second thoughts. Life comes at you every day, ready or not, and you have to deal with the twists and turns and big moments as best you can.

Susie and I had a steak dinner complete with wine at the hospital the night before she and Eric came home. Soon dinners with just the two of us would be rare. Once Eric was home, we fell into an entirely new routine. For the next several months, sleep would be constantly interrupted. When Eric woke up hungry at night, I'd get him, change his diaper, and give him to Susie.

Susie and I became parenting partners. We both changed diapers. We took turns getting up at night when he cried. I won't say that was fun—but in terms of the big picture we were living the dream: I had a great job, and so we decided that she would be a stay-at-home mom. It figured to be tough financially, but we knew we could do it. It was how we were raised. Moms stayed home and cared for the children. That's what we wanted.

BACK IN THE ARMY

Life went on, but I realized that I missed the army. I had thought about joining the reserves for some time. Now, with a new mouth to feed, we needed extra money. Reserve duty only required one weekend of service every month, and members got the equivalent of four days' pay for two days' work.

I enlisted in the army reserves and was assigned to 2nd Battalion, 338th Infantry, 85th Division. Because I was a combat veteran, they did a grade evaluation. When I left the army in 1969, I was a sergeant, E-5. Now, in 1972, I skipped staff sergeant, E-6, and went right to sergeant first class, E-7. I was assigned to A Company as a training NCO. At the next weekend drill, I was named acting first sergeant. Soon the reserves became just another part of our family routine. I liked being back in the army. It gave me a sense of purpose. Overall, things couldn't have been better for Susie and me. Eric was a great baby, who by then was sleeping all night. Susie loved being a mom and I loved being a father.

In April 1973, we moved again, this time to Waukegan, which is five miles north of Downey VA Hospital. Eric would soon be one year old. We found a townhouse to rent in the north part of Waukegan, and between my reserve pay and government salary we were doing well financially. Beyond that, we got involved in the local United Methodist church, attending Sunday school and adult Bible class on Sunday night. I also got involved in the Waukegan American Legion.

THE DRAGON RISES

In the summer of 1973, just a couple of weeks before Eric's first birthday, I was riding the bus back and forth to work at Downey VA Hospital. One hot, muggy evening, I had just stepped off the bus when a severe thunderstorm broke. By the time I got home, I was soaking wet. Susie met me at the door. I stripped off my wet clothes and took them to our basement laundry, then went upstairs to change. I came down just in time for supper. Eric was in his high chair and Susie was bringing the dishes to the table when suddenly there was a flash of lightning and a loud crack of thunder. I found myself on the floor. Susie later said I got a strange look on my face, like I wasn't really there before diving to the floor. I didn't know what to think. I had never done anything like that. I learned later that it was a "startle reaction." Loud noises can cause that reaction in those of us who have been in combat.

For weeks afterward, every sudden noise made me jump. I also started to have what are known as "intrusive thoughts," unwanted and unexpected, about my experiences in Vietnam. Out of the blue, my mind suddenly would be ablaze with thoughts of the war and what I saw there. Over the previous year or so, I had thought about Vietnam and my combat duty, of course; it was impossible not to. But this was different. I didn't want these thoughts and memories just popping up unexpectedly. All sorts of things triggered these damn things: smells, humidity, loud noises. I didn't know what to do. I didn't know how lucky I was not to have flashbacks, sudden vivid memories that are almost like being in your own movie.[3]

At that time, there was no such thing as post-traumatic stress disorder. What we now know as PTSD wasn't classified as a mental health issue until 1980, seven years after my first episode, when the American Psychiatric Association added the illness to the third edition of its *Diagnostic and Statistical Manual of Mental Disorders*. Most veterans experiencing the same symptoms were diagnosed with "anxiety reaction."[4] I did not want a diagnosis, so I kept most of what I was experiencing to myself. I didn't go to any doctors and didn't tell anyone but Susie, but I didn't tell her much. I didn't want her to think I was crazy.

My job with the drug treatment center ended in late 1973 when I was transferred to the hospital side at Downey and got my old title back, veterans benefits counselor. I was tasked with contacting every veteran admitted to the hospital. The work was gratifying and I loved meeting veterans.

In 1974, we bought our first house, in the Grandwood Park housing development in Gurnee, just west of Waukegan. It was a small ranch house with four bedrooms, a living room, and a large combination kitchen and dining room. It had a huge back yard with an above-ground pool and a one-car attached garage. It would be our home until 1986.

I started working on the house. I ran the wiring for our washer and dryer and put in the circuit breaker. I was proud of my electrical work. I also did some remodeling—even took down a wall. I learned more about plumbing than I cared to. Roots from the trees in the front yard constantly got into the sewage tiles. I had to use a Roto-Rooter to get them out of the sewage line. Not pleasant. I also maintained and, when necessary, repaired our cars. In 1974 we had a Honda Civic and a 1970 Plymouth Valiant four-door. I was my father's son: There was nothing I couldn't build, install, or fix.

We loved to entertain and had many family parties at our Grandwood Park home. We also had two more children. Carolyn was born July 4, 1976. We had planned a big party for the 4th. The baby wasn't supposed to come for another couple of weeks. But Carolyn decided that she wanted to share her birthday with the United States of America. Early that morning, Susie went into labor and a few hours later Carolyn was born. She was our firecracker baby. Her personality is much like this country: strong-willed, passionate about issues, and determined. Growing up, she would give us many challenges.

Our third child, Brian, was born May 22, 1979, when Eric was eight years old and Carolyn was about to turn three. I was going into the delivery room this time; I would be right there to see him born. We went through the classes and then came the great day. I was there for hours. Susie and I did all the things they had taught us in class: I made sure she had plenty of ice, I held her hand, I told her to push and pant and all the wonderful things that you're supposed to do. But he wasn't coming. After several long hours, they decided to do a C-section. A couple of hours later the doctor told me I had another son, an 11-pound, 4-ounce bouncing baby boy. "Bouncing baby boy? More like a Chicago Bears linebacker," I thought. We had decided to name him Brian after Jerry Brines, my friend who was killed in Vietnam by friendly fire. Brian would prove to be the family's practical joker. He had a unique sense of humor and would surprise us with the intricacy of his tricks and pranks. Brian was always very loyal to his friends growing up. He was also sports-minded and played football in high school.

When it came to raising children, I was more of a disciplinarian than Susie. We knew our children would eventually leave to make their way in the world. We knew that for them to be successful they

 "I'm not your friend, I'm your father. I'm responsible for how you turn out as an adult."

had to have discipline. I used to say to them, "I'm not your friend, I'm your father. I'm responsible for how you turn out as an adult." Our job was to make sure they would be ready for the world. We were raised with, and believed in, corporal punishment. But we also believed that a spanking should not be given for doing something wrong, but for showing disrespect. I tried very hard not to spank when I was angry. Waiting accomplished two things: It allowed me to cool down and it gave the children time to think about what they had done.

On one occasion when Eric was about five years old, he backtalked and threw something. I don't remember why or what he threw, but I do remember sending him to his room to "await his doom." As I sat on the couch and slowly drank my cup of coffee, I noticed him sneaking down the hall to Carolyn's room then back to his room. He did that four or five times. Finally, I told him I was coming in to give him a spanking. When I walked into his room he stood there waiting—with his butt bubbled out about three inches. It seems he had gotten Carolyn's diapers and stuffed them in his pants. I almost lost it, but managed to hold in my laughter. I calmly put him over my knee and pulled out the diapers one by one. With each diaper, he let out a whimper, and he was crying by the time the last one was removed. Finally, I gave him a very light tap on his butt. He just looked at me. "Is that it?" he asked through his tears. I told him, "I think you've been punished enough." Then we talked about what he did and why it merited a spanking.

Susie and I believed in challenging our children. We knew better than they what they could do and not do. On one occasion, Eric had the job of taking the garbage out to the front of the house for pickup. It had been snowing all day and it was going to be quite a chore for him. But I told him to get it done. He got bundled up, went out, and started lugging the garbage cans to the front. When he came back in the house we had hot chocolate waiting for him. His look of satisfaction from accomplishing such a momentous task was priceless.

Our children were required to clean their rooms and do chores around the house. It gave them a work ethic and the drive to accomplish great things in their lives.

Our life was stable but not entirely satisfactory. In November 1973, I decided to leave the reserves. It seems a crazy decision in retrospect, since I'd only reenlisted a year before. But the reserves were too much with my college classes, work, and parental responsibilities. I thought that with more time I could focus on my studies and my family.

It was a logical decision, but dropping out of the reserves left me with a lot of time to myself. That was also true of my job as a veterans benefits counselor. I worked alone for the most part and became somewhat fixated on my own life. I started wondering whether I was happy or not. I got self-centered and selfish and then slid into depression. Worse, things started to go wrong in my marriage. On the surface I had a lot to be happy about, and yet I suffered from a nagging sense of unhappiness. I didn't know why.

I toughed it out and gradually worked through my funk. I realized that being busy was important, a good thing. The more I had going on in my life, the better. About a year after Carolyn was born I decided I needed to be back in the army. With the new addition, we were running a little low on cash. The army would feed my need to be in an organization and give us some supplemental income. In May 1977, I decided to reenlist in the reserves. I was made a training NCO for a short time. In October, I volunteered for the 85th Division (Training) Drill Sergeant Academy. When I first joined the reserves in 1972, I was in that same unit and admired the drill sergeants for their ability to get up in front of a class and teach. I wanted to do that. I loved marching and teaching my company, so going to drill sergeant school seemed quite logical.

I was back in my old routine. I worked during the day, went to college two nights a week, and had reserve duty one weekend a month back with my old unit in Waukegan. My reserve unit had several Vietnam veterans and after drill, we would head to the Quonset, a local bar near the reserve center. Over beer and pizza, we shared war stories. It was cathartic.

Drill sergeant school took a year to complete. Every weekend drill, my fellow candidates and I attended and presented classes on the skills required to be a drill sergeant. We learned military leadership, drill and ceremonies, and the intricacies of the M16 rifle and M60 machine gun—in short, everything a drill sergeant needed to know to train new recruits.

For the most part, the school was run at battalion level, with some division-wide training. I wanted no one to know I was a Medal of Honor recipient. I didn't want any special treatment. The senior drill sergeants and drill sergeant candidates at the battalion kept my secret. When I graduated during the two-week summer camp at Fort Leonard Wood, Missouri, I was the Distinguished Military Graduate, meaning at the top of my class. When I was awarded that honor, the senior drill sergeant informed everyone that I was a Medal of Honor recipient. That was one of my proudest moments.

My hectic schedule kept my mind active and focused. But after I graduated from drill sergeant school and earned my associate's degree from the College of Lake County in May 1978, I had a lot of time on my hands and started self-obsessing again. That was not good. Memories of my combat duty in Vietnam began to torment me. There was a disconnect between my memories of what had happened on December 15, 1967, in the Battle of Tam Quan, and what my Medal of Honor Citation described. That bothered me. It is common knowledge that there can be no completely accurate account of a military battle. There is too much going on, in too many places, with minds completely stressed, for any one person or handful of people to know what every soldier in a unit was doing at all times.

Several people tried to put my mind at ease by saying, "It's the fog of war." Even so, I couldn't get past the differences between my memories and the citation. I also began to wonder if I had done first aid properly on the guys I rescued. I kept going over it in my mind, especially when I was not involved in other things. Part of me was certain that I knew first aid and felt very confident that I had done the right thing. But then doubt would creep in and I'd agonize about it.

I felt guilty that I had not been wounded in the battle. In my mind, perhaps, I hadn't paid a sufficient price for the Medal of Honor. That bothered me, especially when meeting other MOH recipients who had been wounded—men like Einar Ingman, who earned the Medal in the Korean War. His face was horribly burned. Dick Bush, with whom I worked, lost part of a hand and suffered multiple shrapnel wounds when he jumped on a hand grenade to save fellow marines. He told me he smothered the blast with his steel pot and a sandbag. Friends kept telling me no one wants to be wounded; it's just what happens. Still, I was troubled.

I sank into depression. I hid it well except for those times when I erupted in anger. Then I would usually hit a wall with my fist. Anger would well up inside me and I had to do something to release it, so I'd hit a wall. It was better than hitting a person, but hitting something softer than a wall would have been smarter. I broke a knuckle one day when I struck a wall stud. It hurt like hell. The only benefit was I became very good at repairing holes in the wall. But I could not control my need to strike out. I started drinking too much, and with the drinking came self-pity.

A SENSE OF NORMALCY

In fall 1978, I started an accelerated bachelor of science degree in health care administration at the Southern Illinois University extension at Great Lakes Naval Base. It was a two-weekend-a-month program and I could complete a degree in a year and a half. That got me motivated. Meanwhile, I was an active dad. Eric, by then age seven, had joined the Cub Scouts and started playing both T-ball and flag football. His participation in those activities got me involved with them. I was busy then, which kept my mind off me. Still, I wasn't getting any professional help, and I wasn't on medication. I was just trying to cope with the problem myself as best I could.

On the last day of 1979, I interviewed for the chief ambulatory care position at Downey VA Hospital. It was a midlevel management position that oversaw admissions, outpatient care, central scheduling, and several ancillary staff functions. I was thrilled when they offered me the job. It was a big promotion that meant I would supervise about thirty people. During my first two weeks on the job I worked in each of my areas of responsibility, learning the intricacies of the departments. Meanwhile, Downey VA Hospital was about to become the North Chicago VA Hospital, and change from being mainly a psychiatric hospital for veterans to a general medical and surgical hospital. I thoroughly enjoyed my management job. Life was good. The PTSD was causing some problems, but I was busy and didn't have time for it.

AN EDGY, EMOTIONAL MAN

In the spring of 1980, I earned my bachelor's degree from Southern Illinois. I was so proud. I was the only one in the family to graduate from college. With the parchment in hand, I wanted to devote time to my family. I got more involved with Eric and Cub Scouts and was an assistant scoutmaster for a time. I was also assistant coach of his Little League baseball team.

But I was starting to have trouble again with my Vietnam experiences. Sometime in the early 1980s, my family and I were watching an episode of *M*A*S*H*, the classic TV show about a field surgical hospital during the Korean War. In this episode, a soldier is seriously wounded on the battlefield. When he falls to the ground, a small clock appears on the lower right corner of the TV screen and starts ticking away the minutes. It was a powerful symbol of how fleeting life can be, especially in war. Partway through the episode, I was overcome with emotion and started to cry. Eric and Carolyn were with Susie and me when it happened. They got upset because they didn't understand why I was upset, so I left the living room and went to the bedroom. Susie came in and comforted me. She told me she thought I was seeing what happened to Jerry Brines after he was medevaced. I saw him shot, I saw him on the medevac, but I didn't see him again. The *M*A*S*H* episode was, at least emotionally, what happened after we put him on the chopper. It was closure.

I was fine at work, for the most part. But at home I was edgy and irritable. I became very depressed and thought a lot about my own death. I drank and had angry outbursts. I felt survivor's guilt. I couldn't understand why God had allowed me to come home unscathed while so many others had died or were severely wounded.

I had, in effect, four different personas, each operating in its own silo. There was my work self, my army self, my church self, and my home and family self. Each was separate and all were linked. Through each self, I tried to constrain my simmering PTSD issues. However, there was no congruent me, comfortable with all facets of my life. The army self thrived within the structure and discipline of military work. My church self was a disguise in a way—I could just smile charitably and pretend to be even-keeled and stable. I still studied the Bible and went to prayer group, but that was for a short time and therefore easy to wear my mask. My work self was a little harder. I was under stress a lot, assisting veterans with their problems with the hospital. I was dealing with personnel issues, employees who just couldn't make it to work on time or who were incompetent. But I could disappear into my office or into the hospital if it all got to be too much. The big thing, though, was that I had to control myself; my job depended upon it.

My home self is where the real problems were. I had no mask. At the end of the day, most of my guard came down. I didn't have to watch myself. If I'd had a dreadful day at work, it came out at home.

I remember walking into the house and telling the kids, "Daddy had a bad day." Warning them not to act up. *Nice*, I know.

It was at home where the symptoms of PTSD emerged. That's where the wall hitting happened, where the yelling in frustration happened. Many days I was fine and happy to be home. I enjoyed being with Susan and our family. I loved being a father and talking with the kids, especially with Eric who was becoming a young man. But there were other, darker days.

Emotional disguises are just that—masks that hide the problems lurking behind them. And under stress, my masks fell away. On Christmas Eve 1980, I was getting ready to leave my office around noon. It was a half-day of work for all nonessential personnel. As I was closing my briefcase, the assistant chief of medical administration, Mr. Sally—my immediate supervisor—came into my office. He told me I had to stay at work "in case someone has a question."

I thought he was joking, and when I realized he was serious, I blew up. There was no need for me to stay at work, I told him, and I didn't intend to. He insisted. We got into an argument in the hallway leading to his office. I cussed him out and told him in no uncertain terms what I thought of him. I just lost it. We ended up in his office, where I continued to scream at him. He told me that if I wanted to fight, to go ahead and take a swing. I raised my hand, then I saw that he had a smile on his face. Funny, that smile. In a split second, I knew if I hit him I was going to jail. I stopped inches from his face and stormed out of his office. I walked over to the personnel department and quit. Merry Christmas!

I packed my office stuff in a cardboard box and went home. When I pulled in the driveway, Susie came out of the house to greet me. When she saw me take the box out of the back seat, she said, with a smile, "Did you quit your job?" I replied, "Yes." I went into the house and explained what had happened. Susie was shocked and mad. She was so mad at me that she couldn't speak.

The two of us hardly spoke over the next two days—the entire Christmas weekend. Our families came up to visit—my mom and dad; my sister, Nancy, her husband, and their two children, Rebecca and Tommy; Susie's mom, Mary; Susie's brother, Paul, and his girlfriend, Marcia. We put up a good front. After they left Susie stopped talking to me. I remember walking down Stern School Road to the tollway and sitting on the embankment, thinking about what to do. I saw myself walking up to the overpass and jumping into traffic. Then I walked home. Sunday came and went. I was beside myself. I knew I would have to start looking for a job on Monday. But more than that, I knew I had let my wife down and, if I didn't find a job, my whole family.

Monday morning, I woke up to the grim realization that I was unemployed. I had three children, a very angry wife, a mountain of bills, and no job. I was in turmoil. Then salvation came in the form of a telephone call from the chief of medical administration, Mr. Alexander. He was the head of the department. "Al," he said, "you have three children and a wife and responsibilities. Your job is waiting for you. All I want you to do is apologize to Mr. Sally. I'll see you tomorrow." I was elated—relieved. Tuesday morning, I reported to Mr. Sally's office and apologized. I don't remember what I said, but he was gracious. Everything went back to normal. Most important, Susie was no longer mad at me.

FIGHTING THE DRAGON

I was sitting in my office a day or so later, when one of my friends came in, a hospital social worker named Betty Best. She asked how I was doing and we ended up talking for an hour. I saw her weekly at the hospital for almost a year, and after that, I saw her for another six months in her private-practice office. They were talk sessions—a chance to unload emotional and psychological baggage. I told her what was bothering me. She listened, tried to put my frustrations in context, and helped me through my frequent dark moods.

We started working on my anger issue. I needed to control it. It turned out that she had heard me screaming at Mr. Sally. She suggested I start running after work. It was a good idea—so good that I

 I still suffered from PTSD symptoms but I was learning how to handle them.

put on athletic garb and took to the street in running shoes as soon as I got home from our session that day. I ran regularly and got to a point where I could run three to five miles at a good pace. I always felt better after a good run. I still suffered from PTSD symptoms but I was learning how to handle them. It was good to have a guide like Betty, someone who could help me develop some coping skills. She was a godsend.

The reserves also helped. I was a first sergeant, and my friends who went through drill sergeant school were acting first sergeants. In 1978, we were going through armor retraining at the reserve center and during summer camp at Fort McCoy, Wisconsin. Retraining meant we were going from infantry to armored cavalry. The first sergeants oversaw training and ensured that it conformed to standards. I was happy to serve under our new battalion commander, then Maj. Jim Mukoyama. He was a Vietnam veteran who would later retire as a major general. Maj. Mukoyama was a lead-by-example commander. If we were out in the rain, so was he. He made sure we trained hard. He knew the difference between command and leadership. Simply put, a commander tells you to go to hell; a leader makes you want to go.

Through it all, I kept working and putting on my masks. I gave talks about VA benefits to local veterans organizations. I talked to local school kids about the cost of freedom and the student's responsibility to honor those who serve. No one knew the turmoil that was going on inside me. Because I'd received the Medal of Honor, I had a duty to set an example, but my emotions, the survivor's guilt, kept joy from me. I was like Pagliacci, one person outside, another on the inside. (I'm glad my dad gave me an appreciation for music. I love opera and Pagliacci is one of my favorites because of the emotions it shows.) Only Susie and Betty Best were aware of it all. I tried to keep my problems to myself. I still felt depressed at times, and my anger continued to bubble up. Susie and I were not getting along because I was impossible to get along with. One of my friends described me as "happy being miserable."

Running helped, but it wasn't a cure-all. I could function perfectly well at work or with other people outside, but at home I was a mess. I kept thinking the world would be better off without me and started to wish I had died in Vietnam. I thought about doing away with myself. I even had a plan to make it look like an accident. Then I'd meet with Betty, and she would talk me through it. I was on an emotional rollercoaster, and the drinking didn't help. I fell into the trap that snares a lot of people: Feel bad and take a drink or two or three or more. Big mistake. As a doctor I knew put it, "Stinking thinking leads to stinking drinking and stinking drinking leads to stinking actions." Sadly, his name escapes me.

In January 1981, Susie and I attended President Reagan's inauguration. It was our third, having previously attended the swear-ing-in of President Nixon in January 1973 and President Carter in January 1977. Later that year, in November, we went to a Medal of Honor convention in Honolulu. The convention was held at the Hale Koa Resort, an Armed Forces Recreation Center. It was a great convention, filled with events that make Hawaii, well, Hawaii. Susie and I had never been there before and it was everything we imagined. Hawaii helped to lift my spirits. We visited the USS *Arizona* Memorial and the "Punchbowl," the National Memorial Cemetery of the Pacific. There I walked among the Courts of the Missing,[6] a part of the cemetery that lists the names of those missing in action from World War II, Korea, and Vietnam. The names, as I recall, are etched in gold.

I remember talking to the names. I was having such a good time feeling sorry for myself. Then out of the blue I heard a voice as clear as if someone were standing right next to me. It said: "You should be ashamed of yourself. You have what these men will never have—life, family, children. HOW DARE YOU FEEL SORRY FOR YOURSELF!" It was like a slap in the face. I felt ashamed. I had a duty, as all war veterans—and indeed, all of us—do, to live the life these men in the cemetery never had a chance to live. I started to heal.

CHAPTER 14

PATH TO RECOVERY

WHILE WE WERE IN HAWAII, I OVERHEARD LEO THORSNESS, a Medal of Honor recipient and former POW who was held at the Hanoi Hilton, talk about the Vietnam Veterans Leadership Program (VVLP). It was started by President Reagan and led by Tom Pauken, and its purpose was to dispel the negative image of the Vietnam veteran and to assist those who were unemployed or underemployed.[1]

I wanted, needed, to become a part of it, and my involvement would be life changing. Leo put me in contact with the VVLP in Chicago where I attended a meeting at the Union League Club. There I met executive director Rick Eilert and the board of directors. Rick served in Vietnam with the marine corps and had been severely wounded. He passed away on June 9, 2011, I believe as a result of the wounds received in combat. Rick and I became good friends for the years we were involved with VVLP, but drifted apart when I left the program. The board included Gene Connell, a lawyer who served as the program's counsel; H.G. "Skip" Smith, a real estate broker who served in Vietnam; and Dennis Coll, a West Point graduate who served in Vietnam. Dennis was the chairman of the board.

Rick and I hung out a lot with Gene. Gene loved to drink and party, and he had a heart for helping veterans. He loved Irish bars and Irish music and soon Rick and I loved them, too. Several Irish songs spoke to our hearts: "The Ballad of Willie McBride," also known as "Green Fields of France," and "And the Band Played Waltzing Matilda," both written by Eric Bogle. These songs told of the costs of war and its futility. We dearly loved Irish drinking songs, and when in Washington for VVLP conferences we always ended up at the Dubliner, an Irish bar with live music. We drank Guinness and Black and Tans, and sang our hearts out. Irish music still really speaks to me.

I WAS ASKED TO JOIN THE BOARD IN EARLY 1982. THE VA GAVE me administrative leave to attend conferences in Washington. The conferences featured veterans who'd found good jobs, adjusted well to civilian life, and were determined to put the war in the past where it belonged, while still retaining their allegiance to those who had served. Their presentations and talks inspired me, as did the opportunity to see how successful Vietnam veterans functioned and approached life.

VVLP was innovative and I was excited to be a part of it. The Chicago VVLP's first major event was the dedication of the Chicago Vietnam Memorial and the Vietnam Veteran Art Group show, *Reflexes and Reflections*, which ran in November 1982. It coincided with the dedication of the Vietnam Veterans Memorial in Washington, D.C.

I was selected to give the dedication speech in Chicago on Thursday, November 11. It was a great honor. I had given many talks before, but this would be my first major speech before a large audience that included Chicago mayor Jane Byrne, Illinois attorney general Neil Hartigan, and other dignitaries. When it was my time to speak, I followed Susie's advice and spoke from my heart. I said: "This is for my friends, our friends, and it isn't for their memory, but for all the good times...all the camaraderie and all the kids' confidences we shared all those nights we were scared to death." I went on: "It was twelve months of what some people would consider hell, but I wouldn't trade it for anything. It has given me a perspective on life that other people don't have. I've seen the worst and nothing can ever be that bad again." Then I voiced my opinion of the government: "They should have seen we needed help when we came back—counseling for emotional problems, outreach centers, and help just getting established. It hurts to remember how frustrating it was for us. Now, maybe somehow that wrong will be righted. Especially for those whose bodies are here but whose minds are still in Vietnam."

When the festivities ended, Susie and I went to the art show for a short time before I joined several of the Chicago VVLP board members and other Vietnam veterans for the flight to Washington and the dedication of the national memorial on the Mall. Maya Lin's black granite wall was, and is, deeply poignant. It seems to me a profoundly stark reminder of the human cost of war—with the name of every soldier killed in the conflict etched on The Wall—and the strength of those who gave their lives for a cause.

THE DEDICATION WAS WONDERFUL EXCEPT THAT I COULDN'T FIND the name of Jerry Brines on the monument. In the army as in other services, we called each other by our last names or by nicknames. I couldn't remember Brines' first name, and didn't know how he spelled his family name. I knew him simply as "Brians." It was frustrating and for a time took the joy of the dedication from me. About two years later, I was going through some boxes and found a picture of Jerry. His full name, Gerald R. Brines, was on the back. When the half-scale wall came to Chicago for the 1986 welcome home parades honoring Vietnam veterans, I found his name. Over the years, I've gone to Washington several times, and each time I visit Jerry.

Each military division that served in Vietnam had a hospitality suite in a hotel that weekend. I made my way to the 1st Cavalry's suite. Everyone there was in a great mood and welcomed me, but I saw no one with whom I served, which was disappointing.

Over the years, the Vietnam Memorial in Washington was enhanced with other sculptures. First came the addition of *Three Servicemen*, dedicated on Veterans Day 1984. It was installed partly to allay the complaints of critics who found Maya Lin's dark wall too abstract and untraditional. Next came the Vietnam Women's Memorial, dedicated on Veterans Day 1993. A bronze sculpture by Glenna Goodacre, it shows three uniformed women tending to a wounded soldier. It honors the American women who served in Vietnam, many of them as nurses.

During the 1980s, many other Illinois cities dedicated Vietnam memorials, and I spoke at some of them. My message was typically about the cost of war; the honor owed those sent to fight; the denial of the "veterans preference" in hiring by Illinois state government; and the VA's poor treatment of veterans in the claims process. I also spoke about the meaning of Memorial Day and Veterans Day. I spoke about how this country would not exist if not for those who have defended it, those who wear the uniform. When I spoke at schools, I often spoke of the gift of freedom given by those who lost their lives, and the responsibility of us all to honor that sacrifice through service.

Despite the outpouring of respect and patriotism at those events, each memorial dedication and parade left me feeling ambivalent. I felt good that we Vietnam veterans were finally being honored, but tangible support was still lagging. Veterans like me were still struggling with PTSD. VA hospitals, while transitioning to updated, modern facilities, were still places many Vietnam veterans were afraid to go. They felt that the VA's answer to every problem was medication and more medication.

The Veterans Benefits Administration was still viewed as the "Guardians of the Mint," as we called it derisively. The agency seemed to have a very narrow view of benefits eligibility and was, in my view, extremely conservative in applying the VA rating schedule, by which claims were reviewed and payment amounts determined. In Chicago, the VA regional office was often criticized for low-balling claim ratings, which meant extremely stingy benefits for the veteran and his family.

DAD: AN INTERVENTION

By December 1982, Dad's alcohol problem had become unbearable. A normal person could easily drink a couple of beers, but Dad couldn't. I often marveled as I watched him change from Dr. Jekyll into Mr. Hyde after just two beers. He became verbally abusive, overly sarcastic, and just plain nasty to those with whom he had a grudge, even a small one. To Dad's way of thinking, he worked every day and it was his right to stop off for a couple of beers. He never really believed he had an alcohol problem. But he did and we'd had enough. Finally, three days before Christmas 1982, we decided to take action.

I arranged for Dad to get checked into the alcohol treatment unit at the North Chicago VA Medical Center, where I worked. On December 22, my sister, Nancy, her husband, Tom, Mom, and I were waiting for Dad when he got home from work. We told him his drinking had gotten out of hand and that he needed to get help. He said he knew he was drinking too much but had a plan to cut down. We told him all the arrangements were made, and that he'd be going with me. After some tense discussion, he agreed to go after

Christmas. We told him there wasn't going to be a Christmas if he wasn't in the program. He was angry but finally agreed to go into treatment. He never forgave me for ruining his Christmas. Even on his deathbed, he still held a grudge about it.

Dad completed the alcohol program and started attending Alcoholics Anonymous meetings at the hospital. He got zealous about AA, which was encouraging, and he had his AA group thinking that he was on the straight and narrow, until Mom attended one meeting and blew his cover. She got angry when she heard him lying to the group about his sobriety. She said aloud, and plainly, that Dad was still drinking. He sheepishly admitted that she was right.

In 1981 Dad had bought a camper, what today is called a recreational vehicle. It was his pride and joy. He and Mom went camping during the spring and fall, after our kids were back in school and the campgrounds were empty except for seniors like them. He was always so careful with it. One weekend in the late spring of 1983, after he was discharged from the alcohol program at North Chicago VA, he and Mom went to a family campground in Kankakee State Park. Some of the extended family was also camping there. While there, Dad drank, and he was half drunk on Sunday when he started for home. As he started to back the RV out of the campsite, as Mom and other family members watched, he hit a tree branch and damaged the roof of the vehicle.

The next day, he came to the VA and told the doctor to put him on Antabuse, a drug that prevents the body from processing alcohol and produces very unpleasant side effects when combined with alcohol.[2] When I asked Dad why he'd made the decision, he told me that he'd wrecked his camper: "I said to myself, 'Now, you son of a bitch, you can't drink." Damaging the camper had been the last straw. It made him realize he wasn't as in control of his alcoholism as he'd thought. He had convinced himself that Mom just didn't like his drinking and that he didn't have a problem.

Dad was sober for almost three years, during which time he became a pleasant man again. But his transformation came to an end in August 1985, when he decided to stop taking Antabuse. He resumed drinking and continued to drink for the rest of his life. He would quit for short periods of time, improve a bit, and then fall off the wagon. He struggled with his drinking until he died in 1994. He always blamed his drinking on other people or outside factors—my mom, or the stress of work. He was full of excuses. On his deathbed, suffering the effects of lung cancer, he told Mom he smoked because she stressed him out so much. If I learned anything from Dad—and I learned a lot—it was to be responsible for my own actions and not to blame others for my failings.

LIKE FATHER, LIKE SON?

In September 1983, I left my career with the VA to become the executive director of the Chicago Vietnam Veterans Leadership Program. This decision would change my life in ways I couldn't imagine. Rick Eilert had resigned to go on a promotional tour for his book, *For Self and Country*, which was about to be published. He told me the position was mine if I wanted it. I applied and was accepted by the board of directors.

Becoming the executive director gave me a raise in pay but more important I had a great opportunity to build the program. It was my responsibility to manage our $50,000 grant, raise funds for our program, and provide a means to assist veterans in the employment process. In June 1984, we held our first Salute to America's Heroes weekend. We arranged for the transportation and accommodation of about 40 Medal of Honor recipients in Chicago. It was my first major project and it was a success. I was hungry to do more. Susie helped me organize things then and during my entire time with VVLP.

VVLP was a big responsibility and involved many meetings with board members in various hotels, restaurants, and bars. My drinking increased as our meetings increased. To make matters worse, I was speaking to a lot of veterans organizations and that added to my time away from home. I'd speak at a meeting then end up in the bar, "networking." Of course, I had to have a drink or two with the members, right? Soon I was drinking too much and too often. I was still having problems with PTSD symptoms and that added to the alcohol problem. When I was busy with external matters, I seemed to have few symptoms; when my scheduled slowed, the symptoms would flare.

One of the bars where we did a lot of business was on the South Side of Chicago, in the suburb of Beverly, fifty-five miles from my home in Gurnee. One night, some VVLP colleagues and I ended up there after a meeting. I drank way too much. I had driven home inebriated a number of times, and didn't think twice about doing so on this night. This was before the crackdowns on drunk driving. First, though, I decided to get something to eat. At a local White Castle, I ate ten sliders and drank a large cup of black coffee, figuring the food and coffee would sober me up.

It didn't. I don't remember getting home—but fortunately everyone was asleep when I did. The next morning, I got up and immediately went out to take a look at the car. I had an uneasy feeling that I'd hit something the night before. As I walked around the Plymouth scanning for damage, Susie came out and stood on the porch, watching me with a scornful frown. "It's pretty sad that you were so drunk last night that you couldn't remember if you'd had an accident," she said. I felt terrible. Thankfully, I hadn't hit anything. I was lucky not to have hurt myself or other people. I had three children in school and a wife that depended on me, and I was acting irresponsibly. But I wasn't ashamed enough to stop drinking then. I'd just have to be more careful. Yeah, right.

I was still sure that my drinking was "manageable." I told Susie basically the same thing my dad told my mom. But the truth was, just like Dad, I didn't know when to stop. Worse, Susie couldn't depend on me to be home when I said I would be. All our kids were in school, and she wanted to start college herself. She'd always wanted to be a nurse, and I was fully supportive of the idea. It was her turn. But she was afraid to start school or to take a job for fear that I was not reliable, that I wouldn't be home to take care of the kids when she was out. And she was right: All too often I was late or just forgot to be where I said I would be.

It might have helped if the VVLP didn't meet in bars or we didn't end up in a bar after a meeting. But we all liked a drink or two. I loved the camaraderie of working on a project and having a good time after a meeting or even during a meeting. But the night I drove home drunk and had to look at my car the next day to make sure I didn't have an accident weighed on me.

Then came St. Patrick's Day 1985. I was planning a small VVLP event at a Chicago bar. There was a meeting at the bar before it opened to talk about the details. After the meeting and before the bar opened to the public we had a couple of beers. "I behaved myself," I thought. I had only four beers, then drove back to the office and worked till about 5:00. On my way home I drove through Mundelein, a small town just south of Grandwood Park on Route 45. I was going a little over the speed limit and was pulled over. When the police officer came up to my window, he told me he smelled beer on my breath. I told him my last drink was about four hours earlier. He had me get out of the car and told me to walk along a line on a sidewalk. I stumbled a little bit. He said I seemed inebriated. I told him that the sidewalk was uneven.

I knew it was a stupid thing to say, even though it was true. The next thing I knew, I was in handcuffs and standing in a police station. As it turned out, both the arresting officer and his lieutenant were Vietnam veterans. They saw, as they went through my wallet, that I'd received the Medal of Honor. Yet they had to do their job. The lieutenant looked at me, grabbed a handful of change, and dropped it on the floor in front of me. He said, "I will give you one chance. You will bend over at the waist. You will pick up a coin. You will put it in the palm of my hand and tell me what it is. You'll then reach down and get another coin, put it in my hand and identify it, and keep doing that until I tell you to stop." I was still in the reserves and in very good shape. More important, by then I was stone cold sober. I reached down and grabbed a coin—"nickel." I picked up another coin—"quarter" and then another—"penny." After I'd quickly picked up and handed him about eight coins, he stopped me. He told me that I was sober, but had still been speeding. They couldn't let me drive home. I called Susie and asked her to come get me. I was so embarrassed. I tried to explain the situation to her, but she didn't want to hear it. My credibility was in tatters.

ON THE WAGON

I firmly believe that God sometimes has a good laugh when we fail to heed his first warnings. In our church, we call it "a God thing." I believe it was a "God thing" that I got stopped when I was speeding through Mundelein. Message sent, message finally received. I got it through my head I needed to quit drinking for a while. The next day I told Susie that I was going on the wagon for six months. I would not have any alcohol at all during that period. I told her that I'd be more responsible, too. If I said I'd be home at a certain time, I'd make sure to be home at that time or earlier. I made that promise to her. She was skeptical. She said, "We'll see."

I kept my word. I quit drinking for six months, and Susie got a good husband back, though it took her a while to trust me. When I said I would be somewhere, I was; when I said I'd do something, I did it. Susie came to count on me again. We were back to being a team. I felt good about myself.

During my six months of alcohol abstinence, I learned something about drinking buddies. It turns out that they are just that—people whose friendships revolve around drinking—and if you or someone else in the group stops drinking, the personal dynamics in the group are altered. When I was on the wagon, I still met my drinking buddies in bars. We still ended up in a bar after a meeting. They ribbed me about my sobriety and tried to persuade me to have a drink or two. But after a few weeks, their jokes stopped being good-natured. Some of them got irritated or offended when I refused to drink, as if I wasn't "one of them" anymore.

I stood my ground. During this period, I went to a family wedding. Everyone was drinking and getting "happy" except me. I was drinking club soda with a twist of lime. I was having just as much fun as everyone but I wasn't drinking. One of my uncles came up and berated me. I made it very clear to him that I chose what I put in my body, nobody else. I'm a very stubborn person—and if someone tells me I must do something, like drink, I dig in my heels all the more.

When I came off the wagon, I adopted a strict alcohol limit. I would have no more than three beers or two mixed drinks, and would not drink anything for at least an hour before leaving a bar or restaurant. I developed a habit of having a regular beer followed by a nonalcoholic beer, or I'd have a vodka tonic and then just a tonic and lime. If people didn't see what I was drinking, they left me alone.

One day a friend caught me having a nonalcoholic beer at a Veterans Day celebration. I told him that my new philosophy was to avoid getting drunk off my ass; instead, I aimed to maintain "cruising altitude." Surprisingly, he seemed to understand.

Susie was very happy with the new me. She started college in preparation for nursing school. Meanwhile, I was getting a good reputation as a veterans advocate during the two years I was with VVLP. I gave numerous speeches and talks around Chicago and the state.

 I learned something about drinking buddies. It turns out they are just that.

My son Eric, who was twelve and thirteen at that time, attended a lot of events with me. We went to President Reagan's second inauguration in 1985 and to a Medal of Honor convention, among many other trips. He became my travel buddy—and we became close, much like my dad and I had bonded in my early teen years doing home and car repairs together. Eric and I became great friends.

When Eric got busier with high school and college, I started taking trips with Carolyn. Then, as Brian came of age, he and I traveled to various veterans engagements. As with Eric, I only took them when there was no school. Those were good family times. I enjoyed taking the kids with me on trips. They kept me positive and happy, and I believe the events gave them an education they would not have gotten otherwise. It also gave us a chance to really bond with each other. Those times alone with Eric, Carolyn, and Brian involved a lot of deep discussions. It was a very special time.

VVLP DINNERS AND A PATH TO ADVOCACY

I may have had a drinking problem and PTSD issues, and I may have been on the wagon, but I still had a job to do. One thing my dad had taught me throughout my life was that men work. Shortly after my becoming executive director of VVLP, we added five members to the board: Neal Meehan, CEO of Midway Airlines; John Morrissey, who worked for the Chicago & Northwestern Railroad; Ronald R. Robinson, executive director of a golf club and condo association; and Keith Houston and Steve Denton, both from Springfield, Illinois. We also changed the name of the program from the Chicago VVLP to the Illinois VVLP.

I was starting to develop a positive reputation for my veterans work. Gene Connell, the program's lawyer, was talking with the Illinois attorney general's office about forming a veterans advocacy division. In early 1985 things started happening that would again change my life and direction.

Attorney General Neil Hartigan hired his friend Col. Dick Thomas (Ret.) to assess the idea of a veterans advocacy bureau within his office. Col. Thomas had realized that Illinois veterans were not being adequately served. In statistics provided by the VA he found Illinois, with the nation's seventh largest veteran population, ranked dead last in receipt of VA benefits for compensation. Something was wrong. The state wasn't doing its job advocating for veterans. Further, it was found that many state benefits for veterans were not adequate.

PARTNERSHIP WITH THE ATTORNEY GENERAL'S OFFICE

After several months of investigating these issues, Hartigan decided to give the project the green light. He formed the Veterans Rights Bureau and hired me to be its first chief. I was honored. The Veterans Rights Bureau was the only agency of its kind operating under a state attorney general's office. It was a thrill to work there, and I was breaking new ground in veterans affairs. An assistant attorney general was assigned to the division part time, and Col. Thomas was hired as the bureau's deputy chief. Dick was a World War II and Korean War veteran who had earned the Distinguished Flying Cross in Korea. I hired a secretary, and that was our team.

I would lead the Veterans Rights Bureau for the next 20 years, serving under four attorneys general—Democrat Neil Hartigan (1983-1991), Democrat Roland Burris (1991-1995), Republican Jim Ryan (1995-2003), and Democrat Lisa Madigan (2003-present). I found each one to be very pro-veteran, and each made sure Illinois veterans were treated properly. Neil Hartigan, who had the foresight to create the bureau, will always have a fond place in my memory.

For a couple of years after becoming the chief of the Veterans Rights Bureau, I remained involved with the VVLP. In 1986, Chicago held the Vietnam veterans welcome home parade. It was attended by more than 100,000 veterans. The leadership program had its dinner the same weekend and our special guest was Gen. William Westmoreland. The general was so gracious he even did an interview with the local CBS television affiliate. He gave a great speech and interacted with the medal recipients and other Vietnam veterans attending the dinner. Gen. Westmoreland and members of the VVLP board of directors led the welcome home parade.

The weekend was a success but the capstone for me came Sunday, when Eric and I took the general to the airport. I related how the last time I saw him it was on LZ Laramie in the An Lao Valley in December 1967. We talked like two Vietnam veterans sharing war stories. He told me the 1st Cavalry Division was the best unit in Vietnam. (He was probably "blowing smoke up my skirt.") We also talked about the M16, its positives and negatives. As we were riding and talking, it hit me: "I am talking to General freaking Westmoreland just like I'd talk to anyone!" Eric was suitably impressed with his dad.

At the attorney general's office, I was happy to work at the state level to change things for veterans, and being chief of the bureau gave me the ability to tackle important issues. We started Veterans Senior Advocacy and Awareness Malls (VETSAAM). We invited

 ## "I am talking to General freaking Westmoreland just like I'd talk to anyone!"

federal, state, and county agencies to attend the "malls" to inform veterans and seniors about their rights. For many veterans, this was the first time a state agency did such things. We held VETSAAMs around the state for over fifteen years.

We worked to assist county Veterans Assistance Commissions (VAC). VACs supplied aid to indigent war veterans who served honorably and their dependents. They also assisted with obtaining federal VA benefits. At that time, some VACs were having trouble forming. They ran into local politicians who, contrary to Illinois state law, opposed the VAC because they couldn't control it. The assistant attorney general and I often mediated those struggles.

I'm very proud to have assisted in a small way with the passage of the Veterans Judicial Review Act of 1988. Then Attorney General Hartigan and I both testified before the House Veterans Affairs Committee on behalf of the bill, which passed into law in November. The law established the U.S. Court of Appeals for Veterans Claims.

In 2005, just before I retired from the attorney general's office, I testified in Chicago before then Senator Barack Obama, who served on the Senate Veterans Affairs Committee. I testified on the problems with approval of claims by the Chicago VA regional office.

During my tenure as chief of the bureau, Col. Thomas and I wrote and revised *The Legal Rights of Illinois Veterans*. Unlike the federal pamphlets and booklets, *The Legal Rights of Illinois Veterans* was written from an advocacy point of view. It explained both state and federal benefits and advice on how to obtain them. Col. Thomas wrote the original *Legal Rights* book in 1985. I also wrote pamphlets on several topical issues, including the Soldiers' and Sailors' Civil Relief Act and the formation and function of Veterans Assistance Commissions. I also worked with the Illinois Association of Veterans Assistance Commissions in amending the law that governs them.

Dick Thomas and I created a monthly cable-television program called *The Veteran's Advocate*. It ran from 1989 through 1992, and ended when Dick retired. I believe it served a significant public service. The show brought attention to veterans organizations, including the Montford Point Marine Association (named for the first African American marines, who trained at Camp Montford Point, in North Carolina[3]); the Tuskegee Airmen (the first African American fighter pilots); and the Mexican American Veterans Association.

I interviewed the first African American to sail around the world by way of the five great capes. I interviewed survivors of the USS *Indianapolis*, the ship that delivered parts for Little Boy, the first atomic bomb in history. The sinking of the *Indianapolis* in July 1945 was the largest single loss of life in U.S. Navy history. I interviewed survivors of the Bataan Death March and the ex-POWs who'd taken part in the "Great Escape" from a German prison camp during World War II. I loved doing the program. It brought to light so much overlooked veterans history. It also allowed us to publicize issues of importance to veterans.

MY TRUE CALLING

My most important accomplishment came in 1991 when the AG's office allowed me to become a Vietnam Veterans of America service officer and represent veterans who had been denied their benefits before the Board of Veterans Appeals. As soon as I received my certification, I immediately started assisting veterans who were in appeal. Because I worked in the attorney general's office, I wanted to ensure that I represented my veterans with a high degree of professionalism. To that end, I had an assistant attorney general review my appellate briefs until she determined I was expert enough to write them without assistance. From 1991 until I retired in 2005, I won millions of dollars for veterans. I'm most proud that I didn't cherry pick my cases and take only the easy ones. I thrived on the hardest cases; the more difficult it was, the more I liked it. I especially liked cases that other organizations had failed to win.

My first case was that of a Vietnam veteran who had been denied 100 percent service connection for his PTSD. He had been represented by several veterans organizations but none were able to assist him. I was his last resort. The VA had refused his claim over and over again on the grounds that he was an abused child and therefore half of his PTSD was related to childhood abuse. I thought his many 4-H Club awards and other accolades proved that he was a well-adjusted young man when he went into the army.

I presented his case before the Traveling Board of Veterans Appeals. I showed the hearing officer every award the veteran had won in high school for athletic and academic achievements. I showed his senior yearbook, which had very positive comments. Then I placed each 4-H award before the officer and asked, "Does an abused child win awards for public speaking? Raising animals? Do these awards show a kid with problems or a well-adjusted child?" We won. About three months later, his PTSD was determined to be 100 percent connected to military service and he received over $150,000 in back pay. I had many such successful cases.

I was the one Illinois veterans came to when they had an appeal that seemingly couldn't be won. I lost very few cases. I was very proud of the fact that when we went to appeal, I could write a brief that properly cited case law. My success didn't make me many friends with VA rating specialists or with other service officers. Some were not happy that I would cite case law, and others thought I was invading their turf. But frankly I didn't care what they thought of me. I was focused on helping veterans, and I was having too much fun. I would joke with my clients that it wasn't about their cases, it was all about me winning. "I love winning and I hate losing," I told them. Of course, it was all about their cases. But they got my sense of humor and my determination. I was not just someone who filled out forms; I really was their advocate.

THE DRAGON BARES HIS TEETH

In the 1980s and early '90s, after I left VVLP and went to work for the Illinois attorney general, I was very busy doing advocacy casework for veterans. In preparation for an appeal I'd read medical files about veterans like me who had health and PTSD problems. I couldn't help but think about my own combat experiences in Vietnam. Occasionally, something I read triggered an intrusive thought or a vivid memory. I felt frustrated and angry then. "I thought I dealt with that crap," I would say to myself and my anger would rise. Most of the time I could deal with it by taking a walk, but sometimes that wasn't enough and I'd sink into depression.

I was careful not to drink when I was in these states. I had learned that drinking made things worse and it was just better to work through it. I was running and walking a lot, but exercise wasn't enough. I started to keep a journal. My entries were sporadic but the writing helped. It was a new outlet for my emotional pain. Still, I kept to myself. At home I was becoming reclusive. I'd come home from work and go to the basement to watch TV or read. I disconnected from Susie and the kids. Many times, when I came upstairs for bed, all the lights would be out. I'd get up in the morning and leave before Susie or the kids were up. Or, if they were up, I'd talk very little.

Susie graduated from nursing school in 1986, the year we moved to our current home in Gurnee. She worked from 7:00 a.m. to 3:30 p.m. at Victory Memorial Hospital in Waukegan. She became an oncology nurse, and a good one. She was busy with the kids and learning her job. I traveled a lot. On the outside things looked great, but on the inside I was back to being Pagliacci.

I SLAY THE DRAGON

Finally, in 1992, I filed a claim for PTSD and was given the diagnosis. I first had to go through a compensation and pension examination in which a psychologist or medical doctor examines the veteran to determine whether the diagnosis is appropriate. After the C&P interview, I realized I needed help. I'd spent twenty years helping Vietnam veterans with health and benefits issues—many with the same PTSD issues that I had—and yet had never sought the help I needed. It was crazy and foolish. My old-school stoicism, the attitude my dad's generation took toward dealing with problems, wasn't the answer. It had just prolonged my misery.

I started seeing Betsy Tolstedt, Ph.D., a psychologist and team leader at the Evanston Vet Center, about my PTSD. I saw her once a week for two years. It was the hardest personal work I've ever done.

I had to talk about Vietnam and what was going on at home, everything. She gave me assignments, such as talking to Susie about things that bothered me. Betsy helped me talk through issues with my parents. A lot of it was recounting incidents that happened in Vietnam. We tried EMDR (eye movement desensitization and reprocessing), but I couldn't do it. For me, it was talking through incidents, sometimes over and over again. But I was determined to either kill the PTSD dragon or learn how to live with it. Betsy helped me probably more than she knew. She gave me the tools to keep PTSD in check and then to defeat it when it reared its ugly head.

Betsy was helping me a lot, but I was learning something on my own. When I was focused on helping a veteran or someone else, I felt good. I thought less about my own problems. The answer to many of my PTSD symptoms was so damn simple: I was like a man drowning in knee-deep water who just has to stand up. The answer was right in front of me. But I'd continue to flounder like a drowning man for a few more years.

Over the years, I've heard PTSD sufferers refer to "my PTSD." But for me, declaring ownership of PTSD was a very bad thing. It gave me an excuse for self-destructive behavior. I concluded that the PTSD wasn't mine but an enemy who, just like the Viet Cong, was trying to destroy me. I wanted the weapons to either kill it or disable it so it could no longer control me. When I first started to suffer the symptoms of PTSD in the '70s, I didn't identify the disorder as my enemy. That realization would come after several years of suffering it and through therapy with my psychologist.

Betsy Tolstedt was my drill sergeant in my war with PTSD. Through conversation, we worked through my anger, reclusiveness, intrusive thoughts, suicidal ideation, and such. We didn't solve them, but I learned how to combat them. I learned how to be aware of my moods and how to deal with them before they got out of hand. She didn't know it, but many times she pulled me off a very negative path. One of the best things she did was to give me back my holidays. At some point, I'd told her I hadn't had a good holiday season since returning from Vietnam. I could put on a good face, but essentially found the stretch from Thanksgiving to New Year's to be depressing. She suggested I do something different.

We came up with a plan for the 1993 holiday season, one that might deal with my Vietnam demons and have a beneficial effect on my family. We decided that I should go find the grave of my old friend Gerald R. Brines. I'd always been haunted by the memory of seeing him shot right in front of me. I would travel to Shullsburg, Wisconsin, where Jerry had lived, on December 15—the anniversary of the Tam Quan battle in which I'd earned the Medal of Honor. I'd try to find Jerry's grave and record some of my experiences with a video camera. When I got home, I'd show the images to my family, giving my wife and children a real sense of what I'd been dealing with for years. They, in turn, would share with me what was important to them about the holidays.

About two days before December 15, I told Susie and the kids about the plan and asked them if they'd take part. They agreed. On the morning of the 15th, I got up at 5:00 a.m. and left for Shullsburg. It was only two hours away. I had no information about Jerry other than his hometown. I knew of no family members and had no contacts. When I got to Shullsburg, I drove around, stopping at every cemetery. I scanned headstones for Jerry's name, but had no luck. I realized that this wasn't the most efficient way to locate his grave.

After traipsing through the cemetery of a Catholic church, I asked a priest if he'd heard of Gerald Brines or knew of any veterans groups in town. He suggested that I visit a local pub, where the commander of the local Veterans of Foreign Wars post worked as a bartender. He might know something. It was about 10:30 when I got to the bar. I went in, ordered a beer, and asked the bartender if he knew Gerald Brines. He blanched. "I buried that boy," he said.

I choked up. I told him that Jerry and I were friends in Vietnam, and that I wanted to visit his grave. In a voice cracking with emotion, he told me that Jerry was buried in Warrenville, Illinois, just

 At some point, I told her I hadn't had a good holiday season since returning from Vietnam.

across the border. He told me how to get there. I put five dollars on the bar, but he told me the beer was on the house. I left.

A little more than an hour later, I was standing at Jerry's grave in Warrenville. I had brought a few things with me on the trip—a 1st Cavalry Division patch, my business card, and a note telling whoever read it that I was a friend of Jerry's. I put them on his grave with a rock to hold them down. I took out my camera, put it on a tripod, and stepped in front of it. I told Susie and the kids about Jerry and what he meant to me. I told them how he died and what happened to the guy who'd shot him—how he had got past his tragic mistake and become a better person. Then I turned off the camera and spent some time alone with Jerry. I told him about my life and family.

As I traveled home from Warrenville, I thought a lot about my life and about Jerry, Vietnam, and the events of December 15, 1967. I thought of how lucky I was to have a great family, good, smart kids, and a wonderful wife who'd stuck with me despite my anger and drinking issues and other difficulties. I wanted more than ever to be the best father and husband I could be. I still had a long way to go, but as the Chinese proverb says, "A journey of a thousand miles begins with but one step."

I got home about 5:30 p.m. I set up the camera so that the video would show on our television. I told Susie and the kids about my day and then showed them what I'd recorded. I shared with them how Jerry's life and death had affected me. Susie and the kids were touched. Next, Eric, Carolyn, and Brian did their part. Each of them told me who his or her heroes were—who they admired in life, and why, and what human qualities each valued most. Susie did the same. It was a wonderful family experience.

Finding Jerry's grave, visiting with him, was intensely cathartic. It released years of pent-up anger and stress. That night, after our talks, we had a delicious family dinner—Susie's special beef Stroganoff. That Christmas was the best ever. I haven't had a bad holiday season since that day. I've never heard a word from anyone who may have visited Jerry's grave. I go back there every so often. It's a touchstone for me, a reminder of friendship and fate, and the sacrifices soldiers make. Visiting his grave keeps me grounded and focused on living a good and honorable life. I'm trying to live the life that Jerry couldn't live.

Betsy Tolstedt also helped me deal with the events of December 15, 1967, which had been a source of pride and torment for years. I described to her my memories of the battle, what I did, and how my recollections differed from the account on my Medal of Honor citation. We talked about each part of the day, as I remembered it. In the end, it became clear that my version of the battle could never be fully reconciled with the army's version, and I finally made peace with that reality. Ever since that 1992 session with my therapist, I've described the My An battle as I remember it, however faulty my memory might be.

In retrospect, I truly believe my long personal conflict made me a better, more dedicated veterans advocate. Having received the military's highest medal, I have a duty to represent with dignity all those who serve and have served. My peers recommended me for the Medal of Honor, and I try to honor them with how I live my life and through my service to my fellow veterans.

I will always have problems with PTSD. I retired at age sixty partly because I still suffered from symptoms. But because of the tremendous help of Dr. Tolstedt, I know how to be vigilant and fight it. I've learned to use journaling and physical exercise to relieve stress (funny how pedaling a bike when you need to vent gets rid of anger and frustration). I have learned never to drink alcohol when I'm depressed or symptomatic. I control it; it doesn't control me.

I've learned one simple motto that helps get me centered when I begin to simmer: "Others, not self." I have found that as long as I put others first, I don't fall into depression or self-pity

CHAPTER 15

CAREER AND CHANGE

IT's A FACT OF LIFE: OUR PARENTS ARE INDESTRUCTIBLE UNTIL they're not. My dad was man who, for all his faults, loved life and lived it to the max. He was quick to laugh and play practical jokes and was a great sport when the jokes were on him. He loved camping and fishing with Mom, woodworking and gardening, and dearly loved reading and studying the Bible. He could be tough as nails and never backed down from anyone. He enjoyed his children and grandchildren. Then in 1993 he contracted lung cancer and spent a year dying. When he finally passed away on May 29, 1994, he was a mere shadow of himself.

My mother loved to walk in the woods, to camp and fish with Dad. She was a phenomenal cook and, above all, a loving, giving person. She found ways to help people in need. Like Dad, she studied the Bible and was an example of Christ's love. She loved being with her grandchildren and children. She thrived on visits with friends and family members. In January 1997, she had a major stroke and, eleven months later, she passed away. In her last months she could not talk or communicate. This woman who so often shared her love through cooking and chatting died silent.

Life changes when you lose your parents, and so the 1990s were years of transition for my family and me. It was traumatic and painful to see first my dad and then my mom fall ill. There was a lot of heartache, but in the process, ironically, I learned something of benefit. Thanks to two years of treatment, I had been doing a better job of dealing with my PTSD symptoms. Then, as I started focusing my attention on my parents and their needs, my symptoms practically disappeared. I didn't even realize it for months because I was so busy. In what was a bad time, I physically and mentally felt better. It would take me a few more years to learn the essential lesson: Focusing on others lessens your own problems.

EMPTY NESTERS

By 1997, Susie and I were adjusting to being without children in the house. From time to time our two youngest kids, Carolyn and Brian, would come home to live for a month or two, but they were on their own. Our job as parents wasn't over; it just changed. We went from being authority figures to mentors and advisers.

Eric, our oldest, was already carving out his own life. In June 1997, at age twenty-four, he married Mary Frances Philip. They moved into a house in Lindenhurst, just ten miles from us. Before Mary Frances' death from lung cancer in 2010, she and Eric would have three children, Katherine, Alexandra, and Patrick. Shortly after graduating from Northern Illinois University, Eric got a position with the pharmaceutical company Baxter Laboratories. The company later paid for him to go to graduate school. He got a master's of business administration degree from Northwestern University's Kellogg School of Business. Just after getting his MBA, Baxter reorganized the company. Eric moved to Abbot Laboratory, and when Abbot spun off AbbVie Inc. as an independent biotech firm, Eric joined AbbVie.

By 1998, our daughter Carolyn had earned a degree from Northern Illinois, and after working for a couple of years, she earned a master's degree in education from Trinity International University in Deerfield. She became a sixth-grade teacher and still loves it.

Brian, our youngest, took some time to find his niche. He went to Western Illinois University for a time and then dropped out. He came home and worked, then enrolled at Carroll University in Wisconsin, but dropped out of that school, too. He became a successful job recruiter and amazed his college-graduate friends by making more money than they did, proving that success starts with drive. In September 2006, Brian married Kelly O'Driscoll. In May 2008, they had a daughter, Cailinn. Brian returned to college part-time while working and completed his bachelor's degree. He is now working on a master's degree.

Susie earned a nursing degree from College of Lake County in 1986, then got her bachelor of nursing degree from St. Xavier University while working full time as an RN at Victory Memorial Hospital in Waukegan. She left Victory in 2005 to work as a nurse adviser for a health-care company. It paid more, and there was no weekend work and no lifting of patients. She retired in 2009 to help Mary Frances as she battled cancer. I'm proud of my wife for getting her degrees, for her career, and for helping Mary Frances.

THE HOME FRONT

My home life in the mid-1990s was on a good track, too. It was more stable, because I was more stable. I no longer had the time to hang out at the local bars with my Vietnam veteran friends. I'd still walk over to my buddy Don's garage on Friday nights, and drink a couple of beers with him. Don was a Vietnam veteran who serviced my cars. But beyond that I rarely ventured out. I don't know whether it was age, wisdom, or general life changes, but going to the bar had gotten old. I liked my new routine.

And it was a routine. I caught the train every weekday morning at 7:37. I got off the train in Chicago at 8:40 and walked to the State of Illinois building. I worked all day then caught the 5:07 train home. It arrived in Waukegan at 6:05 and I was in my house by 6:20.

However, I was feeling very guilty about my behavior in previous years. I'd been away from home too much, drank too much, and was irritable too often. At first I tried to shift the blame for my screw-ups. It was Susie's fault, or the children's, or PTSD—everyone and everything was responsible for my mistakes but me. But that didn't work.

In the mid-1990s Susie and I had drifted away from church. I couldn't stand the permissiveness of parents who let their children run rampant during services. Finally, I just walked out of a service and never went back. In truth, after much reflection, I left church because I was having trouble reconciling my life with God. I stopped reading and studying my Bible but I didn't lose my faith. There was always in the back of my mind the idea that God was there for me, if only I'd repent. But I was stubborn. I was at war with myself. Though I tried to rationalize and justify my crappy behavior in years past, I knew only I was to blame. I sought solace by walking alone in the woods with my camera. Photography has been a release for me, especially wildlife photography. There is something wonderful about quietly walking up on an animal and getting a picture of it in its natural environment.

One week in the spring of 2000, Susie told me she missed going to church. That Sunday, she went to Joy! Lutheran Church in Gurnee and was very impressed. She came home, told me all about it, and suggested I attend. The following Sunday, I decided to check out Joy! Lutheran by myself.

I had left the last church because there was too much mayhem during the service. The same thing happened at Joy! The service was noisy, but there were a lot of things I liked about it. The music was contemporary Christian and sung with great enthusiasm. The sermon was right out of the Bible and spoke to me. And perhaps most of all, I liked the pastor, Jeff Marion. He saw me sitting alone and introduced himself. And church members did the same—introduced themselves and asked me how I came to attend. The next weekend Susie and I attended the service together. Over the next seventeen years, we attended services at Joy! almost every Sunday. Carolyn went with us frequently, and even sang in a small group there until she moved away.

One day as I was walking in the woods, I started thinking about my drinking, my reclusiveness, and the way I treated Susie and my kids over the years. I considered all the times I was away from home when I should have been there for them. It was like a lead blanket had been dropped over me. I fell to my knees and found myself praying. I was begging forgiveness for all the wrong I had done over the years—and got it. Some people have a conversion experience and immediately change, but I knew that's not how God dealt with me. I knew my path would be long and slow, but I didn't care. I felt as if a weight had been lifted. I couldn't alter the past but I could do something about the future. I decided to amend my life going forward. To be clear, I wasn't a bad husband or father. I just wasn't the best husband and father I could be. I'm still not. I was missing the "it" factor. Whatever "it" was, I didn't have it. I always felt a great responsibility to be a husband to my wife, father to my kids. Now, I decided, I would actively show my love for them.

I didn't want to say anything to Susie or the children about my intention. I didn't want to make any tearful confession or overt demonstration of my new attitude. It didn't matter whether Susie or the kids ever knew what I was doing. I did not want to emulate my dad, who frequently talked about changing his habits and vowed to make amends, but seldom followed through. I wanted to show my love without making it about me.

RETIREMENT?

In 2000, I turned fifty-five and started to think for the first time of retirement. I knew that at age sixty, I could draw my military pension as a retired first sergeant, E-8, with twenty-one years of service. I could draw my pension from the state of Illinois. I'd also continue to receive my Medal of Honor stipend and my VA compensation. In sum, I'd have a pretty good income when I decided to retire.

I didn't want to wait too long. My dad retired at age sixty-five and at seventy-one he was gone. After working for fifty years, that was a bad deal. I kept working and continued to mull my retirement over the next two years. America's war on terrorism, which started in Afghanistan in 2001, affected me. We had soldiers dying in that country. I attended the funerals of some troops from Illinois. I was getting angry with the antiwar protesters; it seemed every week in Chicago there was some demonstration going on, especially at the start of the war. I was even angrier with the government for again getting us into a war without any idea of what victory would be or how to attain it. Around that time, I made up my mind to retire in 2005, at age sixty. I still worked diligently as a veterans advocate and still cared about their rights. But I was looking forward to the day I could just live the quiet life—go fishing, learn to play golf, and enjoy my family and grandkids.

During 2003 I started to remove all the pictures and plaques from my office. By October 2004, I had exactly one year until retirement—and twelve photos and plaques left in my office. They became my modern short timer's calendar. I removed one picture or plaque a month. By October 2005, I had one picture left that would go with me my last day of work.

Finally, the great day came. I retired on October 28. The attorney general gave me a party at the office. My colleagues came, as did Susie and Brian. The attorney general spoke about my work and how sad they were to see me go. Then the Chicago White Sox gave me a parade! They came right by my party on LaSalle Street. I'm sure it had nothing to do with their winning the World Series two days earlier! Susie and Brian drove me home to a family retirement/ birthday party. It was a great day. I was now fully retired.

'WE PLAN AND GOD LAUGHS'

Well, not quite. I kept helping veterans with their appeals as a volunteer service officer with Vietnam Veterans of America. But that was only a few hours a week. I wanted to get into shape and joined a health club in Gurnee. During the first six months of my retirement I lost 20 pounds, dropping from 255 to 235. I lost two inches on my waist and started looking good, considering. I got tired of paying the same price for a haircut as those with a lot of hair, so I shaved my head. When spring came, I started playing golf. I was thoroughly enjoying myself.

One Sunday before I retired, Pastor Marion gave a sermon about spiritual gifts. I felt moved but didn't want to get involved again in church activities. But I just couldn't get the idea of spiritual giving out of my mind. Every day for the next week, the thought kept coming to me: "You should lead a Bible study." It was like an "ear worm"—one of those songs that you can't get out of your head. Finally, I approached the pastor and told him that I needed to lead a

Bible study. So I did. I led one on Colossians. It was brief—once a week for four weeks. When it was over, I said to myself: "Good, I've done my part. I'm done."

Then the church started a discussion of the book *The Purpose Driven Life*, by Rick Warren. There was pressure within the congregation to join a Bible study or small group as they went through the book. "I'm not doing it," I told Susie. Then one night a member named Mrs. Savage called. She and her husband, Ken, had been in my Colossians study group. She told me her husband would do the study on *The Purpose Driven Life*, but only if I led it. Pressure! I told her I had no time during the week and my Saturdays were busy. But, I added, if people wanted to convene at 7:00 Saturday morning, I'd do it. "There is no way on earth anyone will get up that early on a Saturday morning," I thought. Wrong! I had a full house. I led a study of *The Purpose Driven Life*, and then followed that with a men's Bible study. The Bible study led to a ministry at the Lake County Jail. So much for not getting involved in the church!

Sometime in 2004, my old first sergeant from the 85th Division, Larry Peddle, called. I invited him to our Bible study and he started attending. Often during the winter, when it was snowing and cold, many in our study group would waver about going to the jail. But Larry, who was attached to an oxygen tank on wheels, was always eager to go. He was ready to brave the cold to minister to prisoners, so how could we stay home? At the jail, Larry would be the first to greet the prisoners and give each of them a hug. We all followed suit. I wasn't much of a hugger until then. Now I am. Larry passed away a few years ago, and his legacy lives on with me.

Retirement for me was a joy. I really was living the dream. I loved preparing for the Saturday Bible study and writing my own lessons. I loved working around the house. Susie was still working and I would send her off, clean the house, exercise, and prepare supper. By 10:00 a.m. my chores were done and I could do as I pleased. Life was quiet and simple.

But not for long. In August 2006, I got a call from Ed Tracy at the Pritzker Military Museum & Library. Frankly, it was a call I didn't expect or want. Ed informed me that Col. Pritzker wanted to bring the Medal of Honor convention to Chicago in 2009. He asked me to be involved. On the phone, I was delight itself. When I hung up, I

 She and Eric tried to push decades of family memories into the little time she had left.

turned to my wife and said in my best "Godfather" voice, "Just when I thought I was out, they pull me back in." The last thing I wanted was to be involved with a convention. But I felt duty-bound to help. Once I got involved, I must say that I enjoyed the process. As much as I had dreaded doing more organizational work, I had a good time working with others to pull the convention together. The theme was "Commit to Courage," and it was one of the best I've attended. I met many wonderful people and was proud to be a part of it.

In September 2006, my son Brian married Kelly O'Driscoll. They are a great couple, and it was a wonderful wedding. They honeymooned in Ireland. Kelly is a special woman—we'd all learn just how special very soon. Brian and Kelly both had great careers. Kelly worked at a senior citizen apartment building. She planned events and assisted with the leasing of apartments. In 2007, they bought a house in a small town just west of Milwaukee.

It was not long after Brian and Kelly got married that my other daughter-in-law, Mary Frances, was diagnosed with lung cancer.

The whole family was devastated. We couldn't understand it. She never smoked or hung out in smoke-filled bars; she didn't work in a toxic environment. She was a fine mother and wife, with no bad habits, yet she had lung cancer. It was incomprehensible.

In November 2006, she started chemotherapy. I would often watch my grandson, Patrick, who was two years old at the time. Over the next four years, Mary Frances would show us all the true definition of courage. As the cancer progressed, she and Eric tried to push decades of family memories into the little time she had left. They took their kids to Disney World several times for vacation.

In 2010, Mary Frances knew her time with us was coming to a close. Rather than focus inward, she reached out. She attended Susie and my fortieth wedding anniversary. She sent out thank-you baskets to everyone who'd helped her and Eric over the last four years. They threw a family party in May and another over the 4th of July weekend. Mary Frances spent time individually with each person who attended the July 4 gathering. The next day she went to the hospital and a week later she was gone. She set an example of how one should live and die.

Eric was now a single dad with three small children to support. He and the children struggled trying to make sense of it all. We all did. But Eric could not afford to wallow in self-pity. He stood strong and did his best to fill the roles of father and mother. He became an awesome cook. "It's my therapy," he said. On Sundays he cooked Indian, Pakistani, Italian, and other cuisines. He learned how to grill and smoke meats. He had successes and failures but he never quit doing his best. He learned from his mistakes. The children—Katherine, Alexandra, and Patrick—coped with the tragedy as well as could be expected. Each had some problems adjusting to the loss of their mom, but each has overcome the loss. Katherine, like her father, loves to bake and cook. Alexandra became skilled at soccer, sings in her high school choir, and loves competing in beauty pageants. Patrick is in Boy Scouts and becoming quite the young man.

Susie and I provided support to Eric by watching the children when he traveled on business. We cleaned his home frequently in the first three years. And we grew very close to each grandchild.

In 2014, Eric found a new love, Heidi Litizia, and they got married in 2016. Heidi and her daughter, Delany, are now a part of our family, and we are a part of theirs. She has become a mom to Patrick, Alexandra, and Katherine. She's had a wonderful impact on their lives: Heidi loves them and they know it. Delany now has new sisters, a new brother, and a new dad. We all love her and she knows it.

AMID SORROW, JOY

Amid the trauma of Mary Frances' cancer, a bright spot appeared. In late 2007, Brian and Kelly announced they were pregnant. The whole family was ecstatic. Cailinn was born May 8, 2008. We got the call from Brian early in the morning. We drove to the hospital in Milwaukee, where Brian met us on the ground floor. We were so excited we didn't really "see" him. As soon as we were in the elevator, he became emotional and said, "There is something wrong with her." Tears streamed down his face. He regained his composure and told us that Cailinn was in the newborn intensive care unit.

We soon learned that Cailinn was born with a "translocated gene" and had two large holes in her heart. Only eight children were known to have survived the condition until birth. One died within eight days; several died within the first few years; and one made it to age thirteen. All were severely disabled. We were devastated. The doctors told Brian and Kelly that Cailinn's chances of survival were very slim, that she probably wouldn't make it out of the hospital, and they should just let her go. Brian and Kelly told the doctors Cailinn would write her own book.

Cailinn went through several surgeries in her first year of life. The first, when she was six months old, was to close the holes in her heart. It was successful. She was next given a tracheotomy, so she could breathe better. She had a tough time swallowing, so two tubes were put in, a J-tube for drainage and a G-tube for feeding. She was in and out of the hospital for three or four years. She'd get sick, develop digestive issues, or some other problem and be readmitted.

All the while Kelly was learning to be a special-needs parent and Cailinn's advocate. It wasn't long before Kelly was advising other special-needs parents on how to care for their children and how to deal with a sprawling health-care and social-services network to get every available benefit and service—equipment, therapy, nursing, and more. Soon the hospital was calling on Kelly to make presentations to doctors and nurses. She has a unique ability to explain the myriad issues faced by special-needs parents. Kelly, Brian, and Cailinn even were asked to go to Washington, D.C., to lobby Congress on behalf of special-needs children. They went, and Cailinn was a hit with Wisconsin's congressional delegation.

Susie and I spent a lot of time at Brian and Kelly's house, caring for Cailinn so her parents could work. At first, it was just feeding, diaper changing, and holding her. Then during 2009 she started to get therapy. The machine feeding was ended and we fed her by G-tube. When it was time to feed Cailinn, we'd lay her down and insert the tube into the port in her stomach and slowly poor the liquid food into a cylinder attached to the tube. She loved to kick and so the one who wasn't feeding had to make sure she didn't whack the feeding tube. She was progressing, but we just didn't know how far this miracle child would go.

Susie and I also looked after the family dog, Brophy. He was good company. Dogs are such friends when you are feeling down.

One moment with Cailinn really stands out. We were at a party hosted by Mary Frances and Eric. The guests were getting ready to leave, when Cailinn stood up. She was two years old at the time, and had just started standing, but hadn't yet walked. I motioned for her to come to me. "Cailinn, walk to Grandpa," I said. And it happened: She took four or five good steps to reach me, and then gave me a hug. Kelly's mouth dropped. Then she got on the floor and made the same request: "Cailinn, walk to Mommy." I hoped that she would. I didn't want her walking to me and not to her mother, but thank God, Cailinn took four steps to Mom. Everyone broke out in smiles.

About six months later, the first Christmas after Mary Frances passed away, the family was gathered for a party. At one point, something made Cailinn unhappy and she started to cry. I motioned for Kelly, who was holding Cailinn, to give her to me. "Do you want to go to Grandpa?" Kelly asked. Cailinn, clear as a bell, said "Grandpa." All the guests stopped talking and looked at Cailinn. She had been uttering a lot of baby sounds, but until then had not said a real word. I said, "Cailinn, say 'Grandpa' one more time." And she said, "Grandpa." I took her and held her very close. I have to say I was pleased to get her first steps and her first word. Color me one proud grandpa.

Cailinn is now nine years old. She doesn't talk much but she has learned sign language, goes to school, and she can run. She and Brophy are often partners in crime. She loves to play with Brophy and Brophy just loves her. She likes to play jokes, especially on her dad. Over the last several years Kelly has gone on vacation to Florida to visit one of her girlfriends. While she's gone Brian takes care of Cailinn. After work he picks her up from school and takes her home. On one particular day Brian had a real rough day at work. He told me, "Dad, all I wanted to do was to eat my pretzels and drink a beer before making dinner. Cailinn was on the floor watching her iPad. She got up and came over and motioned that she wanted some of my pretzels. So I gave her a pretzel, which she immediately gave to Brophy. I told her not to do that. She made a face and got back down and started watching her iPad. A few seconds later she got up and

 Brian and Kelly could have allowed Cailinn to pass away. Or they could have put her in a home.

signed that she wanted some milk. As I was getting her special milk ready, I heard a commotion in the living room. Seems that I had been tricked. As I was preparing her milk she was giving Brophy all my pretzels. When I looked out into the living room, I saw Cailinn standing with my pretzel bag in her hands and Brophy's head very deep inside the bag happily munching away. So much for my beer and pretzels. Dad, I didn't know whether to be unhappy that my pretzels were gone or be very proud that she had tricked me."

Cailinn attends school just like any other kid, and her classmates love her. She is writing her own story. Cailinn has shown us that God has a plan for every child. She has been such a blessing, and everyone who comes into contact with Cailinn comes away changed. She brings such joy.

Brian and Kelly could have allowed Cailinn to pass away. Or they could have put her in a home. But they decided they would be her mommy and daddy. Kelly now works as a volunteer at Children's Hospital in Milwaukee. She is a peer to other new parents with special-needs children. In addition, she has started her own business, Cailinn's Creations. She makes and sells weighted blankets for autistic children, children with attention-deficit disorder, and for those suffering from post-traumatic stress syndrome. I bought one and love it. It helps me sleep when the dragon is active.

Brian dotes on Cailinn. He's six two and athletic—he was a bouncer at one time—but he's as gentle as a lamb when it comes to his daughter. He's been known to do handstands just to get Cailinn to eat. When he wants Cailinn to continue doing something, he says: "What do Lynches do? One more." And Cailinn will always do one more. Brian is still working as a business recruiter and, in his spare time, plays the Irish sport of hurling. He was a team captain for several years. He is a man of faith and was president of his church council for several years.

In 2009, Susie had her own health issue. She had such pain in her back that she could hardly walk. She'd had back problems most of her adult life, but now she needed surgery. The operation was set for the first week of July. We were told it would be a simple procedure, and that she'd be able to return to work within a week. The surgery was successful but the recovery was hell. Within two weeks of being sent home her incision opened, and blood and puss oozed out. We rushed her to the doctor, who told us that the problem was not uncommon. His nurse taught me how to clean and pack the wound.

I had learned a lot about wound care with Cailinn, so I was prepared for my new job. Before Cailinn could leave the hospital, all of her caregivers (or potential caregivers) had to learn how to clean a tracheotomy tube, stoma care, how to change the J/G-tubes, and a whole lot more. So I knew I could take care of Susie—and that's what I did for two and a half months. I did everything for her. It wasn't fun but it was gratifying. Carolyn, Eric, and Brian helped, too, but they had their families. In many ways it was a wonderful experience for me. It was an opportunity to show her how much I loved her. By mid-September, when the Medal of Honor convention was imminent, Susie was able to walk without assistance for the first time since July.

That year after the convention, I started getting more and more speaking engagements. My quiet life was over, and though I miss it sometimes, I'm thankful for all the opportunities I have to share my faith and life experiences, and to motivate young people.

LEGACY

In 2008, I started going to Rockford, Illinois, to serve veterans who needed assistance with their claims. There I met two outstanding veterans advocates, Mark Lawrence and Jeff Metheny. They worked tirelessly on behalf of veterans. Jeff would become one of the best service officers I've known in forty-five years of veterans work. It was Mark, however, who defined for me why service to others is so rewarding. "It is more fun to hang out with givers than takers," he said to me one day and I agree. Hanging out with people like Mark and Jeff make a life in service so damn much fun.

In 2012, John Schwan, a successful businessman and friend of mine, suggested we do something for veterans who needed help getting over bumps in the road of life. John had been a first lieutenant with the 1st Cavalry in Vietnam. He and I had been raised in lower-middle income families, and, thankfully, were now in a position to give back. John and I talked about how we could best assist veterans. We decided to form a foundation, the Allen J. Lynch, Medal of Honor, Veterans Assistance Foundation. We got it up and running in October 2012. We decided that every member of the board of directors must be a veteran or have a direct connection to a service member. Bruce Peterson, a retired lieutenant colonel who'd served as a helicopter pilot with the 1st Cavalry in Vietnam, was elected vice president. He would handle all the claims casework for the first two years, and do so much more. John was made secretary and would assist with fundraising. Paul Brian, a Vietnam-era veteran turned Chicago radio personality, agreed to help with fundraising. I served as president.

We assisted our first veteran in December 2012, and have helped hundreds more in the past five years. We offer a hand up, not a handout. Our motto is: "We are veterans helping veterans help themselves." In 2014, we became part of Operation Support our Troops–America. Through the Allen Lynch MOH Veterans Assistance Program, we provide financial assistance to veterans and their immediate family members. We also help veterans seeking employment through the Veterans Employment Exchange, a part of the Lynch program. Our parent organization, Operation Support Our Troops–America, provides care packages to those who are deployed and conducts "Leap of Faith" seminars for Gold Star family members.

In 2013, I got very sick and ended up in the hospital. I had an infection in my left foot that required surgery. I ended up on intravenous antibiotics for a month. I couldn't get around much. Susie became my caregiver, and she was amazing. She did everything for me and got me healthy just in time to participate in the foundation's first major fundraising event, a sporting clay shoot. Every year, on the first Friday in June, we host the Allen J. Lynch, Medal of Honor, Sporting Clay event. Then in late August, we host a golf-outing fundraiser named Swinging for the Vets. Both events help us continue to serve veterans in need of a helping hand. It is my hope and expectation that the foundation will go on for many years. I can't imagine having a better legacy.

EPILOGUE

WASN'T BORN TO A LIFE OF PRIVILEGE. I WAS AN AVERAGE, WORK-
ing-class, Midwestern guy. As many people do, I went through some
tough times. I could have let my difficulties drag me down—and at
times they almost did. But I pushed through the emotional pains
and other challenges, and looked for avenues that might help me
overcome the pains and meet the challenges.

Who could have anticipated that service in the army and fighting in Vietnam would be my road to a better life?

I was so adrift that I took a risk and actually volunteered to go
and fight in Vietnam. There, I followed orders and did all I could
to survive and defeat the enemy, and made sure to assist my fellow
1st Cavalry troopers in any way possible. They became my brothers.
That I came out of the war with the Medal of Honor was happen-
stance, as I see it. One day, I went to the aid of wounded soldiers in
a firefight. I believe that any man in my company would have done
the same—and indeed lots of men in my company risked their lives
to rescue me and the two wounded troopers with me that day. My
platoon leader was killed and our company commander seriously
wounded trying to save us. That's a thought guaranteed to keep a
guy humble—and grateful.

Getting ahead in life is not easy. It's just the opposite. I have learned that you have to do a lot of things that are unpleasant in the vague hope that life will be better in the future. You put in your time, pay your dues, explore alternatives, and try to make wise decisions.

Anyone who's been in the army knows how hellish it can be. That's the point. That's the whole idea of basic training—you get up early, you get yelled at all day, you are challenged physically and psychologically, you wash dishes and clean latrines, and go to bed exhausted before resuming the grind at dawn the next morning. You do it because you have to, because you've chosen to, and through the process you acquire mettle—that's a word I like. The work improves your mental toughness and your character—and people with mettle tend to achieve their goals. It has worked for me.

Even earlier in my life, I didn't like going out in the cold to help my dad clean out clogged sewer lines at our house in Indiana, or adding coal to an apartment furnace in Chicago before school, or spending more than an hour getting to a school in another town. I didn't have a choice. That was my life. Nobody said I had to like it; I just had to do it. That's what real men and women do—they face life directly with all its trials and tribulations. And then they pass that trait on to their children. My dad worked hard and was self-sufficient, he taught me to be the same, and I tried to teach my children to be the same. Life, to a large degree, is about making sacrifices: You make them to improve yourself, and then you make more to help your kids get a leg up. Parents make decisions that their children don't always like—mine certainly didn't—hoping that they'll learn lessons and values and grow up to be kind, wise, successful adults.

My wife, Susie, is a special person who has stuck by me through my darkest times. She has never given up on me. Together we've raised three wonderful children, Eric, Carolyn, and Brian, who have made us very proud. Each of them has had to face his or her own crisis, and each has pushed through it with dignity, courage, and honor.

Getting ahead usually involves being bold and never accepting that you've reached your personal potential. In my career as an advocate for veterans, I accepted new responsibilities when they were offered, even though I wasn't certain I could handle them. When I was a veterans assistance counselor and assigned to Icarus II, a drug treatment unit at the VA hospital, I realized I needed more education. I was not a good student in my youth, but as an adult, I recognized that I needed to learn more, took college classes part-time, and finally earned my degree. That was a proud moment.

When I was serving in the army reserve, I thought about becoming a drill sergeant. The idea appealed to me, but I didn't know if I had the personality and skills to do it. I was nervous about it but gave it a go, went to drill sergeant school, and finished at the top of my class, earning the Distinguished Military Graduate award. A lot of ideas or ambitions like that one don't pan out. But, as we've all heard, you won't know until you've tried.

When I was first asked to speak to school groups and to other organizations about earning the Medal of Honor, I wasn't sure I wanted to do it. I felt a lot of trepidation about speaking in public. But I felt a responsibility to represent the military and veterans, and so I started giving talks and telling my story. I wasn't very polished to start, but got better with practice. You can't shy away from challenges and expect to have a fulfilling life. It took me years to stand up to the guys who were bullying me. I was weak. I was afraid. I withdrew from social contact, until eventually, I screwed up enough courage to start defending myself.

Everybody fails at one thing or another—or at multiple things. My personal failings, and failures, are numerous. But I believe that getting to success often means passing through failure first. As my favorite coach, Mike Ditka of Chicago Bears fame, once said: "Success isn't permanent and failure isn't fatal."[1] I've experienced both.

There is a tradition in the military of giving out "challenge coins"— medallions or coins that have the insignia of a unit on one side and some personal message on the other. Officers sometimes give challenge coins to soldiers to acknowledge an action well done. They are an informal gesture to promote camaraderie and enhance morale. Other groups have challenge coins as well. One year after I gave a talk at a Rotary Club, one of the club members gave me a challenge coin. On one side was written the Rotary's Four-Way Test for personal integrity and ethical behavior. It read:

Is it the Truth? Is it Fair to All concerned? Will it Build Goodwill and Better Friendships? Will it be Beneficial to all Concerned?

I memorized the four tests and carried that coin with me for years. Most Medal of Honor recipients have their own challenge coins, which we give out to individuals as a symbol of friendship or appreciation for something special they've done. When I created mine, I put my name, date and location of MOH action, and military branch on one side, along with my personal motto: "Others, not self." On the reverse, because it means so much to me, I put the Rotary Four-Way Test.

I am a spiritual man, and I've learned that there is a God who loves me in spite of myself. A Savior who sees me as I am and loves me anyway. I've learned that he is constantly seeking me. My most important life lesson came from the first line in Pastor Rick Warren's book *The Purpose Driven Life*: "It's not about you." In our "me first" culture, that is a counterintuitive thought. It is so simple, yet can be difficult to grasp or to apply to our own lives. We passed that idea along to inmates at our men's ministry at the Lake County Jail. When one of the inmates heard that line, his response was: "What do you mean, it's not about me? I thought it was, until making it all about me ruined my life and put me in prison."

I believe selfishness is the cause of many social problems. It certainly has been at the root of most of the problems in my life. I often acted selfishly rather than selflessly. I've learned, as my friend Mark Lawrence says, "Hanging out with givers is a hell of a lot more fun than hanging out with takers." Had I been aware of that idea early on, during my selfish period, and taken it to heart during my struggles with PTSD and drinking, I would have saved my family and me a lot of heartache.

"Others, not self" has become my core value—selflessness rather than selfishness—and that has made me a happier person. I don't always live by my own motto even now; I still have my "I"-centered moments. But I try hard to avoid them and return to the idea of being of service to others, to my family, my friends, and fellow veterans. When I fail, I try again. I am happiest when I am serving others and not myself.

Writing this autobiography has been one of the toughest things I've done. It brought back a lot of memories. I had to look at these memories from two perspectives: that of a child and that of an adult. Through my child's eyes many challenges I faced growing up seemed insurmountable. But from an adult perspective they didn't seem so great. It's like when as an adult I went back to visit Lake Eliza. I remembered the lake being really big, but when I viewed it as an adult it was really small. The lake had not changed; it was simply a matter of perspective. That's the way my problems were growing up. When I was going through them they seemed enormous but now, looking back through more experienced eyes, the problems of my youth seem very small.

Writing this book I wanted to visit the child of my youth, to tell him that after all his struggles he was going to have an amazing life: that this chapter of his life would end when he graduated from high school and went into the army; that all the hardships, all the things the bullies put him through would make him tougher and more resilient; that in his later years he would have wonderful friends who would be closer than family.

I also wanted to visit my adult self as he struggled with post-traumatic stress disorder. I wanted to tell him that he would eventually beat PTSD and though it would always be with him he would always win the battles. I wanted to shake him to his senses when he was drinking too much and explain that he was better than that. I wanted to slap him on the back of the head to remind him that he had a strong and steadfast wife who would always be there. I wanted to tell him that he should be grateful that the later years of his life would be the best years of his life.

To my readers. You do not know what the next chapter of your life will bring. No matter how far down you may feel today every valley is surrounded by mountains whose peaks hold new and wonderful experiences. Throughout the toughest times in my life, I have held onto this one Scripture verse, "I can do all things through Christ who strengthens me." Philippians 4:13.

ENDNOTES

Chapter 11: Moment of Truth at Tam Quan

1   Combat After Action Report—Battle of Tam Quan, 30 Dec 1967, page 3

2   Ibid., page 23, sketch map

3   In the 1st Cavalry Division, companies are often referred to as troops, A Troop meaning A Company in army lingo.

4   Combat After Action Report—Battle of Tam Quan, 30 Dec 1967

5   *Spooky* was an AC-130 gunship armed with two 20mm M61 Vulcan cannons, one Bofors 40mm cannon, and a 105 Howitzer. https://en.wikipedia.org/wiki/Lockheed_AC-130

6   Combat After Action Report—Battle of Tam Quan, 30 Dec 1967, page 4

7   TOT barrage means all munitions arrive on the target at the same time.

8   Air rocket artillery were Huey gunships armed with two 2.75" Folding Fin Aerial Rocket pods holding 24 rockets each and two M60 machine guns.

9   Combat After Action Report—Battle of Tam Quan, 30 Dec 1967, page 4

10 Ibid., page 5

11 http://www.rjsmith.com/glossary.html#Z

12 Rigo Ordaz's comments on the Battle of Tam Quan, http://www.ichiban1.org/html/news_pages/news_36.htm

13 Combat After Action Report—Battle of Tam Quan, 30 Dec 1967, page 5

14 Rigo Ordaz's comments on the Battle of Tam Quan, http://www.ichiban1.org/html/news_pages/news_36.htm

15 Daily Staff Journal or Duty Officer's Log, 9 Dec 1967

16 This is in some conflict with the AARs for the same date.

17 Daily Staff Journal or Duty Officer's Log, 10 Dec 67

18 Combat After Action Report—Battle of Tam Quan, 30 Dec 1967, page 6

19 Ibid., page 7

20 Donald Orsini Journal, page 40

21 Ibid.

22 Ibid., page 41

23 Ibid.

24 Daily Staff Journal, 15 Dec 67

25   Orsini Journal, page 41

26   Ibid.

27   Ibid.

28   Ibid., pages 45-53

29   Ibid. See also Morning Report, 15 Dec 1967

30   Orsini Journal

31   Ibid., page 49

32   Ibid.

33   Ibid., page 52

34   Ibid., page 53

35   Ibid.

36   Combat After Action Report—Battle of TAM QUAN, 30 Dec 67, page 10

37   Ibid., page 13

38   Daily Staff Journal, 15 Dec 1967

39   Ibid.

40   Lt. Gen. John J. Tolson, *Vietnam Studies: Airmobility 1961-1971* (Washington, DC: Department of the Army, 1973), pages 150-51

Chapter 13: My Family and My PTSD

1   https://www.biblegateway.com/blog/2016/09/evangelism-the-romans-road-to-salvation/

2   Psalm 51 is the best I've found.

3   Romans 8:15

4   https://en.wikipedia.org/wiki/Flashback_(psychology)

5   http://www.dictionary.com/browse/anxiety-reaction

6   https://www.findagrave.com/cgi-bin/fg.cgi?page=cr&CRid=1990395

Chapter 14: Path to Recovery

1   https://en.wikipedia.org/wiki/Tom_Pauken

2   https://www.drugs.com/antabuse.html

3   https://en.wikipedia.org/wiki/Montford_Point_Marine_Association

Epilogue

1   https://www.brainyquote.com/quotes/quotes/m/mikeditka357619.html

ACKNOWLEDGMENTS

I want to start by thanking Col. Jennifer Pritzker, founder of the Pritzker Military Museum & Library. She is the prime reason that this book has been printed. She is a staunch supporter of veterans and our history. And the Museum & Library and its staff are a tremendous resource for those who wish to study military history and affairs. The Museum & Library is also the publisher of this book, and I want to thank everyone there who helped make this book possible.

Special thanks to Ken Clarke, former President and CEO of the Museum & Library, and executive editor of the book, for his constant motivation and for "talking me off the ledge" when I became frustrated in writing this book. He kept me focused on the reasons for completing my story.

Many thanks to John Schwan, Interim President and CEO of the Museum & Library, who for years encouraged me to tell my story. It was John who helped me understand why I needed to write this biography. He made me understand that there are many people, kids and veterans alike, who would benefit from my story. John is a major reason this book has been written.

Thanks to Richard Ernsberger, my co-author, for teaching me so many things as we struggled through producing the book. He kept me focused on times, places and locations, and the reasons for being clear and specific. He helped me understand why it was necessary to explain the hows and whys of certain things military—even as I frequently drove him crazy with my overuse of commas and double spacing.

Thanks to Michael Robbins for editing this entire work, and for putting up with and understanding my strange sense of humor. He provided great assistance and guidance in reorganizing some of the chapters to achieve a better flow.

And my deepest gratitude to She Who Must Be Obeyed, my wife, Susie, who listened to my ranting and raving as I worked through chapter after chapter. She was constantly called to my office to read what I wrote. She listened as I dictated paragraph after paragraph when my hands were sore from typing. She was patient when I screamed at the computer for not understanding the words I spoke. I thank her for her silence as I turned the air blue when frustrated. And I thank her for guiding me up the stairs to get back to work.

My thanks to all those people who did the heavy lifting for the Lynch Program, giving me the time to write: To Leon Mangum, our director, for his vision and for leading us to places we never dreamed of. To Paul Brian, our publicity guru, whose postings on Facebook and Twitter about our fundraising events helped to make them successful. To Mark Lawrence, who taught me it is more fun to hang out with givers than takers. To Jeff Metheny, for being a veterans advocate who made me very proud to have had a part in his development. To Bruce Peterson, who was there at the start of the Lynch Foundation, for all his help and hard work in getting our program off the ground. To John Schwan, who first had the idea for the Lynch Foundation and for all his hard work in fundraising— and most of all for his being closer than a brother to me. To Janna Schwan, John's daughter, for her unwavering support in our fund-raising efforts and for liking beer almost as much as I do. To John DeRue and his wife, Gennie, for chairing the golf outing committee from its beginning, and to Allan Ayres and Mike Peck for doing so much of the work to make our golf outings a success year after year.

Finally, my heartfelt thanks to all the friends and family who encouraged me and would not let me give up completing this work. If I've missed anyone I will fall back on the excuse that I think I've earned and used and abused, "I'm old." And by the way this excuse can only be used if you're over 65.

PRITZKER MILITARY MUSEUM & LIBRARY STAFF
Martin Billheimer, Library Clerk
Olivia Button, Digital Collections Coordinator
Kenneth Clarke, Transition Consultant,
    Immediate Past President & CEO
Leah Cohen, Oral History & Reference Manager
Mary Dickey, Customer Service & Sales Coordinator
Dustin DePue, Special Collections Librarian
Teri Embrey, Chief Librarian
Paul Grasmehr, Reference Coordinator
Brad Guidera, Production Manager
James Hansley, Customer Service & Sales Representative
John LaPine, Collection Services Manager
Kat Latham, Director of Collections Management
Nathan Magnuson, Administrative Assistant
Lee May, Development Officer
Andrea Martinez, Archivist
Tina Louise Mead, Associate Chief Librarian
Bianca Milligan, Customer Service & Sales Representative
Ana Lovado, Customer Service & Sales Representative
Angel Melendez, Production Coordinator
Chris Meter, Adjutant to President & CEO, Operations Specialist
Javier Rangel, Customer Service & Sales Representative
Antina Redmond, Director of Administration & Operations
John Schwan, Interim President & CEO
Linda Sterling, Development & Membership Coordinator
Katie Strandquist, Special Events Manager
Lindsey Sturch, Librarian
Megan Williams, Director of External Affairs

Sonya Sindberg, Corporate Project Coordinator,
    Tawani Enterprises, Inc.

INDEX

1st Cavalry Division (Airmobile), 2–3, 157–64
ambush patrols, 175–77
assignment to, 150, 157–58
Battle of Tam Quan, 225–53.
See also My An battle
casualties, 252–53
company assignments, 160–61
C-rations, 167–68
Dak To, 165, 198–201
death of Jerry, 183–89
first combat, 181–82
at LZ English, 165–67
misdirected gas attack, 191–93
Operation Dragnet, 177–80
return to platoon after rescue, 253–55
search-and-destroy missions, 3, 183–91, 193, 196–201, 254–55
searching hooches, 172–75
training school, 161–64
2nd Armored Division, 264–65
4th Infantry Division, 159, 160, 199
8th Cavalry Regiment, 225
8th Infantry Regiment, 199
9th Cavalry Regiment, 158, 225
12th Cavalry Regiment, 1, 3, 225
22nd NVA Regiment, 3–4, 225–31, 234, 237 52, 239
40th ARVN Regiment, 225, 228–30, 237, 252
48th Infantry Regiment, 132–52
50th Infantry Division, 3, 225

85th Division (Training) Drill Sergeant Academy, 294–95
85th Infantry Division, 101, 108, 288–89
173rd Airborne Brigade (Separate), 159, 160

Abbot Laboratory, 329
AbbVie Inc., 329
Advanced infantry training (AIT), 117–19
Afghanistan, 333
African American soldiers, 103, 109, 110, 146, 148, 319
Agent Orange, 96, 201
"Airborne shuffle," 106
Airmobile concept, 158
Alcoholics Anonymous (AA), 309
Algebra, 71
Ali, Muhammad, 110
Allen J. Lynch, Medal of Honor, Veterans Assistance Foundation, 343–44
Allen J. Lynch Day, 281
Altgeld Gardens, 5, 67
Ambush patrols, 171, 175–77, 196, 198
American Psychiatric Association (APA), 290
An Khe, 3, 189–90, *214*
An Lao Valley, *212*, 254
ANPRC-25, 174–75, 232–34
Antabuse, 309–10
Anti-war protests, viii, 265–66
"Anxiety reaction," 290
Apple trees, 52
Armed Forces Examining and

Entrance Station (AFEES), 96–97
Army, U.S. *See also* 1st Cavalry Division
   advanced infantry training, 117–19
   enlistment, 91–92, 94–96
   in Germany, 132–53
   Officer Candidate School, 2, 115,
      116–17, 121–27
   reenlistment, 2, 139–41
   signing up for Vietnam, 150–52
Army Air Corps, U.S., 7–8
Army of the Republic of Vietnam
   (ARVN), 225, 227, 228–30, 237, 252
Army Reserve, U.S., 288–89, 293–94,
   301–2, 347
Army Signal Corps, U.S., 116
Article 15, 148–49, 150
Article 91, 144–45
Autry, Gene, 27, 36

B-1-A meals, 168
Barracks at Fort Knox, 101
Bartlow, Vail, 9
Baseball, 57
Basic training, 2, 96–116, *208*
   chow, 105–6
   Christmas leave, 114–15
   drills begin, 100–108
   first "duty day," 97–99
   graduation day, 115–16
   grenades and bayonets, 112–14
   growing tensions, 109–11
   guard duty, 111–12
   Thanksgiving, 108–9
Basketball, 57
Bataan Death March, 319
Bathing, 109–10
Battle of Iwo Jima, 260
Battle of Tam Quan, 3, 225–53.
   See also My An battle
   aftermath of, 226, 251–52

casualties, 252–53
   Delta company joins the fight,
      229–32
   first engagement, 227–29
   "hammer and anvil" operation,
      234–35
   radiotelephone operator, 232–34
   units involved, 225–26
Baxter Laboratories, 329
Bayonets, 114
BB guns, 49
Bees, 47–48
Bell H-13 Sioux, 236
Bell UH-1 Iroquois "Huey," 3, 158,
   167, 203
Berlin, 143–47
Best, Betty, 300–301
Bible study, 13, 266–67, 284–85, 298,
   328, 334–36
Bike business, 75–76
Bikini Atoll nuclear testing, 31
Binh Dinh Province, 9, 177, 179, 193,
   226, 253
Birth of Allen, 5–6
Bleeding ulcers, 8
Board of Veterans Appeals, 320–21
Boeing CH-47 Chinook, 158, 165, 183,
   193, 229
Bogle, Eric, 305
Bolda, Chester, 69–70, 82, 151
Bolda, Thomas "Beau," 42, 300
Bolda, Tommy, 42, 300
Bong Son City, 165, 166, 182–83, 253
Bong Son Plain, 3, 179–80, 226
Boy Scouts, 65, 296, 297
"Breaking squelch," 174–75
Brewery, Barry, 253
Brian, Paul, 344
Brines, Gerald R. "Jerry," *211*
   death by friendly fire of, 183–89, 298

name on Vietnam Veterans
Memorial, 306–7
naming son in honor of, 292
search for gravesite, 324–26
Brophy (dog), 340–41
Bullying, xii, 1–2, 20, 45, 55–61,
63–66, 74
effects of, 56–61
Bum Town, 35–36
Burris, Roland, 317
Bush, Richard E., 260, 282–83, 296
Byrne, Jane, 305

C-4 (explosive), 162–63
Cadence, 106–7
Cailinn's Creations, 341–42
Camp Radcliff, 158–65, 196, 257
Cam Ranh Air Base, 156–58, 260
Captain Video and His Video Rangers
(TV show), 36
Career counselor, 268, 270
Carroll University, 330
Carter, Jimmy, 303
Casares, Javier, 4, 240–52
Catholic Church (Catholicism), 76–79,
82, 266–67, 274–75
"Cherries," 170–71
Chess, 135, 148, 149
Chicago Bears, 283, 348
Chicago & Northwestern Railroad, 316
Chicago riots, viii, 265–66
Chicago Vietnam Memorial, 305–6
Chicago Vietnam Veterans Leadership
Program, 304–6, 310–13, 316–17
Chicago White Sox, 334
Childhood of Allen. *See* Early life of
Allen
*Choosing Courage: Inspiring True
Stories of What It Means to Be a
Hero* (Collins, ed.), 72

Chores, 43–44
Christmas, 81–83, 114–15, 275, 299–
300, 309
Christopher, St., 266–67
CIDG (Civilian Irregular Defense
Group), 184–85, 186
Cinnamon rollups, 41, 262
Civil Rights Act of 1964, 85
Civil rights movement, 146
Civil War, 42
Clark Air Force Base, 155
Claymore mines, 162–63
Clerical duties, 143–44
Coal-burning furnaces, 68–69
Coal dust, 24, 25
Cockfights, 44
Coconut milk, 179–80
"Coke girl," 190–91, *214*
Cold War, 32–33, 34–35, 79–81
Coleman Kaserne, 132–41
Coll, Dennis, 304
College of Lake County, 286, 295, 330
Collette, Jim, 75–76, 91, 92, 121, 261,
263
Combat landings, 159
Combat memories, 235–36, 326–27
Comic books, 13–14, 45, 119–20
Communion, 77
Confession, 77–79
Connell, Gene, 304–5, 316
Constitution, U.S., 97
Cookies and milk, 18, 73, 262
Cordon missions, 178–79, 181–82,
191–93
Corporal punishment, 11, 18–19, 24–25,
26, 37–38, 54–55, 293
Court of Appeals for Veterans Claims,
U.S., 318–19
C-ration coffee, 176
C-ration matches, 246–47

C-rations, 168, 171, 173
"Crotch rot," 168–69
Cuban Missile Crisis, 80–81

Dai Dong, 229, 231
Dak To, 165, 198–201, *213, 215*
"Danger close," 173–74
"Delta tangos," 173–74
Denton, Steve, 316
Depression, 6, 296, 298
"Depression soup," 19
Diagnostic and Statistical Manual of Mental Disorders, 290
Dirty cadence, 107
Disciplinary reprimands, 2, 144–45, 148–49
Distinguished Flying Cross, 317
Distinguished Service Cross, 271–72, 279
Ditka, Mike, 348
Doberman pinscher, 29–30
Dolton, Illinois, 67–92, 151–52
Donuts, 24
"Double-digit midget," 258
Downey VA Hospital, 286, 289, 296–97
Drill sergeants, 100–101
Drinking
    of Allen, 311–15, 321–22
    of father, 14–15, 21, 32, 42, 276, 283–84, 285, 308–9
Duke (dog), 43, 193, *207*, 258
Dulles, Allen, 94
Dulles, John Foster, 94
Dutch Huguenots, 16
Dynamite, 118

Early life of Allen, 23–66, *204–7*
    in Dolton, 67–92
    in Homewood, 32–40

in Lake Eliza, 42–66
    in Roseland, 5–6, 23–31
East German military ranks, 134
Eddie (friend), 44–45
Education of Allen, 27–28, 34, 42, 58–59, 63, 70–75, 88–89, 286, 296, 297
Eilert, Rick, 304–5, 310
Electro-Motive Diesel, 5–6, 12, 33
Eli's Trailer Camp, 32, 33–40
EMDR (eye movement desensitization and reprocessing), 323
Enlisted Men's Club (EM Club), 135–36
Enlistment, 91–92, 94–96
Esparsa, Joe, 240–52
Evans, Dale, 36
Evanston Vet Center, 322–23

"Falling into" formation, 97–98
Ferreira, Leonard, 243–49, 253
Field training exercise (FTX), 138–39, 146
Fights (fighting), 44, 54–55, 56, 59, 65, 110
Firecrackers, 49
Fish fries, 47
Fitzgerald, Tommy, 51–52
Flores, Sgt., 253
FNG (f**king new guy), 164, 169–71
"Fog of war," 295
Foley, Paul, 75–76, 91, 92, 121, 261, 263
Ford, Rudolf H., 243–49, 253
For Self and Country (Eilert), 310
Fort Benning, 121–27
Fort Dix, 128, 129, 132
Fort Gordon, 116–20
Fort Hood, x, 263, 264–65
Fort Knox, 97–116, *208*
Fort Leonard Wood, 295
Fort McCoy, 301–2

Fort Ord, 151, 153–56, 260
Fort Sheridan, 272, 279–80
"Forward fire bases," 165, 197
Forward observer (FO), 173–74
"Foxhole strength," 229–32, 234–35, 252
Frankfurt, prostitute incident, 141–43
Frankfurt Main Airport, 141
Fred, 184–86, 188
Fred N Guy (dog), 258
French, Daniel W., 237–38, 244, 247, 253
Friendly fire, 183–86

Gail (girlfriend), 91, 114, 121, 129–30, 151, 261, 262–63, 273
Gambling, 135–36
Gas chamber, 108
Gatelys Peoples Store, 24–25
Germany, Allen stationed in, 132–53
Gettysburg Replies: The World Responds to Abraham Lincoln's Gettysburg Address, 72
G.I. party, 118
"G.I. showers," 110
Godfather, The (movie), 286
"God thing," 313–14
Goldfinger (movie), 99
Gold Star families, 344
Goldwater, Barry, 93–94, 95
Gomez, S. Sgt., 167–68, 169, 186, 188, 192, 202, 210
Goodacre, Glenna, 307
Gordon, John Brown, 116
Gorges, William E., 233, 243–46, 248, 253
Grandwood Park, 290–91
Great Depression, 10, 19, 31
Great Lakes Naval Hospital, 260, 282–83, 286

Gronholm, Mary, 20–21, 275, 278, 283, 300
Gronholm, Paul, 276, 278, 283, 300
Guarding bridges, 189
Gulf of Tonkin incident, 85, 94
Gulf of Tonkin Resolution, 94

Hale Koa Resort, 303, 304
"Hammer and anvil" operations, 234–35
Hand grenades, 112–13, 118
"Hard Core," Capt., 200–201
Hartigan, Neil, 305, 316, 317, 318
"Heat tabs," 163, 170, 171
Herby (neighbor), 26
Hill 724, 199–201
Hines Veterans Administration Hospital, 8
Ho Chi Minh Trail, 182
Hoffman Estates, 283–84
Homewood, Illinois, 32–40
Homewood Elementary School, 34–35
Honor, 10, 53, 347, 348
Honor code, 122
Hooches, 172–75
Houston, Keith, 316

Illinois Association of Veterans Assistance Commissions, 319
Illinois Vietnam Veterans Leadership Program, 316–17
Indiana Boulevard, 151–52, 277
Indianapolis, USS, 319
Ingman, Einar, 296
Ivanhoe United Methodist Church, 218, 275
Izaak Walton League, 35

Jody cadence, 107
Johnson, Lyndon, 84–85, 93–94, 95, 266

Joy! Lutheran Church, 331–32, 334–35

Kankakee State Park, 309
Kennedy, John F., 79–81, 93
    assassination of, 83–85
Kennedy, John F., Jr., 84
Khrushchev, Nikita, 81
Killeen, Texas, 267, 269
Kjos, Tom, xiii, 226–27, 236
"Klick," 169
Kon Tum City, 183–84
Kon Tum Province, 165, 182, *211*
Korean War, 32–33, 297
Kuala Lumpur, 194–96

Laird, Melvin, 280–81
Lake County Jail, 349
Lake Eliza, Indiana, 8, 42–43, 46–47
Lake Eliza Road, 42–66, 67
Lake Saint Germain, 39–40
Landing Zone Apache (LZ Apache),
    197–98
Landing Zone Becky (LZ Becky), 201–3
Landing Zone English (LZ English), 3,
    165–67, 182, 194, 229, 232, 235,
    251, 253
Landing Zone Laramie (LZ Laramie),
    254, 317
Landing Zone Tom (LZ Tom), 227, 231
Landing Zone Two Bits (LZ Two Bits),
    165, 253, 254
LaRue, Alfred "Lash," 37
Latrines, 100, 101–2
Laundry, 23–24
Lavizzo Elementary School, 27
Lawnmowing, 75–76
Lawrence, Mark, 343
"Leech checks," 187
Legal Rights of Illinois Veterans, 319
Leos, Pedro, *211*

Letizia, Delany, 338
Libby, McNeill & Libby, 90–91, 271,
    272–73, 279, 283
Lin, Maya, 306, 307
Little League baseball, 57
Loan sharking, 8
Logistical flights ("logs"), 167
Lohr, Germany, 141
Lucid, Father, 267
Lung cancer, 15, 21, 310, 328, 336–38
Lynch, Alexandra, 329, 337–38
Lynch, Alva, 7
Lynch, Art, 8–9
Lynch, Bob, 8
Lynch, Brian, *220*, 334
    birth of, 291–92
    early life of, 315, 330, 336
    education and career of, 330
    father's PTSD and, 326
    marriage and daughter Cailinn,
        330, 338–43
    travels and friendship with father,
        315
Lynch, Cailinn, *222*, 330, 338–43
Lynch, Carolyn, 329, 332
    birth of, 291
    early life of, 291–93, 297–98
    education and career of, 330
    father's PTSD and, 297–98, 326
    travels and friendship with father,
        315
Lynch, Daniel, 42
Lynch, Eric, *220*
    birth of, 286–88
    early life of, 289, 291, 292–93,
        296–99, 315
    education and career of, 329
    father's PTSD and, 297–99, 326
    marriage and family, 329, 336–38,
        340

travels and friendship with father,
315, 317–18
Lynch, Heidi Litizia, 338
Lynch, Katherine, 329, 337–38
Lynch, Kelly O'Driscoll, 330, 336,
338–43
Lynch, LeRoy James, 5–16
Allen in the Army, 120–21, 130–32,
195–96
Allen's early life and, 24–31, 33, 34,
37–38, 43, 46–53, 56, 58–60,
62–64, 65, 68–72, 83, 88–90,
205, 206, 207
Allen's enlistment in Army, 96, 115
Allen's Medal of Honor and, 219,
278, 280–81
Allen's return from Vietnam,
261–62, 263–64, 270, 271–72
appearance of, 7–8
background of, 6–7
Bible study of, 13, 284–85
death of, 15–16, 21, 310, 328
disciplinary standards of, 1, 11,
18–19, 24–25, 26, 37–38,
39–40, 72, 74–75
drinking intervention by family,
308–10
drinking of, 14–15, 21, 32, 42, 276,
283–84, 285, 308–9
education of, 13–14, 88–89
employment of, 1, 5–6, 9, 12–13,
33, 34, 85–88, 141
home improvement projects of,
12–13, 50–51
lung cancer of, 15, 21, 310, 328
meeting Susie and, 274
parenting style of, 9–11
personality of, 6, 7, 14, 18, 53
religious conversion experience of,
284–85

siblings and family of, 8–9
traditional role of, 11–12, 34, 41,
52–53
during World War II, 7–8
Lynch, Mary Frances Philip, 329,
336–38, 340
Lynch, Nancy
Allen in the Army, 120–21
Allen's Medal of Honor and, 278,
280–81
Allen's relationship with, 41–42
Allen's return from Vietnam,
261–62, 264
birth of, 40, 42
children and family life, 42, 300
early life of, 41, 47–48, 49–50,
52–53, 70, 141, 206, 207
mother as role model and mentor, 17
Lynch, Patrick, 329, 337–38
Lynch, Ruth, 9
Lynch, Simon, 9
Lynch, Susan Gronholm "Susie," x–xi,
346–47
Allen's drinking and, 311–15
Allen's Medal of Honor and, 219,
278, 280–81
Allen's PTSD and, 297–300, 302,
324, 326
children and family life, 7, 220,
283, 286–88, 289, 291–92,
293, 297–98, 299–300
dating Allen, 273–75
as empty nester, 329
first meetings of Allen, 272–73
honeymoon of, 279
marriage proposal and engagement,
275–76
nursing career of, 315, 322, 330
wedding of, 218, 277–79
Lynch, Viola Van Heel, 1, 5, 6, 16–22

Allen in the Army, 120–21, 130–32, 195–96

Allen's early life and, 24–31, 33, 34, 39, 48, 49–50, 52–53, 56, 59–60, 61–63, 68–73, 83, *205, 207*

Allen's enlistment in Army, 96, 115

Allen's Medal of Honor and, *219,* 278, 280–81

Allen's return from Vietnam, 261–62, 263–64, 270, 271–72

background of, 16

cooking of, 19, 52

devotion to family, 20

husband's drinking and, 14–15, 21, 32, 42, 276, 308–10

JFK's assassination and, 84–85

parenting style of, 11–12, 18–19

personality of, 6, 16–18, 20–21

religious faith of, 18, 76–77

stroke and death of, 21–22, 328

traditional role of, 17, 19

M14 rifles, 113–14

M16 rifles, 161–62, 166–67

M60 machine guns, 118

M79 grenade launchers, 166–67

M113 armored personnel carriers (APCs), 133–34

M203 grenade launchers, 166

McNair Kaserne, 143–47

Madigan, Lisa, 317

"Mad minute," 176

Malaysian peppers, 195

Marine Corps, U.S., 8

Marion, Jeff, 332, 334–35

M*A*S*H (TV show), 297

Massages, 190

McLagan, Don, 330–31

Medal of Honor, vii–viii, ix–xi, 302

announcement of, 279–80

anxiety about receiving, 295–96

the ceremony, 219, 280–81

notice of, 277–78

recommendation for, 253–54, 256, 268

Medal of Honor Convention (2009), 336, 343

Meehan, Neal, 316

Memorial Day, 307

Merrill's Marauders, 118

Metheny, Jeff, 343

Mexican American Veterans Association, 319

Michigan Avenue, Chicago, 24

Midway Airlines, 316

Migraine headaches, 17

Military draft, 91–92

Military dress code, 134–35

Military occupational specialty (MOS), 115

Montagnards, 186, *210*

Montford Point Marine Association, 319

Morrissey, John, 316

Mortars, 133

Mosquito repellent (bug juice), 161–62, 187, 254

"Mox nix" time, 134

Mukoyama, Jim, 301–2

"Mules," 159

Multiple sclerosis, 270

Murphy's Law of combat, 234

My An battle, xiii, 3–4, 235–51

See also Battle of Tam Quan

Allen's recollection of, xiii, 235–36, 326–27

endgame, 249–51

Medal of Honor citation, ix–x, xiii

pinned down in a trench, 240–44

rescue attempt, 244–47

second rescue attempt, 247–49

Napalm, 250
National Memorial Cemetery of the
Pacific, 303
Naughton, Father, 77, 78, 79
NCO Club, 268-69
Nett, Robert, 126-27
New Year's Eve, 83, 275
Nixon, Julie, 280-81
Nixon, Richard, ix-x, xi, 79-80, 127,
219, 280-81
North American F-100 Super Sabre,
249-50
North Chicago VA Medical Center,
297, 308-9
Northern Illinois University, 329, 330
North Vietnamese Army (NVA), 171,
172-73, 176, 177, 200
22nd Regiment and Battle of Tam
Quan, 3-4, 225-31, 234, 237-52
Tet Offensive, 226-27, 257
Northwestern Community Hospital, 287

Oakland Airport, 155
Obama, Barack, 318-19
Observation posts (OPs), 174-75, 176
Officer Candidate School (OCS), 2, 115,
116-17, 121-27
exit from, 125-28
Ogilvie, Richard, 281
O'Hare Airport, 261
One Million Years B.C. (movie), 232
Opera, 302
Operation Dragnet, 177-80, 189
Operation Pershing, 189
Operation Support our Troops—
America, 344
Ordaz, Rigo, 226-27, 228-30
Orsini, Donald A., xiii, 201, 232-34,
236-38, 240, 243-49, 252, 253
Oswald, Lee Harvey, 84

Owens-Illinois, 90

Pagliacci (opera), 302
Panamint, USS, 31
Panda bear, 28-29
Pauken, Tom, 304
Peddle, Larry, 335
Penthouse, 168, 267
Perseverance, xii
Peter, St., 79
Peterson, Bruce, 343-44
Photography, 140, 331
Physical Training Formation
(PT Formation), 104-5, 106
Pizza party, 123-24
Playboy, 86, 267
"Pogey bait," 123-24, 125-26
Pontiac Catalina, 91
Post-World War II period, 31
Prayer, 332
Presidential election of 1960, 79-80
Presidential election of 1964,
93-94, 95
Pritzker, Jennifer N., vii-viii
Pritzker Military Museum & Library,
336
Prostitute incident in Frankfurt, 141-43
Prostitution, 190
PTSD (post-traumatic stress disorder),
xii, xiii, 289-90, 297-303, 320-21,
322-27
Pullman Company, 5
Punji stakes, 172, 232
Purpose Driven Life, The (Warren),
335, 348-49

Racism, 103, 120-21, 146, 148
Radcliff, Donald G., 158
Radiotelephone operator (RTO), 3,
232-34, 239

Reagan, Ronald, 302–3, 304, 315
Red Cross, 148, 149
Reenlistment, 2, 139–41
Reflexes and Reflections (show), 305–6
REMFs (Rear Echelon Motherf**ks), 256–57
Republic of Vietnam National Police Field Force, 177–78, 192
Reserve Officer Training Corps (ROTC), 112
Retirement of Allen, 333–34
Rice paddies, 4, 173, 177–78
Robinson, Ronald R., 316
Roman Catholicism. *See* Catholic Church
Roseland, Chicago, 5–6, 23–31, 32, 68–69
Roseland Community Hospital, 5
Rotary Four-Way Test, 348
Ruby, Jack, 84
Ryan, Jim, 317

Saint Germain Lake, 83
St. Jude Catholic Church, 77
St. Patrick's Day, 312
St. Xavier University, 330
Sally, Bob, 299, 300
Salute to America's Heroes, 310–11
Sandbags, 156–57
Schwan, John, 343–44
Scott, Richard T., 244–47, 253
Search-and-destroy missions, 3, 183–91, 193, 196–201, 254–55
Second Vatican Council, 79
Segregation, 120–21
Self-confidence, 10, 13
Self-image, 1–2, 15
Selfishness, 349
Septic systems, 50–51
Sewing, 140

Shellie, Darrell A., *216*, 256–57
Sherwin-Williams, 6
Shoplifting incident, 61–63, 142
Sims, Marvin, 253
Sleep habits, 171
Smith, H.G. "Skip," 304
Smoker's cough, 268–69
Smoking, 83, 268–70, 310
"Snatch missions," 177–78
Socialism, 16
Soldier of the Quarter Competition, 269–70
Soldiers' and Sailors' Civil Relief Act, 319
Song Lai Giang, 193
South China Sea, 197
South China Sea coastline, 169–72
Southerland, Roy Edward, 4, 233–34, 235, 239–40, 243–53
Southern Illinois University, 296, 297
Soviet Union, 32–33, 34–35, 79–81
Special Forces, 184–85, 186
Special-needs children, 339–43
Spiritualism, 18
Squad leaders, 102
"Square meal" technique, 122–23
Standard Oil, 6, 12, 48
"Stand downs," 165–66
"Steel pots," 179
Stern School Road, 300
Strong's Exhaustive Concordance, 13
Struck, Gary, 23–24
Summary of Maneuver: Second Battle of Tam Quan (Kjos), xiii
Supernumerary, 111–12
Survivor's guilt, 253, 298, 302
Sytsma, Laura, 6–10, 51, 60–61, *206*
Sytsma, Simon, 7, 10

Table of Organization and Equipment

(TOE), 234–35
Tactical formation, 238–39
Target-pulling duty, 136–38
Task Force Dolphin, 229 30
Tastee Freeze, 33
Tear gas, 108, 191–93
Tetco Metal Products, 12, 85–88, 89–90, 141
Tet Offensive, 226–27, 253, 257
Thanksgiving, 81, 108–9, 275
Thomas, Dick, 316–17, 319
Thornridge High School, 68, 69–75, 80, 83–84, 88–89
Tierno, James, 244, 245, 252
Tolson, John Jarvis, III, 252–53
Tolstedt, Betsy, 322–23, 326–27
Tomb of the Unknown Soldier, 281
Tommy (friend), 44 45, 46–47
Totalitarianism, 63
Tracy, Ed, 336
"Trainees," 100
Training, advising, and counseling (TAC), 122
Traveling Board of Veterans Appeals, 320–21
"Trench foot," 168–69
Trinity International University, 330
Trip flares, 163
Truman, Harry, 32
Turk (friend), 75–76, 91, 121, 261
Tuskegee Airmen, 319
TV (television), 27, 36

Union Carbide, 6, 9, 12, 33, 85
Union Center School, 42, 53–56
Unionism, 16
Union League Club, 304
United Parcel Service (UPS), 271–72, 279
U.S. Steel, 6

USS Arizona Memorial, 303

Vacations, 39–40, 83
Vaccine shots, 98–99
Valparaiso incident, 61–63, 142
Valparaiso University, 45
Van Heel, Alida, 16, 20
Van Heel, Debbie, 33, 47–48
Van Heel, Dick, 31, 33, 47, 67, 68, 69, 73, 82, 275
Van Heel, Harry, 16, 20
Van Heel, Jack, 31, 263, 264, 279
Van Heel, Jay, 33, 47, 52, 67, 68, 73
Van Heel, Laurie, 82, 275
Van Heel, Marty, 69–70, 82
Van Heel, Ricky, 33, 47–48, 207
Van Vlissingen Elementary School, 27–28
Veteran's Advocate, The (TV program), 319
Veterans Affairs (VA) hospitals, 307–8
Veterans Assistance Commissions (VAC), 318, 319
Veterans assistance counselor, 286, 347
Veterans Benefits Administration, 308
Veterans benefits counselor, xi, 282–83, 286, 290, 293–94
Veterans Day, 307
Veterans Judicial Review Act of 1988, 318
Veterans Rights Bureau, 316–19
Veterans Senior Advocacy and Awareness Malls (VETSAAM), 318
Victory Memorial Hospital, 322, 330
Viet Cong (VC), 171, 200
    ambush patrols, 175–77
    first combat, 181–82
    misdirected gas attack, 191–93
    My An battle, 236–37, 240
    Operation Dragnet, 177–80

searching hooches, 172–74
Tet Offensive, 226–27, 257
Vietnam memorials, 305–8
Vietnam Veteran Art Group, 305–6
Vietnam Veterans Leadership Program
    (VVLP), 304–6, 310–13, 316–17
Vietnam Veterans Memorial (Chicago),
    305–6
Vietnam Veterans Memorial
    (Washington, D.C.), 305, 306–7
Vietnam Veterans of America, 320–21,
    334–35
Vietnam War. *See also* 1st Cavalry
    Division; Battle of Tam Quan
Allen's arrival, 1, 2–3, 156–57
Allen's fatalistic attitude about,
    164–65
Allen signs up for, 150–52
Allen's return home, 258–81
casualties, 95–96
Christmas truce, 254
friendly fire death of Jerry, 183–89
Gulf of Tonkin incident, 85, 94
Johnson and, 85, 93–94, 266
Operation Dragnet, 177–80
troop numbers, 95–96
Vietnam Women's Memorial, 307
Viss, Marcia, 300
Vittori, Rebecca Bolda, 42, 300

War on Terror, 333
Warren, Rick, 335, 348–49
Washington National Airport, 280
Wasps, 48
Watkins, Lt., 196–97
Waukegan American Legion, 289
Western Illinois University, 330
Westmoreland, William, 254, 280,
    317–18

Wheeler High School, 42, 53, 63–64
Wildflecken Training Area (WTA),
    146–47
Wilhelms, Irving, 4, 240, 252
"Willie Peter," 166–67
World War II, 7–8, 12, 26, 63, 132,
    145–46, 260, 319
Wright, Sgt., 100–101, 102–3, 105, 107,
    111, 113

"Zippo Tracks," 228